D1118645

RENAISSANCE
WOMEN
WRITERS

৶৹

Marie-Madeleine écrivant by a painter conventionally called
"Le Maître des Demi-Figures de Femmes." First half of the
sixteenth century (Antwerp[?]).
Permission to reproduce from "La Fondation des Princes
Czartoryski." Muzeum Narodowym, Krakow.

RENAISSANCE WOMEN WRITERS

French Texts / American Contexts

Edited with an Introduction by
ANNE R. LARSEN
and
COLETTE H. WINN

WAYNE STATE UNIVERSITY PRESS DETROIT

Copyright © 1994 by Wayne State University Press,
Detroit, Michigan 48202. All rights are reserved.
No part of this book may be reproduced without formal permission.
Manufactured in the United States of America.

99 98 97 96 95 94   5 4 3 2 1

Library of Congress Cataloging-in-Publication Data

Renaissance women writers : French texts, American contexts / edited with an introduction by Anne R. Larsen and Colette H. Winn.
p.   cm.
Includes bibliographical references and index.
ISBN 0-8143-2473-8 (alk. paper)
1. French literature—16th century—History and criticism.
2. French literature—Women authors—History and criticism.
3. Women and literature—France—History—16th century.
4. Renaissance—France.   I. Larsen, Anne R.   II. Winn, Colette H.
PQ239.R46   1994
840.9′9287′0903—dc20   93-26577

Designer: Joanne E. Kinney

FOR OUR MOTHERS

Contents
✌

Acknowledgments
გა

The editors wish to thank Matthew Ballast, Karen J. Barber, Mary Jane Bosker, and Allison A. Craig for their invaluable help in typing the manuscript, and Donna Nix for her help with the index. Thanks go as well to the friendly cooperation of the interlibrary loan personnel at Hope College and Washington University in St. Louis.

We wish to express our gratitude to the anonymous reviewers for their insightful comments and to those colleagues, friends, and family who have given us counsel and encouragement.

Anne R. Larsen
Colette H. Winn

Introduction
ဢ

The title of this volume, echoing that of a special 1981 issue of *Yale French Studies* on "Feminist Readings," enables us to measure the ground that has been covered since this collaborative "(ad)venture" took place a decade or so ago.[1] The reader will find that many of the crucial preoccupations of the 1981 Yale issue reappear in the present volume. Both then and now relational issues are foremost—those between author, text, character, reader, literary tradition, and reception. Yet these issues are viewed from a somewhat different angle, and similar questions are reopened to be explored and taken further. The title also calls attention to continuity in scholarly activities. It situates our endeavor in the context of a mutual support and collaboration in the process of discovery.

The 1981 Yale issue is not exclusively devoted to Renaissance women writers; only one article on the subject, "Assimilation with a Difference . . ." by Ann Rosalind Jones, focuses on two female lyricists of the "Ecole lyonnaise." Nonetheless, this issue has provided a major invigorating stimulus for similar collaborative effort in Renaissance studies.[2] Furthermore, Jones's excellent article has inspired many scholars concerning women's revisionary practices. And Marianne Hirsch's contribution on the mother-daughter bond in *La Princesse de Clèves* has proved a useful tool, especially for those among us who similarly explore the relationship between women, sisters, mothers and daughters, mentors and "protégées."

This project is borne out of our own readings of works by Renaissance women and our mutual desire to engage in a dialogue with scholars sharing these similar interests. When the idea for this volume originated, we were responding to an existing need rather than seeking to stimulate new interest. Indeed, although several recent anthologies pertaining to the

Renaissance examine one or several works by French women,[3] no book-length publication, as far as we know, is entirely dedicated to the study of French texts. François Rigolot's special 1990 issue of *L'Esprit Créateur* is the first on French texts and the problematics of writing in the feminine.[4] The reader will find here many sympathetic voices.

Originally we aimed at a volume that would bring together the current research of scholars from France and the United States. Our enthusiasm was matched by that of our colleagues on both sides of the Atlantic; in fact so much interest followed that we were forced, owing to limitations of space and, in some cases, time, to exclude several articles of great interest. The high number of articles received and the difficulty of publishing a bilingual collection also compelled us to revise our initial project.

The essays in this volume deal with authors and texts spanning the century that have gained a growing recognition on the part of scholars here and abroad. The genres examined include sonnets (Louise Labé, Catherine des Roches), elegies (Louise Labé, Pernette du Guillet), memoirs (Marguerite de Valois), novellas (Marguerite de Navarre), translations, plays, and dialogues (Catherine des Roches, Marguerite de Navarre), dedicatory epistles (Louise Labé, Hélisenne de Crenne, Jeanne Flore, Marie de Gournay), and novels (Marie de Gournay). The essays mirror, furthermore, a broad range of topics and approaches that reflect current trends in Renaissance scholarship in the United States. Several readings meet here, sometimes overlapping within the same essays: historical, textual and intertextual, political and feminist, psychoanalytic, or drawing on structuralist and post-structuralist theories of narrative and reader reception. Although the essays differ considerably in critical approach, each views the text through a feminist lens. They are all informed by a common concern, a recurring question aimed at uncovering the veil of mystery still surrounding these too-long forgotten authors: What does it mean to write through the prism of gender in early modern France? Other questions raised are closely related: How, under adverse circumstances, did women gain access to the public sphere? How did the "entourage factor" or coterie collaboration serve their growing cultural and literary presence? And from these questions more follow as to the link between gender and writing, gender and genre, and issues related to this problematic: intertextuality, authorization and appropriation, translation, mythopoeia (or the feminization of male myths), and so forth. Indeed, one may rightly ask, can we claim a "distinctive mode" for Renaissance women's writing? As Cathleen Bauschatz points out, in an era advocating the imitation of celebrated (male) models so as to resemble the (male) writer imitated, the issue of difference, when it comes to aspirant women writers, becomes central.[5] In whose enabling name does the woman write? To whom? How does she forge a literary identity? And how does she address institutions of power mediated through literary codes and genres?

We have grouped the essays into three sections that reflect major characteristics of Renaissance women's writing practices.

The first essay of part one opens with the question of exclusion on the basis of gender, but here the question is posed differently. In her study on Renaissance writers' "exclusionary poetics," Deborah N. Losse demonstrates that literary women tend to exclude men from the community of readers whom they are addressing, a pattern especially striking in their prefaces. For example, in her "Epître dédicatoire à M.C.D.B.L.," Louise Labé proceeds, by juggling with linguistic markers, to relegate man to the mute state her sex has previously experienced. Her dedicatory remarks to a woman may be owing to a fundamental reluctance in many women writers to address directly a large mixed audience. And as has been shown elsewhere female literary friendship legitimizes women's publication.[6] When there is a shift in address (from female to male readership) in Labé's epistle, the topos of authorial humility (inability, inexpressibility, untranslatability) resurfaces. This topos calls attention to her "difference," yet another strategy to court approval so as to promote her publication. Losse further observes that, while the prologues of the "conteuses" generally tend to adhere to the Boccaccian model by addressing a purely female readership and stressing the pleasurable and/or the profitable in their works, they also reveal women's strategies to distance themselves from the discourse of the Other. By displacing key elements in the Boccaccian text—which Losse aptly names an "ungrammaticality in the adaptation of the intertext"—Hélisenne de Crenne and Louise Labé minimize the inspiration of the male *auctor* and elevate the woman writer as intellectual equal.

This section contains another three essays that further illuminate the process of "re-vision." They cause us to think anew the link between gender and writing through their specific focus on the feminization of translation and classical myths.[7] They shed new light on the position of women who wish to integrate themselves as subjects into a traditional script.

Kirk D. Read poses the question as to what become of Diana and Actaeon in the works of a woman lyricist? For Pernette du Guillet and Louise Labé, appropriation of the myth, he contends, reflects the individual needs as well as the personal choices confronting female poets in their respective private/public life, and in Labé's case, her awareness of the politics of reception. Rachel Blau Du Plessis argues that:

> The poet's attitude toward the tale as given determines whether there will be a displacement of attention to the other side of the story, or a delegitimation of the known tale, a critique even unto sequences and priorities of narrative. Narrative displacement is like breaking the sentence, because it offers the possibility of speech to the female in the case, giving voice to the muted. Narrative

delegitimation "breaks the sequence"; a realignment that puts the last first and the first last has always ruptured conventional morality, politics, and narrative. (108)

The "lyonnaise" lyricists use both strategies of narrative displacement and delegitimation. Louise Labé retells the tale of Diana and Actaeon in a woman's perspective. Rather than informing the male poetics of confrontation and abandonment, her story speaks to cooperation and the privilege of female community. Pernette du Guillet's speaker refuses to metamorphose her lover, thereby relinquishing Diana's threatening power. As Lawrence Kritzman has recently expressed it, Du Guillet demystifies the illusion of mastery.[8] Her ethics of love allow for an exchange that rejects the Petrarchan requirement of love-sick masochism. She thus realizes her own status as subject by ensuring her lover's.

For Catherine des Roches, the myth of Ceres and Proserpina is particularly appealing as it echoes her own closeness to her mother—a closeness, Tilde Sankovitch explains, that had made possible her creativity. Des Roches's translation of Claudian's *De Raptu Proserpinae,* which includes quite a few "creative variations," expresses her emotional response to male intrusion (she, herself, decided never to marry), and her desire to participate in the humanist enterprise of *translatio studii.* Here again, a woman writer chooses a myth that reflects the dilemmas directly confronting her in her public/private life. She inserts in her translation a personal statement that empowers her to fashion a precursor for those who follow.

Marguerite de Valois's memoirs reopen the question of gender and genre. As Luce Irigaray explains, "Woman's social inferiority is reinforced and complicated by the fact that woman does not have access to language, except through recourse to 'masculine' systems of representation which disappropriate her from the relation to herself and to other women."[9] How is a woman to use or reuse what has been put into forms by, and for, men such as the memoir genre? In writing her *Mémoires,* explains Patricia Cholakian, Marguerite found herself in a double bind—to adapt either the exclusively male model to her story or her story to the traditional givens of the genre. Interestingly, she adapted the genre to her own ends by giving precedence to the "private" (her spiritual and intellectual development) over the "public" realm (political events), to autobiography (HER-story) over HIS-toriography (although, as Cholakian notes, she certainly took great pains in making her story sound like his!).

———

In Part two the issue of the relation between language and body—a leitmotiv in contemporary debates on feminine writing—is explored further.[10] Forbidden to speak, woman is equally estranged from her body: "le corps au cachot, l'esprit au silence" (her body imprisoned, her spirit si-

lenced), writes Hélène Cixous in *Entre L'Ecriture*.[11] Coming to writing
thus becomes synonymous with the rediscovery of the body, both essential
to the affirmation of self. The specificity of women's writing is founded on
the relation of language to body, each a metaphor of the other: "mon corps
est mots" (my body is words), notes Madeleine Gagnon.[12] The contemporary attention to language and body presents a new critical vantage point
for studies on women's writings in the sixteenth century.

Paula Sommers traces in Louise Labé's sonnets and elegies the problematic relationship between the female poet/persona and the body—a
relation, she argues, characterized by insecurity and tension. For Labé, the
body is both the locus of desire (and frustration) and the object of the
male gaze. It remains an "outer self" that is seldom in tune with the inner
perception of self; that is why she "assumes a body only to dress it in poetic
texts." Here, Sommers concludes, "femininity lies not in the body alone
but in the combination of body with discourse that articulates and transcends the body."

Likewise, for Marguerite de Navarre, as Colette H. Winn shows, the
relation to the body is far from free of tension. Indeed, in the Neoplatonic
context, the body is conceived as both the starting point of the ascending
process (human love is the means by which to attain divine love) and a
constant obstacle between man and God (the body is the prison out of
which the soul wishes to break free). Convinced of the necessity to negate
the body, Marguerite continually deplores her strong attachment to earthly
matters. This is the subject of a letter she wrote in 1522 to her spiritual
father, the bishop of Meaux, and signed "la trop en corps" (she who is too
embodied). However, while she condemns the transgressive body that puts
the soul in oblivion and celebrates the chaste and silenced body, she comes
to realize, through her own experience as a woman (as a mother in the
Dialogue en forme de vision nocturne, and a lover/sister in the *Navire* and
the *Chansons spirituelles*) that the body cannot, and in fact must not, be
silenced. For to deny the body is to reject what Christ redeemed when he
became flesh and fail to perceive the mystery of the incarnation.

In analyzing language and corporeality from a fresh perspective, Cathy
Yandell explores the treatment of time in relationship to gender, taking as
examples the Horacian *exegi monumentum* and carpe diem topoi. She does
not go so far as to claim the existence of a consistent female ideology of
time in early modern France, but she shows that both Pernette du Guillet
and Catherine des Roches depart from their male counterparts by refuting
"visionary versions of the future" in favor of an "everlasting present."

Finally, Carla Freccero argues the challenge that feminine desire and
subjectivity, figured by the maternal, pose for both Freud's and Girard's
oedipal models of the structuring of the novel. "Early novels," she writes,
"include mothering in their motives (rather than 'fathering' alone)." Freccero reopens the debate on women writers and the maternal by examining,

in the light of Marguerite de Navarre's *Heptaméron*, the mother-daughter struggle for authority and, more particularly, the ambivalent position of the mother under patriarchy. The mother's stance is one of both subjection and authority. To the extent that she collaborates with patriarchy by enforcing/reinforcing the culture of oppression, the mother may exercise power over less empowered feminine subjects; yet, her authority is precarious, continually undermined and challenged by her daughter's rebellion.

———

The essays in part three deal for the most part with "the politics of reception"; they focus on how women writers maneuver within the social restrictions of their time to negotiate their entry into the public world of print.

Gary Ferguson's essay opens this section by highlighting gender differentiation in narrative and society. Examining "the male rhetoric of seduction" as opposed to "the female rhetoric of resistance" in the *Heptaméron* of Marguerite de Navarre, Ferguson describes how male protagonists and *devisants* manipulate the rhetoric of a particular ideology so as to empty it of its usual meaning, while women tend to reaffirm conventional meanings and values. By opting for a code of *courtoisie* based on the "bourgeois principles of thrift" and the deferral of pleasure, women undermine the "seigneurial morality of *jouissance.*" But while aristocratic writers were adopting a "rhetoric of resistance," a woman writer of the bourgeoisie, Louise Labé, was claiming the right to sexual expression and aristocratic *jouissance.* How did Labé write her way through the constraints on women's speech?

Breaking through these constraints is the subject of Tom Conley's "Engendering Letters: Louise Labé Polygraph." Conley explores Labé's use of the graphic medium to "produce an illusion of space, volume, and unending movement" in the representation of desire. By drawing on contemporary typographers and cartographers, he shows how Labé's poetry shares much with the period's view of the letter as a perspectival object.

The reception of Catherine des Roches's *Tragicomedie de Tobie,* one of the few female-authored French Renaissance plays, is Anne R. Larsen's focus. Des Roches's rewriting of the Apocryphal Book of *Tobit,* in which Sarah, the heroine, and her mother daringly critique the biblical erotic and marriage plots, is ironically echoed in Odet de Turnèbe's comedy *Les Contens.* Turnèbe wrote this play shortly after his 1579 visit to Poitiers, the Dames des Roches's hometown. Larsen argues that Turnèbe, by taking position with Des Roches, underscores the divide separating her from contemporary male writers: to her threatening impulse to power and control—he opposes the male erotic economy in which women are primarily seen as objects of exchange.

Cathleen M. Bauschatz explores issues of power relations and the daughter's struggle to establish her identity as woman writer.[13] As Sandra Gilbert and Susan Gubar indicate, a woman writing has anxiety projecting herself as an author; she experiences a "fear that she cannot create, that because she can never become a 'precursor' the act of writing will isolate or destroy her."[14] Marie de Gournay surmounts this fear owing to a growing sense of authority which Bauschatz traces through the changes that appear in the preface of the 1626 edition of *Le Proumenoir de Monsieur de Montaigne* and in the novel itself. Her focus is Gournay's relation to her new readers (mostly women), and to the sources or authors she has drawn from. In each case, Bauschatz argues, Gournay regains the "Empire" the Father(s) once had over her. Where she had invested her readers—Montaigne in particular—with "excessive power over her," Gournay is able in 1626 to develop a strong narrative persona, project a positive rather than merely negative relation to her reader, and fully affirm her status as woman writer.

Can we claim a distinctive mode for Renaissance women's writing? Judging from these essays, it appears so.

Part one encompasses three revisionary practices in relation to dominant codes: women writers define a female reading community to empower the female speaker; demystify the illusion of mastery inscribed in male myths and encode these myths with the topos of female creative bonding; and privilege the "private" over the "public" in a genre such as the memoirs that was hitherto limited to narrating public events. These practices complement the views that Renaissance women writers express on the body and feminine desire.

Hence in part two, the female body, an object mastered and seduced in male ideology, a locus of dread as it reflects the ravages of time, is deemphasized and ultimately transcended. The body is affirmed only in a spiritual climate, as in Marguerite de Navarre's oeuvre. The relation of the body to amorous time is also perceived differently: the female poet privileges amorous plenitude in the present, her male counterpart victory over time through idealized beauty and fame. Likewise conflicting feminine mother/daughter desires are mediated in the service of feminine subjectivity rather than merely in that of patriarchy.

A rhetoric of resistance and camouflage in part three best characterizes Renaissance women writers' relation to narrative and society. Marguerite de Navarre and Catherine des Roches share a common strategy of undermining the prevailing "morality of *jouissance*." Louise Labé claims the right to *jouissance* but embeds her claim in cautionary forms: she uses the polymorphous experimentation with the graphic medium to dispel an illusion of totality. Resistance for Marie de Gournay means eventual empowerment as woman writer.

Other women writers now remain to be discovered, their works edited and interpreted. Evelyne Berriot-Salvadore's recent study of the status of women in Renaissance France mentions some twenty published women writers in the sixteenth century.[15] Eight, the most frequently read, are discussed here. Others include Marie de Romieu, Anne de Marquets, Gabrielle de Coignard, Marie Le Gendre, Jacqueline de Miremont, Marie Dentière, Marie de Costeblanche, and Nicole Estienne. All, with the exception of Romieu, have never been edited. And the complete works of Marie de Gournay, the Dames des Roches, and Hélisenne de Crenne are still unavailable in modern critical editions. Moreover, as Berriot-Salvadore indicates, a high number of letters, memoirs, diaries, and account books by women are still buried in the archives. An important priority remains the ongoing recovery of the past.

Further work should be done on socio-historic aspects of women's production discussed only tangentially in these essays. For example, we need to know more about women's participation in the polemical debates of their time such as the "Querelle des Femmes" and the marriage controversy. The impact of female court patronage on women writers and the role that the Valois queens played require additional study, as do also the ways in which the salons, the *académies,* and coterie collaboration in the late sixteenth and early seventeenth centuries served women writers' growing intellectual and political presence.[16] Finally, although the link between gender and genre has been a major concern here, much more could be done to appreciate the rich and diverse contributions of French women. Special attention should be given to the subjects they chose (religion and faith, the female experience, bonds between women), and the genres to which they turned—letters, theater, treatises, spiritual meditations, and "minor" poetic genres (*rondeaux,* songs, debate poems, dialogues, *songes*), still too often relegated to the category of the "Underread."

A collective awareness of the determining role of gender marks the essays in this volume. We hope that these will provide fresh insights into the works of Renaissance women writers and new directions for future creative scholarship.

NOTES

1. Colette Gaudin et al., eds., "Feminist Readings: French Texts/American Contexts," Special issue of *Yale French Studies* 62 (1981).

2. See, for example, the anthologies of Margaret W. Ferguson, Maureen Quilligan, and Nancy J. Vickers, ed., *Rewriting the Renaissance: The Discourses of Sexual Difference in Early Modern Europe* (Chicago: University of Chicago Press, 1986); Nancy K. Miller, ed., *The Poetics of Gender* (New York: Columbia University Press, 1986); Mary Beth Rose, ed., *Women in the Middle Ages and the Renaissance: Literary and Historical Perspectives* (Syracuse: Syracuse University Press, 1986); Carole Levin and Jeanie Watson, eds., *Ambiguous Realities: Women in the Middle Ages and Renaissance* (Detroit: Wayne State University Press, 1987).

3. These anthologies examine works by French women as critical documents that raise questions concerning gender relations, as well as religious, economic, and political structures. See those edited by Mary Beth Rose; Margaret W. Ferguson et al.; Katharina Wilson, ed., *Women Writers of the Renaissance and Reformation* (Athens: University of Georgia Press, 1987); and Sheila Fisher and Janet E. Halley, ed., *Seeking the Woman in Late Medieval and Renaissance Writings: Essays in Feminist Contextual Criticism* (Knoxville: University of Tennessee Press, 1989). See also Ann Rosalind Jones's study, *The Currency of Eros: Women's Love Lyric in Europe, 1540–1620* (Bloomington: Indiana University Press, 1990), which includes chapters on Pernette du Guillet, Louise Labé, and Catherine des Roches.

4. François Rigolot, ed., "Writing in the Feminine in the Renaissance," Special issue of *L'Esprit Créateur* 30 (Winter 1990).

5. Cathleen Bauschatz, "Imitation, Writing, and Self-Study in Marie de Gournay's 1595 'Preface' to Montaigne's *Essais*," in *Contending Kingdoms: Historical, Psychological, and Feminist Approaches to the Literature of Sixteenth-Century England and France*, ed. Marie-Rose Logan and Peter Rudnytsky (Detroit: Wayne State University Press, 1991), 356.

6. On women's prefatory strategies, see Evelyne Berriot-Salvadore, "Les Femmes et les pratiques de l'écriture de Christine de Pisan à Marie de Gournay. 'Femmes sçavantes et sçavoir féminin,'" *Réforme, Humanisme, Renaissance* 16 (1983): 52–69; François Rigolot, with Kirk D. Read, "Discours liminaire et identité littéraire," *Versants* 15 (1989): 75–98; and Anne R. Larsen, "'Un honneste passetems': Strategies of Legitimation in French Renaissance Women's Prefaces," *L'Esprit Créateur* 30 (1990): 11–22.

7. For a sampling of studies on mythopoeia and women writers' revisionary poetics, see Monique Wittig, *Les Guérillères* (Paris: Minuit, 1969); Hélène Cixous, with Catherine Clément, *The Newly Born Woman*, trans. Betsy Wing (Minneapolis: University of Minnesota Press, 1986); Tilde Sankovitch, *French Women Writers and the Book: Myths of Access and Desire* (Syracuse: Syracuse University Press, 1988); and Rachel Blau Du Plessis, "'Perceiving the Other-Side of Everything': Tactics of Revisionary Mythopoesis," in *Writing Beyond the Ending: Narrative Strategies of Twentieth-Century Women Writers* (Bloomington: Indiana University Press, 1985), 105–122.

8. Lawrence Kritzman, *The Rhetoric of Sexuality and the Literature of the French Renaissance* (Cambridge: Cambridge University Press, 1991), 28.

9. Luce Irigaray, *This Sex Which is Not One*, trans. Catherine Porter, with Carolyn Burke (Ithaca: Cornell University Press, 1985), 85.

10. For a sampling of studies on language, the body, and *écriture féminine*, see Susan Rubin Suleiman, "(Re)Writing the Body: The Politics and Poetics of Female Eroticism," in *The Female Body in Western Culture: Contemporary Perspectives*, ed. Susan Rubin Suleiman (Cambridge: Harvard University Press, 1985), 7–29; Nancy K. Miller, "Rereading as a Woman: The Body in Practice," in *The Female Body in Western Culture*, 354–362; Ann Rosalind Jones, "Writing the Body: Toward an Understanding of 'l'écriture féminine,'" *Feminist Studies* 7 (1981): 247–263; and Cécile Lindsay, "Body/Language: French Feminist Utopias," *The French Review* 60 (1986): 46–55.

11. Hélène Cixous, *Entre L'Ecriture* (Paris: des femmes, 1976), 12. Translations are our own.

12. Madeleine Gagnon, "Mon corps dans l'écriture," in *La Venue à l'écriture*, ed. Hélène Cixous, Madeleine Gagnon, and Annie Leclerc (Paris: Union Générale d'Editions, 1977), 62.

13. See as well Maryanne C. Horowitz, "Marie de Gournay, Editor of the *Essais* of Michel de Montaigne: A Case-Study in Mentor-Protégée Friendship," *The Sixteenth-Century Journal* 17, no. 3 (1986): 271–284.

14. Sandra Gilbert and Susan Gubar, *The Madwoman in the Attic: The Woman Writer and the Nineteenth-Century Literary Imagination* (New Haven: Yale University Press, 1979), 49.

15. Evelyne Berriot-Salvadore, *Les Femmes dans la société française de la Renaissance* (Geneva: Droz, 1991).

Anne R. Larsen and Colette H. Winn

16. See Sharon Kettering, "The Patronage Power of Early Modern French Noblewomen," *The Historical Journal* 32 (1989): 817–841; Margaret Ezell, *Writing Women's Literary History* (Baltimore: The Johns Hopkins University Press, 1993); and Erica Harth's *Cartesian Women: Versions and Subversions of Rational Discourse in the Old Regime* (Ithaca: Cornell University Press, 1992).

Coming to Writing

Women's Exclusionary
and
Revisionary Practices

WOMEN ADDRESSING WOMEN
The Differentiated Text
৶৶

Deborah N. Losse

An examination of the liminary pages of the Renaissance storytellers brings to light a curious anomaly present in the works of three women writing *contes* and *débats* in the third, fourth, and fifth decades of the sixteenth century. Shunning the more current prefatory forms of the *conteurs*—the prologue and the *avis au lecteur*—Jeanne Flore, Hélisenne de Crenne (born Marguerite de Briet), and Louise Labé show a predilection for the dedicatory epistle addressed sometimes to a single woman: "à madame Minerve sa chère cousine" (to Madame Minerva her dear cousin) (Flore, *Les Contes Amoureux*) or "à M.C.D.B.L. (Mademoiselle Clémence de Bourges lionnoize) (Labé, *Le Débat de Folie et d'Amour*), or to a collectivity of women: "à toutes honestes Dames" (to all honorable Ladies)(Hélisenne de Crenne, *Les Angoysses douloureuses qui procedent d'amours*).[1]

Addresses to clearly defined social groups, such as Bouchet's prefatory remarks to the merchants of Poitiers in the *Serées* (1584), are rare among the Renaissance *conteurs*. Rabelais's readers may choose to include or exclude themselves from the ranks of the "beuveurs/verolez" (boozers/poxy ones). He progressively widens the circle of his audience in the prologues from the "chevaleureux champions, gentilz hommes et aultres" (chivalrous champions, gentlemen and others) he addresses in *Pantagruel* to the "beuveurs/verolez/goutteux" of *Gargantua* and the *Tiers Livre,* and finally, the "gens de bien" of the *Quart Livre*. Des Périers and Marguerite de Navarre address their readers in the gender-free *vous,* with Des Périers calling upon the ladies to read boldly on or to let their brothers and cousins censor the "off-color material" ("passages trop gaillars").[2] He

23

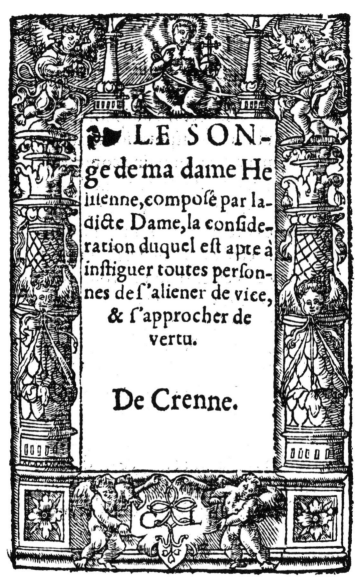

LE SON-
ge de ma dame He
lienne, composé par la-
dicte Dame, la conside-
ration duquel est apte à
instiguer toutes person-
nes de s'aliener de vice,
& s'approcher de
vertu.

De Crenne.

Title page of Hélisenne de Crenne's *Songe,* in her
Oeuvres, Paris, 1544 (courtesy of the Newberry
Library, Chicago).

extends readership to include both sexes, sometimes evoked in the masculine, "mon amy" (my friend), sometimes in the feminine, "Lisez hardiment, dames et demoyselles" (Read on boldly, ladies and young ladies), and to the young and the more mature, "entre vous femmes/entre vous fillettes" (among you women/among you, young girls). Likewise in the *Heptaméron,* gender parity among the inscribed storytellers—five men and five women—and among the historic figures mentioned in the prologue, "le roy François, premier de ce nom, monseigneur le Daulphin, madame la Daulphine, madame Marguerite" (King Francis, first of this name, Milord the Dauphin, Madame the Dauphiness, Madame Marguerite) implies that the sparing *vous* with which the narrator addresses the reader includes readers of both sexes.[3] Philippe de Vigneulles ends his prologue by begging "tous ceulx et celles" (all those [men] and those [ladies]) who read his tales to take the good that is in them and to correct the flaws.[4] Many *conteurs* choose the gender-distinct form "au lecteur" (to the reader) or "aux lecteurs"/"aux liseurs" (to the readers) to address their readers. We cite Noël du Fail, Philippe d'Alcripe, Cholières, La Motte-Messemé in this regard.[5] But is the address "au lecteur" really a gender-distinct form? A case can be made, as Monique Wittig does with the pronoun subject *ils,* for assuming that the masculine form "au lecteur" or "aux lecteurs" does not exclude women, but that it is simply an *unmarked* form to address a general readership.[6] In contrast, the feminine form "aux lisantes" (to the women readers) used by Hélisenne de Crenne in the liminary *dizain* preceding her dedicatory epistle to the *Angoysses douloureuses,* is a *marked* form set apart for two reasons: first, because of the infrequency of its usage in the prefatory discourse of Renaissance storytellers, and second, because in French a feminine form is never the "bearer of a universal point of view."[7] Similarly, Jeanne Flore's *Contes amoureux* begin with a poem addressed by madame Minerve to the "Nobles Dames amoureuses" (Noble Ladies in Love).[8] Louise Labé follows in the tradition of narrating to a feminine audience in her *Débat de Folie et d'Amour.* She addresses her prefatory remarks to a woman, Clémence de Bourges, and her use of personal pronouns suggests that she is speaking to an exclusively feminine audience. This one-to-one exchange between "Dames Lionnoises," as François Rigolot and Kirk D. Read remark, signals a common front and a community of interest.[9]

Labé's dedicatory epistle is an appeal to women not only to take up studies and writing—areas from which they had formerly been excluded by the "severes loix des hommes" (stern laws of men)—but also to surpass or equal men in the same enterprise: "mais en science et vertu passer ou egaler les hommes" (18) (but in knowledge and eminence surpass or equal men) (Wilson 148). The preface opens by highlighting exclusion on the basis of gender: "Estant le tems venu, Madamoiselle, que les severes loix des hommes n'empeschent plus les femmes de s'apliquer aus sciences et disciplines"(17, ll. 1–3)(The time having come, Mademoiselle, when the stern laws of men no longer bar women from devoting themselves to the sciences and disciplines) (Wilson 149). She urges women to take up letters to show men the harm they have done to women by excluding them:

> il me semble que celles qui ont la commodité, doivent employer cette hon-
> neste liberté que *notre* sexe ha autre fois tant desirée, à icelles aprendre:et mon-
> trer aus hommes le tort qu'*ils nous* faisoient en *nous* privant du bien et de
> l'honneur qui *nous* en pouvoit venir. (ll. 3–8, emphasis added)

> it seems to me that those who are able ought to employ this honorable liberty,
> which our sex formerly desired so much, in studying these things and show
> men the wrong they have done us in depriving us of the benefit and the honor
> which might come to us. (Wilson 149)

The reader notes with some irony that Labé's grammar is as exclusionary as the harsh law of men about which she is complaining. Systematically throughout the preface, she uses the first person plural *nous* to embrace both her readers—those whom she is exhorting to action—and herself. The men, referred to either as "les hommes" or *ils,* are evoked but not addressed in her preface. Prefatory discourse, which with few exceptions during the French Renaissance tended toward inclusion rather than exclusion, is transformed into an instrument of exclusion on the basis of gender. Learning, as distinct from jewelry and sumptuous clothing, is not a gift from the patriarchy—fathers, suitors, and husbands—but once acquired, belongs to women: "Mais l'honneur que la science nous procurera, sera entierement notre" (17, ll. 13–15) (But the honor which knowledge will bring us will be entirely our own) (translation mine).

Established at the outset of the preface, the bipolar opposition of *nous* (the community of women) and *ils* (the men) continues to function throughout. There is no reason why the second part of the preface, in which she talks about the benefits of writing to the well-being of the individual, could not include common, non–gender specific experiences shared by all writers. But the appropriation of *nous* and *notre* by the female community of writers ensures the exclusion of the male writer and reader:

> Mais quand il avient que mettons par escrit nos concepcions, combien que
> puis après notre cerveau coure par une infinité d'afaires et incessamment re-
> mue, si est ce que long tems après, reprenans nos escrits, nous revenons au
> mesme point, et à la mesme disposicion où nous estions. (19, ll. 61–67)

> But when we happen to put our thoughts into writing, even if afterward our
> minds race through no end of distractions and are constantly agitated, never-
> theless, returning much later to what we have written, we find ourselves at the
> same point and in the same state of mind we were in before. (Wilson 150)

In preferring the now gender-specific *nous* to the inclusive, nongendered *on*, Labé relegates the male sex to the mute state previously experienced by women under the "severes loix des hommes." Once empowered—in poetics, if not yet in legal matters—the female voice does not resist exclusionary grammatical practices.

The men whom Labé has barred from participating in her observations on the value of writing (ll. 38–82) make a surprise reappearance in the last lines of the preface. They have encouraged her to publish her work: "Mais depuis que *quelcuns* de mes amis ont trouvé moyen de les lire sans que j'en susse rien, et que (ainsi comme aisément nous croyons ceus qui nous louent) *ils* m'ont fait à croire que les devois mettre en lumiere" (ll. 82–86, emphasis added) (But since some of my friends found a way to read them without my knowing anything about it, and [thus we easily believe those who praise us] since they have persuaded me that I should bring them to light) (Wilson 150). Lest we interpret *quelcuns* to include men and women, we have an example of *quelcune,* the feminine form, used earlier in the preface, when she speaks of some women achieving fame and honor in letters: "Et si *quelcune* parvient en tel degré, que de pouvoir mettre ses concepcions par escrit, le faire songneusement et non dédaigner la gloire" (ll. 8–10) (And if anyone reaches the stage at which she is able to put her ideas into writing, she should do it with much thought and should not scorn glory) (Wilson 149). The friends who urged her to publish are male.

In spite of her exclusionary poetics in reserving her prefatory remarks for women and excluding men from the community of writers and readers whom she is addressing, Labé claims that her own voice would have remained silent—or at least unpublished—had it not been for the encouragement of her male friends. "Mettre par escrit nos concepcions" is one thing, making them public is another, and for that she needed two things: first, the encouragement of her male friends, more used to venturing out alone in public, and second, the presence of another woman as guide because women do not go out alone in public of their own free will: "Et pource que les femmes ne se montrent volontiers en publiq seules, je vous ay choisie pour me servir de guide, vous dediant ce petit euvre" (ll. 88–91) (And because women do not willingly appear alone in public, I have chosen you to serve as my guide, dedicating this little work to you) (Wilson 150). Clémence de Bourges serves the role of guide, and her reputation as a "jeune fille aux moeurs très pures" (young girl with very pure morals) will help protect the reputation of the author of the *Débat de Folie et d'Amour.*[10]

Along with their expressed reluctance to address a large, mixed audience, another characteristic that marks the prologues of the *conteuses* mentioned above is a tendency to adhere more strictly to the Boccaccian model than we notice in the prefatory discourse of the *conteurs*. These two traits are in fact interrelated in that Boccaccio addresses his work to the "graziosissime donne . . . quelle che amano," the refined ladies who love and seek relief from their suffering.[11]

Boccaccio assumes the posture of a kind of agent of justice, writing to redress the unequal treatment of the female sex by Fortune, who was so stingy in meting out relief and support to women who are unhappy in love.[12] He describes himself as a champion of the cause of the weaker sex, forcibly confined by the will of fathers, mothers, brothers, and husbands. In contrast to the harsh rule of the family, Boccaccio offers the "dilicate donne" entertainment and uplifting advice. Help comes from outside the restricted circuit of female discourse. Boccaccio's work is a lifeline held out to save the foundering women. That help could come from within the confined area of their rooms ("nel piccolo circuito delle loro camere") does not occur to Boccaccio. Inspiration must be sparked from without; the confinement is synonymous with silence and suffering.[13]

In adapting Boccaccian prefatory strategies to their particular circumstances, Jeanne Flore, Hélisenne de Crenne, and Louise Labé find their inspiration from within the confines of feminine company. From Madame Minerve, to whom Jeanne Flore dedicates her prefatory remarks, to the feminine circle of "cousines et amyes"—both tellers and listeners of the love tales told at the wine harvest—Jeanne Flore's narrative cadre is distinctly feminine. The allegorical names of the tellers—Madame Meduse, Madame Sapho, Madame Andromeda, Madame Cassandre—lend the weight of antiquity, but a distinctly feminine antiquity, to the *Contes amoureux*.

The impetus for writing down and publishing the tales does not extend beyond the pleasure and instruction of female readers. Unlike Boccaccio, Flore gives primacy to the pleasure factor: "Puis tout soubdain je me suis advisée que je feroys chose tres *agreable* et *plaisante* aux jeunes Dames amoureuses, lesquelles loyaulment continuent au vray service d'Amour, et lesquelles se *delectent* de lire telz *joyeulx* comptes, si je les faisois tout d'ung train gecter en impression" (*Contes Amoureux* 97, ll. 14–17, emphasis added) (Then suddenly I realized that I would do something very pleasant and agreeable for women who faithfully persist in love's loyal service and who take joy in reading merry tales, if I had them published at once).

She makes but one reference to a wider range of readers, in the context of an apology for her rough and disorganized style: "neantmoins soubs espoir que vous, et les humains lecteurs excuserez le rude et mal agencé langaige. C'est oeuvre de femme, d'où ne peult sortir ouvraige si limé, que bien seroit d'ung homme discretz en ses escriptz" (97, ll. 19–21) (Nevertheless, in the hope that you and other understanding readers will excuse the rough and poorly constructed language, it's woman's work from

which cannot be produced a work as polished as the writings of an unob-
trusive man). Going beyond the humility commonly found in most prefaces, Flore expresses concern that once her tales reach the world outside
the circle of women for whom and by whom they were conceived, they
will meet with disapprobation. The outer circle of "humains lecteurs" is
perhaps less humane and more critical. The *préfacière* is coming to grips
with reader expectation, and here unquestionably the well-fashioned
(*limé*) discourse of male authors sets the standards. Jeanne Flore is faced
with what Hélène Cixous calls the "tourment de la venue à la parole,"
woman's distress at realizing that when she speaks, she commits a transgression.[14] In so doing she suffers a double anguish, for while she speaks, she
violates not only the order that would have woman confined to silent listening but also the expectations of the audience whose ear is attuned to
the male voice. Set against the discourse of "un homme discretz," the female voice is by extension "indiscreet." Woman's literary production calls
attention to itself by the very fact of its status as "oeuvre de femme," while
man's work inserts itself unobtrusively in the mainstream of literary tradition.

Renaissance *conteurs* were not exempt from prepublication jitters.
Philippe de Vigneulles begs his readers to pardon his errors and to supply
their own corrections.[15] Flore sets apart her remarks with the statement
that her discourse is marked by faulty structure and can be differentiated
from that of "ung homme discretz en ses escriptz." Gender, as well as expectations established on the basis of gender, informs the reception of literary discourse.

Hélisenne de Crenne makes no mention of potential male readers in
her dedicatory epistle. Addressing her remarks to "toutes honnestes
Dames," she is specific in restricting her audience to the aristocracy: "c'est
à vous mes nobles Dames, que je veulx mes extremes douleurs estre com-
municquées. Car j'estime que mon infortune vous provocquera à quelques
larmes piteuses, qui me pourra donner quelque refrigeration medica-
mente" (*Angoysses douloureuses* 3, ll. 7–9) (it is to you, my noble ladies,
that I wish to communicate my extreme sorrows. For I believe that my
misfortune will draw from you pitying tears which will be a cooling medi-
cation to me) (Wilson 197). On her readers, Hélisenne places expectations
again based on gender and, more specifically, the female capacity for compassion. She seeks help from within the closed group of female listeners
and only from this group.

Marking her difference from Boccaccio, who writes to comfort others
only after his love has lost its force, Hélisenne writes out of self-interest in
the hopes that the tears and compassion of a sympathetic audience will
chill her passion.[16] Of secondary interest is her hope that the sight of her
suffering will serve as a warning to other women, that they may avoid love's
snares ("eviter les dangereux laqs d'amour," ll. 16–17).

Ending her epistle with an invocation to the Mother of Christ, "celle qui est mere & fille de l'altitonant Plasmateur" (4, ll. 22–23) (she who is mother and daughter of the high-thundering Creator) (Wilson 197), Hélisenne de Crenne makes it clear that help can come only from within the closed network of communication among women. By replacing the classical muses with a Christian muse, Hélisenne is substituting one feminine source of inspiration for another. The weak hand ("debile main") with which she writes must learn to write well ("bien escrire") under the tutelage of the Virgin Mary. Her act of omission—her refusal to admit the male agents of her suffering onto the prefatory pages of her work—effectively silences the male voice and obstructs the flow of either understanding or criticism from the male sector. She passes over in silence the role of the male *auctor* as source, model, and inspiration, a role that neither of her contemporaries Jeanne Flore or Louise Labé fail to acknowledge. Refusing an audience whose expectations she might disappoint, Hélisenne prefers not to compete with a group more experienced than she in public discourse; instead, she confines her audience to a group whose ear is attuned to a woman's halting efforts at self-expression.

Hélisenne retains the dedicatory address to her female readership in the second part of her *Angoysses,* dedicated "A toutes nobles & vertueuses dames." It becomes clear, however, that she envisions but does not yet directly address another audience made up of modern gentlemen—"les gentilz hommes modernes," who might be inspired to pursue "martial exercice" by the example of her *amy* Guenelic, whose voice she assumes in the second and third parts of the work (Secor, *Seconde Partie,* 147, l. 25). Preparing herself to speak in his voice ("parlant en la personne de son Amy Guenelic"), she evokes, as she had not done in the initial dedicatory epistle, the ultimate male *auctor,* Homer, and the authority of the *Iliad* in inspiring Alexander to virtuous action. She hopes that her "petit livre" will have the same effect. If Guenelic was importunate and overly persistent in pursuing his lady, his virtue should not be called into question, but the essence of the male sex, "car telle est l'humaine virile condition que durant le temps qu'ils n'ont encours jouy de la chose aymée, ilz ne pardonnent à aulcuns perilz puis que c'est pour parvenir d'avoir de leurs desirs contentement, comme vous aultres jeunes hommes le scavez" (Secor 149, ll. 87–92) (for such is men's natural bent that as long as they have not yet possessed the beloved, they spare no danger in seeking the satisfaction of their desires, as you other young men know). At the very moment in which she attacks a major flaw in the male character, she expands her readership to include the young male reader in her prefatory remarks.

The liminary voice immediately embraces a male readership in the opening of the third part of the *Angoysses.* In the second book, addressed to the noble and virtuous ladies, she had changed the opening address from the "lecteurs benevoles" to "mes dames benevoles"; thus she opted for a gender-specific form of address in lieu of a general address (Secor 146, l. 1, note). In the third book, she retains the inclusive "nobles lecteurs," but, as in the example above, inclusion has its price—criticism of man's character. Adam, not Eve, is held responsible for man's fall from grace: "Car si le premier homme n'eust esté ingrat envers celluy qui est autheur de tout—duquel il avoit receu tant de benefices,—il ne fust succumbé en la mortelle ruyne pecheresse dont en sont contaminez tous ses posterieurs" (ll. 4–8) (For if the first man had not been ungrateful to him who is the author of all things—from whom he had received so many blessings—he would not have given in to the fatal, sinful ruin by which all his descendants are tainted).

The goal of the third book aspires higher than the virtuous pursuit of martial arts. To help reinforce her plea to men not to give in to their sensual nature, she invokes the authority of Saint Paul—that apostle so often cited by men to criticize the inconstant nature of woman's virtue: "La chair & concupiscence, est adversaire de l'esperit ; & l'esperit est adversaire de la chair" (ll. 34–36) (Flesh and lust are the enemy of the mind; and the mind is the enemy of the flesh). Hélisenne's rhetorical trick is to appropriate the mind for women: "Mais qui sera ce, qui donnera port & faveur à l'esperit si ce n'est dame raison" (ll. 36–37) (But who will be the one to give bearing and favor to the mind if not Lady Reason). Intellect, so long thought to be a male province—as we see in Labé's preface—is here placed squarely in the female domain of Lady Reason. Sensuality is left as a male problem to be overcome through the reading of her *Angoysses* and with the female tutelage of Dame Raison: "Parquoy, je vous obsecre que d'elle ne vous distinguez aulcunement affin que par elle la sensualité succumbe & soit domptée" (ll. 40–42) (Wherein I implore you not to distance yourself from her, so that by her, sensuality may give way and be overcome). The *préfacière* has reversed the customary equation man = head, women = body.

Hélisenne's willingness to enter into the *Querelle des Femmes* is evident in not only the *Angoysses* but also her *Epistres invectives*. In Epistre IV, she denounces her correspondent Elenot for assuming letters and intellectual matters to be the province of men: "& par especial tu increpes & reprens la muliebre condition. Et parlant en general, tu dis que femmes sont de rudes & obnubilez espritz : parquoy tu conclus, qu'autre occupation ne doivent avoir que le filer" (*Epistres invectives*, ed. Grouleau, O iiii r°) (and you especially blame and disparage the female condition. And speaking in general terms you state that women's minds are uncultivated and obscured, wherefore you conclude that their only occupation should be spinning) (Wilson 209). She will not watch silently while woman is relegated permanently to the spinning wheel.

Louise Labé, in her turn, inverts Boccaccio's evocation of woman's preoccupation with spinning. In the midst of her appeal to women to take up studying and "en science et vertu passer ou egaler les hommes" appears a curious echo of an authoritative text:

> je ne puis faire autre chose que prier les vertueuses Dames d'eslever un peu leurs esprits par dessus leurs quenoilles et fuseaus, et s'employer à faire entendre au monde que si nous ne sommes faites pour commander, si ne devons nous estre desdaignées pour compagnes tant es afaires domestiques que publiques, de ceus qui gouvernent et se font obeïr. (18, ll. 26–33)

> I cannot do otherwise than beg virtuous Ladies to raise their minds a little above their distaffs and spindles and to exert themselves to make it clear to the world that, if we are not made to command, we ought not to be disdained as companions in domestic and public affairs by those who govern and command obedience. (Wilson 149)

It is not simply the allusion to distaffs and spindles that brings to mind the *proemio* to Boccaccio's *Decameron,* but what Michael Riffaterre refers to as an ungrammaticality in the adaptation of the intertext.[17] Boccaccio as prologuist writes to offer support, help, and refuge to those women who love ("quelle che amano"). For other women, the needle, distaff, and spinning wheel offer sufficient diversion ("per ciò che all'altre è assai l'ago e 'l fuso e l'arcolaio").[18] In Labé's image, the woman, not the man, is the productive scholar and writer, while the man is a passive witness to her creative activity and will in turn be inspired by her example: "Et outre la reputacion que notre sexe en recevra, nous aurons valu au publiq, que les hommes mettront plus de peine et d'estude aus sciences vertueuses, de peur qu'ils n'ayent honte de voir preceder celles, desquelles ils ont pretendu estre tousjours superieurs quasi en tout" (18, ll. 33–38) (And in addition to the recognition that our sex will gain by this, we will have furnished the public with a reason for men to devote more study and labor to the humanities lest they might be ashamed to see us surpass them when they have always pretended to be superior in nearly everything) (Wilson 149). Boccaccio, we remember, wrote for women because they were cooped up and had no outlet for their sorrows, while men could find distraction in hunting, fishing, riding, and other outdoor activities. Such constraint on woman's freedom to choose her own pastime is precisely what Labé refers to as the "severes loix des hommes" at the outset of her prefatory epistle. Yet the activities cited by Boccaccio are the pastimes of nobles—physical activities. Louise's ladies will use their new-found freedom to exercise the mind, not the body: "pour aquerir cet honneur que les lettres et sciences ont acoutumé porter aus personnes qui les suyvent" (18, ll. 42–44) (to acquire the honor that literature and the sciences are accustomed to bring those persons who follow them) (Wilson 149).

Her dialogue with the authoritative text and author continues as she argues that the pleasures of the senses—the subject of both the *Decameron* and her own book—pass quickly. Recording our thoughts provides a double pleasure, for we not only relive a pleasurable moment but also reflect on our state of mind at the moment the pleasure was experienced.

Even while generating a text that seeks to appropriate discursive practices for and by women, Labé implicitly engages a formidable *auctor* in a dialogue that might go unperceived without the play of the intertext. By appropriating the spinning motif or hypogram from Boccaccio and reversing key elements, she convincingly argues the case for woman's place as intellectual role model.[19] The demonstrated authority of the intertext only strengthens the weight of her argument. The prefatory epistle of Labé's *Débat* offers an example of the strategy of evoking a well-known authority—the storyteller of storytellers—to facilitate the appropriation of discourse by women.

Of the four most noteworthy *conteuses* of the first half of the sixteenth century, only Marguerite de Navarre breaks with the other women storytellers in insisting upon, in the first instance, an audience that includes both sexes. She, in a more explicit manner than Jeanne Flore, Hélisenne de Crenne, and Louise Labé, acknowledges her source of literary inspiration—Boccaccio and his *Decameron*—but rejects his address to an exclusively female audience. As stated earlier, the *je* who addresses the reader resists calling attention to the gender of either the sender or the receiver of the prologue. The unmarked voice of the primary narrator unveils the narrative frame with singular objectivity. The emotional suffering of the narrator, such an integral part of the prologues of Boccaccio and Hélisenne de Crenne, plays no role. If gender remains unmarked at the primary level, a fact that reinforces Philippe de Lajarte's notion of the transcendental character of the first narrative instance in the *Heptaméron*, gender assumes a prominent role at the fictional level of the frame.[20] Hircan clearly delineates the difference between male physical activities—the hunt—and female activities: handwork and dancing. Gender difference creates problems in choosing a common activity, as evidenced when Parlamente blushes as Hircan mentions his preferred pastime. In fact through dialogue agreement is reached in spite of evident differences in personality. We are far from the confined space of a uniquely feminine community, and attitudinal differences enrich the dialogue.

Within the fictional frame of the *Heptaméron,* efforts are made by the storytellers to respect everyone's right to speak. Hircan's comment at the outset that at play men and women are equal ("car au jeu nous sommes tous égaux") sets the tone (*L'Heptaméron* 10). The storytellers alternate spinning tales on the basis of gender. When Saffredent fears that parity between the sexes has not been respected, he comments that he has been granted the honor of beginning two days of storytelling and fears that the ladies will be wronged if one of them does not start off two more days: "Vous m'avez faict l'honneur d'avoir commencé deux Journées; il me semble que nous ferions tort aux dames, si une seulle n'en commençoit deux" (421) (You have given me the honor of beginning two days, and it seems to me that we would be committing an injustice toward the ladies if one of them did not in turn begin two).

Equal right to self-expression is thus foregrounded in the frame of the *Heptaméron*. Repeated reference to respecting woman's right to speak, the parity of numbers of both sexes within the fictional and historic context, mention of doing injustice to women—these are signs of an authorial strategy to put men and women on an equal footing. Such a strategy is supported on the narrative level by the events of individual tales.[21]

Why does Marguerite de Navarre shun the female circle of discourse preferred by Jeanne Flore, Hélisenne de Crenne, and Louise Labé in favor of a frame that establishes everyone's right to express an opinion? We noticed earlier that the primary narrator takes pains to avoid details that would call attention to the gender of either the prologue's sender or receiver. We can only speculate that, unlike the other *conteuses,* Marguerite de Navarre is an empowered voice, used to speaking out and to being heard. Details within individual tales show the influence of the Queen of Navarre in intervening politically on behalf of people who, through no fault of their own, have run afoul of an unjust authority.[22]

It is fitting that her work should refuse the Boccaccian tradition of addressing a purely female audience. Writing is presented as an activity open to participation and appreciation by both sexes, as evidenced by the narrator's mention that the *Decameron* was admired by Francis I, the Dauphin, his wife, and Marguerite herself (9). The historic effort by members of the court to generate a new work along the lines of Boccaccio's is not delineated along gender lines.

Marguerite's remarks make it clear that for her, literary production is an open line of communication. Whether she perceived that by clearly excluding male readers at the outset of the work, women writers were marginalizing their literary efforts, we can only speculate. But by refusing to call attention to the gender of either the originator or the receiver of her discourse, by failing to mention woman's lack of skill or practice in writing for publication, Marguerite de Navarre inserts her work in the mainstream of sixteenth-century literary discourse and secures for it a firm place among her fellow *conteurs*. In contrast, the works of her contemporary female *conteuses* are only beginning to emerge from the margins to which they had been relegated as a *discours de femme*. Had these women been speaking from the empowered position of the Queen of Navarre, they too may have used different prefatory strategies.

NOTES

1. Jeanne Flore, *Contes amoureux par Madame Jeanne Flore,* ed. Gabriel Pérouse et al. (Lyon: Presses Universitaires de Lyon, 1980), 97; Louise Labé, *Oeuvres complètes,* ed. Enzo

Guidici (Geneva: Droz, 1981). There are several editions of the works of Hélisenne de Crenne: *Les Oeuvres de Madame Hélisenne de Crenne* (Paris: Estienne Grouleau, 1560; reprint, Geneva: Slatkine, 1977); *Les Angoysses douloureuses qui procedent d'amours, Première Partie,* ed. Paule Demats (Paris: Belles Lettres, 1968); *Les Angoysses douloureuses qui procedent d'amours, Première Partie,* ed. Jérôme Vercruysse (Paris: Lettres Modernes, 1968); and Harry Rennell Secor, Jr., "Hélisenne de Crenne: *Les Angoysses douloureuses qui procedent d'amours* (1538). A Critical Edition based on the Original Text with Introduction, Notes, and Glossary," Ph.D. diss., Yale University, 1957. I cite from the Secor edition and note variants where pertinent. The *Contes amoureux* and the *Angoysses douloureuses* were published in 1537 and 1538, respectively. See the Pérouse edition of the *Contes amoureux* for an explanation of the date of publication, 22. The preface of the recent edition of the works of Louise Labé by François Rigolot (Paris: Flammarion, 1986) offers some insightful comments on the *Débat de Folie et d'Amour.* English translations of the works of Hélisenne de Crenne and Louise Labé are those of: Jeanne Prine, "Louise Labé: Poet of Lyon" and Kittye Delle Robbins-Herring, "Hélisenne de Crenne: Champion of Women's Rights," in *Women Writers of the Renaissance and Reformation,* ed. Katharina M. Wilson (Athens: University of Georgia Press, 1987), 136–157, 177–218. Other translations are mine unless specified to the contrary. I would like to express my thanks to Diane Wood of Texas Tech University for her suggestions on an earlier version of this paper.

2. Bonaventure Des Périers, *Nouvelles Récréations et joyeux devis,* ed. Krystyna Kasprzyk (Paris: Champion, 1980), 17.

3. *L'Heptaméron,* ed. Michel François (Paris: Garnier Frères, 1967), 10. The English text is taken from Marcel Tetel, "Marguerite de Navarre: The *Heptaméron,* a Similacrum of Love," in *Women Writers of the Renaissance and Reformation,* 99–131. All quotations in English from the *Heptaméron* are from this text.

4. Philippe de Vigneulles, *Cent Nouvelles Nouvelles,* ed. Charles H. Livingston with Françoise R. Livingston and Robert H. Ivy (Geneva: Droz, 1972), 58, l. 48.

5. Noël Du Fail, *Propos rustiques de Maistre Leon Ladulfi,* in *Conteurs français du XVIe siècle,* ed. Pierre Jourda (Paris: Gallimard, 1956); Philippe d'Alcripe, *La Nouvelle Fabrique,* ed. Françoise Joukovsky (Geneva: Droz, 1983); J. de Cholières, *Les Apres-disnées du Seigneur de Cholières* (Paris: Jean Richter, 1587); François Le Poulchre de la Motte-Messemé, *Le Passetemps* (Paris: Jean le Blanc, 1595).

6. Monique Wittig, "The Mark of Gender," in *The Poetics of Gender,* ed. Nancy K. Miller (New York: Columbia University Press, 1986), 63–73.

7. Wittig makes this point in her discussion of the subject pronoun *elles* as opposed to *ils;* see "The Mark of Gender," 69.

8. The editor notes that the rhymes of the dizains are all feminine, *Contes amoureux,* 95. For a discussion of the possible identity of Jeanne Flore and whether she existed in flesh and blood bearing the actual name Jeanne Flore or was a pseudonym invented by a group of men and women writing in Lyon, see the introduction to the edition of the *Contes amoureux par Madame Jeanne Flore* by Pérouse and his team of editors (Lyon: Presses Universitaires de Lyon, 1980), 42. They categorically oppose the identification of Jeanne Flore as Hélisenne de Crenne on the basis of major stylistic and ideological differences, 43–44. Most important to our argument, however, is that Jeanne Flore sought to address an exclusively feminine audience. In "Madame Jeanne Flore and the *Contes amoureux,*" *Bibliothèque d'Humanisme et Renaissance* 51, no. 1 (1989): 123–133, Régine Reynolds-Cornell suggests mixed authorship of the *Contes amoureux,* with active participation by Clément Marot. The fact that the work presents itself as a woman's work, with all the appropriate characteristics, suggests that the group, if indeed it was jointly authored, had in mind a distinct set of characteristics of feminine discourse.

9. François Rigolot (in collaboration with Kirk D. Read), "Discours liminaire et identité littéraire," *Versants* 15 (1989): 75–98. See also Rigolot, "Louise Labé et les Dames Lionnoises: les ambiguïtés de la censure," in *Le Signe et le texte: Etudes sur l'écriture au XVIe siècle en France,* ed. Lawrence D. Kritzman (Lexington, Ky.: French Forum Publishers, 1990), 13–25.

10. See Guidici's notes on Clémence de Bourges in Labé's *Oeuvres complètes,* 94. In *Renaissance Feminism, Literary Texts and Political Models* (Ithaca: Cornell University Press, 1990), Constance Jordan notes that Labé's appeal to women is less a direct challenge to male authority to command than an appropriation for herself, and ideally for other women, of the intellectual resources previously reserved for men (177).

11. Giovanni Boccaccio, *Opere di Giovanni Boccaccio,* ed. Cesare Segre (Milano: U. Mursia, 1978), 8. For the English translation, see Giovanni Boccaccio, *The Decameron,* trans. Mark Musa and Peter Bondanella (New York: W. W. Norton, 1982), 2.

12. *Decameron* 8: "Adunque, acciò che per me in parte s'ammendi il peccato della Fortuna, la quale dove meno era di forza, si come noi nelle dilicate donne veggiamo, quivi piú avara fu di sostegno, in soccorso rifugio di quelle che amano" (Therefore I wish to make up in part for the wrong done by Fortune, who is less generous in the support where there is less strength, as we witness in the case of our delicate ladies. As support and diversion for those ladies in love) (3).

13. In 1572, Jacques Yver closely takes up the Boccaccian model to dedicate his preface to the "belles et vertueuses demoiselles de France," *Le Printemps d'Yver* (Anvers: Guillaume Silvias, 1572), f. 2. In addressing the ladies as either "vertueuses, gracieuses, et bien apprises demoiselles" or "gentilles demoiselles," he shows his tie with the *Decameron.* Like Boccaccio, he writes to bring relief to the gentle ladies who find themselves confined by the religious wars and faced with too much leisure time: "lors que le trop de loisir vous ennuyera et s'efforcera de tromper cest ennuy" (f. 4) (when too much leisure time annoys you and moves you to while away the tedium). Again, the male from outside brings the ladies relief in the form of entertainment.

14. Hélène Cixous, "Le rire de la méduse," *L'Arc* 61 (1975): 43.

15. *Les Cent Nouvelles Nouvelles,* 58, ll. 39–43: "Sy prie et supplye à tous ceulx et celles qui les liront ou orront qu'ilz preignent le bien qu'ilz y verront et fuyent le mal qu'ilz y trouveront et qu'ilz me pardonnent les faultes qui y sont et les mettent à leurs corrections et amandement et veullent supplyer mon ygnorance et mon simple entendement" (So I beg and beseech those [men] and those [women] who will read them or hear them to take the good that they see in them and flee the bad that they find there, and may they pardon the flaws which are there and apply their corrections and changes along with my ignorance and simple mind).

16. *Decameron* 7: "il mio amore . . . per se medesimo in processo di tempo si diminuí in guisa" (my love . . . diminished by itself in the course of time) (2).

17. "Il s'agit d'une intertextualité que le lecteur ne peut pas ne pas percevoir, parce que l'intertexte laisse dans le texte une trace indélible, une constante formelle qui joue le rôle d'un impératif de lecture, et gouverne le déchiffrement du message dans ce qu'il a de littéraire, c'est-à-dire son décodage selon la double référence. Cette trace de l'intertexte prend toujours la forme d'une aberration à un ou plusieurs niveaux de l'acte de communication: elle peut être lexicale, syntaxique, sémantique, mais toujours elle est sentie comme la déformation d'une norme ou une incompatibilité par rapport au contexte. Donc une nongrammaticalité," "La trace de l'intertexte," *La Pensée* 215 (1980): 5–6 (It is a matter of intertextuality that the reader cannot fail to notice because the intertext leaves an indelible trace in the text, a formal constant that plays the role of a reading imperative and governs the decoding of the message in its literary content, that is its deciphering according to the double reference. This trace of the intertext always takes the form of an irregularity—on one or several levels—in the act of communication: it can be lexical, syntactic, semantic, but it is always experienced as a deformation of a norm or an incompatibility in relationship to the context. Hence an ungrammaticality). My thanks to François Rigolot for bringing this article to my attention. See also his article, "Gender vs. Sex Difference in Louise Labé's Grammar of Love," in *Rewriting the Renaissance: The Discourses of Sexual Difference in Early Modern Europe,* eds. Margaret W. Ferguson, Maureen Quilligan, and Nancy J. Vickers (Chicago: University of Chicago Press, 1986), 287–298.

18. *Decameron,* 8. In the translation of the *Decameron* ordered by Marguerite de Na-

varre and completed by Antoine Le Maçon, the same passage is translated into French as "Je veulx et entendz pour le secours de celles qui ayment (car il ne fault aux autres que lesguille, le fuzeau et le rouet)," *Le Decameron de Messire Iehan Bocace Florentin, nouvellement traduict d'italien* . . . , trans. Antoine Le Maçon (Paris: Roffet, 1545), f. 2.

19. For a description of the hypogram as the word's descriptive system, see Michael Riffaterre, *Semiotics of Poetry* (Bloomington: Indiana University Press, 1978), 43.

20. Philippe de Lajarte, "Le Prologue de l'*Heptaméron* et le processus de la production de l'oeuvre," in *La Nouvelle française à la Renaissance,* ed. Lionello Sozzi (Geneva: Slatkine, 1981): "Le *Je* transcendantal de l'Auteur *s'aliène* dans les *ils* des actants du récit (les sujets de l'énoncé) qui deviennent à leur tour des *je/tu* (destinateurs et destinataires) de l'énonciation . . . Au discours *monologique* de l'auteur-Sujet (discours centré autour d'un Signifié unique et absolu) se trouve substitué le discours *dialogique* des actants narratifs (discours décentré incluant l'altérité et la contradiction)," (402). (The author's transcendental "I" gets lost among the third person plural of the nominal phrases ["actants"] of the story [i.e. the subjects of the utterance] which in turn become the first and second person singular forms [senders and receivers] of the speech act . . . The dialogical discourse of the narrative nominal phrases [a decentered discourse that includes alterity and contradiction] substitutes to the monological discourse of the Subject-Author [a discourse centered on an absolute and sole signified]).

21. See my article, "The Representation of Discourse in the Renaissance French *Nouvelle:* Bonaventure Des Périers and Marguerite de Navarre," *Poetics Today* 3 (1985): 585–595.

22. Tale 22, the story of Sister Marie Héroët, is one such example.

Poolside Transformations
Diana and Actaeon Revisited
by French Renaissance Women Lyricists

ॐ

Kirk D. Read

J'allois resvant comme fay maintefois,
Sans y penser: quand j'ouy une vois,
Qui m'apela, disant, Nynfe estonnée,
Que ne t'es tu vers Diane tournée?

I was wandering dreamily along as
is my wont,/ With no thought in
mind: when I heard a voice,/
Which called out to me, saying,
"Poor, shaken Nymph,/ Why have
you not returned to Diana?"
(Louise Labé, Sonnet XIX, ll.
4–7)

During the French Renaissance, many writers turned (or returned) to the mythology of Diana as a rich source for poetic illustration and inspiration. For male poets in particular, Diana's infamous involvement in the transformation of Actaeon (as retold by Ovid) provided the highly suggestive framework of the lone, Petrarchan, lyric lamenter and the idealized, unattainable, perfect lover. Forever drawn to the dazzling, bathing Nymph, countless poets-as-Actaeon arrived at Diana's fountain only to each be metamorphosed, and then devoured by their own dogs. Maurice Scève, in his twenty-second dizain, makes the link between the all-powerful Diana and his "Délie" most explicit:

Comme Diane au Ciel me resserrer,
D'où descendis en ces mortels encombres;

. . . .

comme Lune infuse dans mes veines
Celle tu fus, es et seras DÉLIE,
Qu'Amour a jointe à mes pensées vaines
Si fort que Mort jamais ne l'en délie.[1]

M. P. Revoil, Portrait of Pernette du Guillet, 1830
(courtesy of Bibl. Municipale de Lyon).

To clench me like Diana of the skies,
From whence you descend to this mortal prison;

 · · · · · · · · · · · · ·

like the Moon infused into my veins
Thus you were, are and will ever be my "DELIE,"
Which Love has joined to my thoughts in vain
So tightly that Death shall never part us.

The spellbinding Diana-lover figure holds sway over each moment of the poet's emotions: "Celle tu fus, es et seras DELIE" (Thus you were, are and will ever be my "DELIE"). His every encounter tinged with the threat of instant annihilation, the poet makes of this impossible situation the poignant material of his lyric craft.[2]

In his praise of current scholarship that has investigated the appropriation of such myths in the works of early modern artists and writers, Leonard Barkan declares that "when he [the artist] depicts or alludes to a mythological story, he chooses the story and chooses an iconography that will serve his aesthetic and thematic purposes."[3] Though Barkan departs from this question to investigate the genesis and evolution of myths as entities unto themselves, we remain with the ideas of authorial intent for reasons which Barkan invites in his choice of pronouns. To look at this question through a gendered lens is to ask what happens when *she* "depicts or alludes to a mythological story" that may serve *her* "aesthetic and thematic purposes." Thus, we ask here, what become of Diana and Actaeon in the hands of a woman lyricist? How could (or *would*) a female contemporary of Maurice Scève appropriate this spectacularly threatening, yet attractive deity and her victim to describe a woman's poetic stance? While the modern feminist might easily imagine the empowering possibilities of such a bold and indomitable female deity as Diana, what of a sixteenth-century woman poet writing in a decidedly more proscriptive and judgmental milieu than her male counterparts?[4] Some answers can be found in the works of two of Maurice Scève's Lyonnaise compatriots: Pernette Du Guillet, the woman reputed to be his "Délie," and Louise Labé.

Published posthumously in 1545, Pernette Du Guillet's *Rymes* include a poem entitled by the editors "Elégie II" wherein she reenacts the Ovidian myth with a significantly modified conclusion. Ten years later, Louise Labé's "Sonnet XIX" from her *Euvres* treats the Diana-Actaeon story as well with important and telling changes in perspective. Individually, they represent two highly distinct responses to the material at hand. Collectively, however, they betray an evolution of sorts. With Pernette Du Guillet's *Rymes* very much in mind, it would seem, Louise Labé tells a different version of the events as a woman might experience them; she teaches us much of the potential of Diana and her community of Nymphs for the Renaissance woman poet. In the tradition of Ovid's *Metamorphoses* in general and of the Diana-Actaeon story in particular, these women betray a great attraction to the myth and enact startling transformations of their own.

Pernette Du Guillet's second elegy is most direct in its appropriation of Diana's divine power for her own ends. She begins with an expression of longing to take on the huntress's persona: "Combien de fois ay-je en moi souhaicté / Me rencontrer sur la chaleur d'esté / Tout au plus pres de la clere fontaine"(ll. 1–3) (How many times have I secretly wished / To find myself during the heat of summer / At the site of that clear fountain).[5] She is unquestionably virtuous, "bien accompaignée / D'honnesteté"(ll. 9–10), and she delights in the creative (and recreative) activity of her companions: Apollo, the Muses, and her nymphs. Her poet/lover, a trespassing mortal male, troubles this tranquil setting, however, and thus begins the all-important act of transformation.

Quite self-consciously, Du Guillet explicates her *translatio* of the Ovidian myth. Having plunged into the pool and splashed the approaching intruder with the fateful water, she first enacts the literary metamorphosis: "O qu'alors eust l'onde telle efficace / De le pouvoir *en Acteon muer*" (ll. 28–29, my emphasis) (If only this spray had such powers / As to transform him *into Actaeon*). Before any Ovidian metamorphoses can transpire, Du Guillet must first recast her lover in the person of Actaeon; only then can she begin her own transformations of the myth. In a first deferential move, the author decides (relying on a convenient play of words) that Actaeon will not become a stag (Cerf) but a servant (serf): "Non toutefois pour le faire tuer, / Et devorer à ses chiens, comme Cerf: / Mais que de moy se sensist estre serf" (ll. 30–32) (Not, however, in order to have him killed / And devoured by his own dogs, like a stag: / But that he be made to be my servant). For a brief moment, Du Guillet revels in the heady excitement of her newly acquired powers. Overcome with the enjoyment of this transformational feat, she feels herself surpassing its mythical potential: "Tant que Dyane en eust sur moy envie, / De luy avoir sa puissance ravie. / Combien heureuse, et grande me dirois! / Certes Deesse estre me cuyderois" (ll. 35–38) (Such that Diane would envy me, / For having stripped her of her powers. / How happy and great I would feel! / Certainly I would think of myself as a goddess).

The conclusion of the elegy, however, represents a gradual undoing of her fantasy wherein concern for her lover's livelihood and doubts about her own worthiness lead her to release the Actaeon/poet figure who may then live free to write the poetry of his unlimited, unfettered desire.

> Vouldrois je bien faire un tel deplaisir
> A Apollo, et aussi à ses Muses,
>
> .   .   .   .
> Ostez, ostez, mes souhaitz
>
> .   .   .   .
> Laissez le aller les neuf Muses servir,
> Sans se vouloir dessoubz moy asservir,
> Soubz moy, qui suis sans grace, et sans merite.
> $\qquad\qquad$ (ll. 40–41, 45, 47–49)

> Would I want to do such a disservice
> To Apollo, and to his Muses,

.   .   .   .
Take away, take away my desires
.   .   .   .
Let him go off to serve the nine Muses,
Without having to serve under me,
Under me, who am without grace and without worth.

Pernette Du Guillet abdicates the deific powers and resubjugates herself to
this lover. Her posturing as Diana is but a flight of fancy into which she
coyly enters and dutifully exits, retreating to a position wherein her lover
retains the power of authorial subjectivity.

In her insightful analysis of this poem, JoAnn DellaNeva sees Du Guillet's literary act here as crucial and highly indicative of harsh, sociohistorical
realities: "Du Guillet's fantasy was doomed to failure. Elegy two thus represents a moment of crisis for the female lover/poet, as she comes to realize that her rightful place is that of the silent object, not speaking maker,
of poetic discourse, by virtue of her sex alone."[6] DellaNeva partially tem-
pers this analysis of Pernette Du Guillet's elegy by suggesting that her decision to put pen to paper at all "in the face of conventions that could only
discourage the heterosexual female poet" (55) was heroic.[7]

Aside from reading Du Guillet's timidity here as symptomatic of every
Renaissance woman's struggle with poetic agency, however, we may consider her rewriting of Diana as a transformation of the myth that responded
to a personal, private, literary relationship with Maurice Scève. Du Guillet's
posturing as Diana, the goddess of the moon, is consistent with her repeatedly voiced portrayal of herself as the Moon or Night to Scève's ever
illuminating Sun or Day. She concludes "La Nuict" (Elégie III) with

Si m'esjouys en la clarté plaisante
De mon cler Jour, que je veis apparoistre,
Pour esclarcir ma nuict tresmal plaisante,
Comme il se faict assez de soy congnoistre.[8]

And so do I revel in the pleasant light
Of my bright Day, which I see appearing,
Which will illumine my unpleasant night,
As he appears more recognizable in the sky.

Du Guillet's gesture can be read as a logical and fitting transformation of
the Diana-Actaeon story that Scève could only have found responsive and
moving. How better to complement her lover/mentor than to take on the
identity of the goddess that Scève had assigned to her—the unattainable
goddess with which he has struggled so arduously—and to offer her back
to him in a fantasized union. Scève's dizain 383, "Plus croît la Lune et ses
cornes renforce," demonstrates, with the metaphor of the doctor and patient, the transformational power of his Délie's moon over his health. He

concludes: "Et quand je vois ta face à demi nue, / De patient en mort tu me transformes" (And when I see your half-naked face / From sickness to death you transform me). Thus, in Du Guillet's poem, her lover comes upon her naked in the pool, approaches, and *is set free;* he is cured of this life-threatening lovesickness.[9] In a poetry that often prescribes a poet's subjugation to her or his beloved regardless of gender, Du Guillet is answering a wish, both personal and monumental, of her long-suffering, literary companion.[10]

In so doing, Pernette Du Guillet describes the regular celestial phenomenon wherein the moon and sun appear in the sky together, neither's radiance obscuring the other. Thus, reading in a more positive vein, Pernette Du Guillet's decision *not* to metamorphose her lover is a most active transformation of the myth that leaves both she and he free to continue to write. Ultimately the fears she expresses of her lover's demise or subjugation may be in fact her own. Keeping him alive and unbound in her poetry perpetuates the conditions that occasion *her* poetic voice as well.

If we are tempted to despair over Pernette Du Guillet's retreat from Diana's transformational wiles as sadly indicative of her silenced voice, it may be useful to recognize the degree to which such abdication allowed for her poetry. By inscribing herself quite consciously into the Sun-Moon, Apollo-Diana construct already in place, she situates herself in a dialogue with one of the premier poets of Lyon, a desirable position for any poet at the time. Her controversial ending crowns this relationship by fulfilling her lover's dreams of an unthreatened life with his Délie/Diane, a solution to the Ovidian myth that leaves *both* lovers engaged in the literary debates and poetic conventions of the day.

Such a reading requires us to take Pernette Du Guillet on her own terms. If Antoine Du Moulin's introductory remarks to the *Rymes* hold true, Du Guillet's husband found her "petit amas de rymes" (small pile of rhymes) "parmy ses brouillars en assés povre ordre, comme celle, qui n'estimoit sa facture estre encor digne de lumiere"[11] (among drafts in rather poor order, as of one who did not yet find her work worthy enough to bring to light). Although it is reputed that she may have sung and performed various of these works in public, she never sought publication. Had not Du Moulin enthused so greatly, and presented them with such inspirational prefatory prose—that is, "Antoine Du Moulin Aux Dames Lyonnoizes"—her work and renown might well have died with her. Neither a polemicist nor a pacifist in the question of her right as a woman to create poetry, Du Guillet goes about her business. With no aspiration to please publishers, Pernette Du Guillet's primary forum is her private, scholarly companionship with Maurice Scève. Du Guillet's metamorphosis of Diana into a more sympathetic goddess is directly in keeping with the circumstances of her chosen, private, literary life.

Ten years later, in 1555, Jean de Tournes, who had published Pernette

Du Guillet's *Rymes,* brought to light the works of another well-known Lyonnaise figure, Louise Labé. Despite the similarities in provenance, gender, poetic genre, and publication, one may easily distinguish these women's works, particularly with respect to the treatment of the story of Diana and Actaeon.

From the very beginning, Louise Labé's *Euvres* betray the spirit of a woman conscious and proud of her publication—literally, the printed, public display of her passion and opinions. Her dedicatory letter to Clémence de Bourges defends her will and right to be heard in a highly polemic tone. She begins her work: "Estant le tems venu, Madamoiselle, que les severes loix des hommes n'empeschent plus les femmes de s'apliquer aus sciences et disciplines" (Now that the time has come, Mademoiselle, that the harsh laws of men no longer exclude women from the sciences and disciplines).[12] Such self-assurance often combines with unapologetic rhapsodies of visceral passion, nowhere more clearly witnessed than in her famous sonnet XVIII which begins

> Baise m'encor, rebaise moy et baise:
> Donne m'en un de tes plus savoureus,
> Donne m'en un de tes plus amoureux:
> Je t'en rendray quatre plus chaus que braise.

> Kiss me again, and again, and once more:
> Give me one of your most delicious ones,
> Give me one of your most amorous:
> I'll return you four that are hotter than coals.

When one contemplates, therefore, what such an unbridled and uninhibited voice might do with the power and playfulness of Diana, the temptation to revel seems irrepressible. What Labé does in her very next sonnet, however, is something quite different. Conventions are stretched, and roles and attitudes are questioned, explored and bemoaned, yet all in a much more quiet and cunning manner than might be expected.

Sonnet XIX is quoted and translated in full:

> Diane estant en l'espesseur d'un bois,
> Apres avoir mainte beste assenée,
> Prenoit le frais, de Nynfes couronnée:
> J'allois resvant comme fay maintefois,
>   Sans y penser: quand j'ouy une vois,
> Qui m'apela, disant, Nynfe estonnée,
> Que ne t'es tu vers Diane tournée?
> Et me voyant sans arc et sans carquois,
>   Qu'as tu trouvé, o compagne, en ta voye,

Qui de ton arc et flesches ait fait proye?
Je m'animay, respons je, à un passant,
   Et lui getay en vain toutes mes flesches
Et l'arc apres: mais lui les ramassant
Et les tirant me fit cent et cent bresches.

   Diane, hidden in the thick forest,
Having killed many a prey,
Sat relaxing, surrounded by her Nymphs:
I was wandering dreamily along, as is my wont,
   With no thought in mind: when I heard a voice,
Which called out to me, saying, "Pour shaken Nymph,
Why have you not returned to Diana?"
And seeing me with neither bow nor quiver,
   "What did you come across, my friend, on your way,
Who did away with your bow and arrows?"
"I attacked a passer-by," I replied,
   "And threw all of my arrows at him in vain
And then my bow: but he, picking them all up
And shooting them at me, wounded me over and over."

To characterize sonnet XIX as a "quiet" work within the entire *Euvres* is to claim that, initially, it bears great resemblance in tone to many of the other twenty-three sonnets. The lament over the injustices of unrequited love tinged with bitterness and a sense of hopelessness are part and parcel of the majority of poems from this section. Labé's particular retelling of the Diana-Actaeon material, however, opens the way for an interpretation that goes far beyond the personal, private commentary we saw privileged in Pernette Du Guillet's elegy. In this briefly sketched encounter, Louise Labé may well offer a broader critique of the conditions of women writers in the public sphere.

Sonnet XIX begins by invoking the powerful deity in all her posthunt splendor. The initial description of the weary huntress, deep in her wooded grotto, surrounded by attendant nymphs, closely mirrors the tone of the Ovidian version.

Vallis erat piceis et acuta densa cupressu,
nomine Gargaphie succinctae sacra Dianae,
cuius in extremo est antrum nemorale recessu
arte laboratum nulla

.   .   .   .

hic dea silvarum venatu fessa solebat
virgineos artus liquido perfundere rore.
Quo postquam subiit, nympharum tradidit uni
armigerae iaculum pharetramque arcusque retentos,
altera depositae subiecit bracchia pallae,
vincla duae pedibus demunt.

There was a vale in that region, thick grown with pine and cypress with their sharp needles. 'Twas called Gargaphie, the sacred haunt of high-girt Diana. In its most secret nook there was a well-shaded grotto, wrought by no artist's hand. . . . Here the goddess of the wild woods, when weary with the chase, was wont to bathe her maiden limbs in the crystal water. On this day, having come to the grotto, she gives to the keeping of her armour-bearer among her nymphs her hunting spear, her quiver, and her unstrung bow; another takes on her arm the robe she has laid by; two unbind her sandals from her feet.[13]

The fourth line of the sonnet reveals, however, that the narrator does not present herself as the goddess Diana, but as someone else. The speaker states, "J'allois resvant comme fay maintefois, / Sans y penser" (I was wandering dreamily along, as is my wont, / With no thought in mind). Recalling Ovid, we are most certainly meant to see in her an Actaeon figure—a hunter lost, half dreaming, on the edge of some sort of encounter. Ovid tells,

ecce nepos Cadmi dilata parte laborum
per nemus ignotum non certis passibus errans
pervenit in lucum: sic illum fata ferebant.

Io! Cadmus' grandson, his day's toil deferred, comes wandering through the unfamiliar woods with unsure footsteps, and enters Diana's grove; for so fate would have it. (ll. 174–176)

Rolfe Humphries's translation compares closely as well to the description in Labé. Actaeon arrives, "with no more thought of hunting, / Till the next day, wandering, far from certain, / Through unfamiliar woodland."[14] Curiously, then, we find Labé approaching the myth—and Diana—from a male perspective. Our expectations about the fate of this errant hunter (huntress?) are all the more troubled and uncertain.

In the poems preceding sonnet XIX, Labé has not shied away from Diana's powers. In her first elegy, presenting herself as the armed huntress, she admits to the cruel force of her lyre-become-bow: "O dous archet, adouci moy la voix, / Qui pourroit fendre et aigrir quelquefois" (O sweet bow, soften my voice, / Which can stab and bite at times) (ll. 17–18). Diana's fatal vision is summoned most explicitly in sonnet VI:

Tant emploiray de mes yeux le pouvoir,
Pour dessus lui plus de credit avoir,
Qu'en peu de temps feray grande conqueste.

I will use the power of my eyes so keenly,
Upon him in order to dominate him,
So that in little time I will have made my conquest.
(ll. 12–14)

Nonetheless, however willing Labé has been in the past to don Diana's deadly gaze, here in sonnet XIX, the most direct retelling of her adventures, she slips, at first, into the posture of Actaeon, the hunted. Labé's version of the story, however, is quickly redirected.

The most dramatic tension in the Ovidian myth is created during the moment of the actual encounter between the lost, unsuspecting trespasser and Diana. From Ovid,

> qui simul intravit rorantia fontibus antra,
> sicut erant nudae, viso sua pectora nymphae
> percussere viro subitisque ululatibus omne
> implevere nemus circumfusaeque Dianam
> corporibus texere suis.

> As soon as he entered the grotto bedewed with fountain spray, the naked nymphs smote upon their breasts at sight of the man, and filled all the grove with their shrill, sudden cries. Then they thronged around Diana, seeking to hide her body with their own. (ll. 177–181)

The Humphries translation states even more emphatically the crux of Actaeon's transgression: "The nymphs, all naked, saw *him,* saw a *man*" (62, my emphasis). Thus, Actaeon's sex alone generates first the frenzied screams and panic of the nymphs and then his eventual metamorphosis and destruction. At this crucial juncture in Labé's version, she exits the Actaeon mode and makes a further transformation of her character and our expectations for her fate.

Her dreamy wanderings are interrupted, she states, "quand j'ouy une vois, / Qui m'apela, disant, Nynfe estonnée, / Que ne t'es tu vers Diane tournée?" (when I heard a voice, / Which called out to me, saying, "Poor, shaken Nymph, / Why have you not returned to Diana?"). In great contrast to the Ovidian tale to which she has been so closely alluding, the wanderer in Labé's version is neither shunned nor greeted with panic or surprise. Rather, she is called out to and accepted as one of Diana's own. The newly delineated circumstances of their meeting make of this moment a decidedly more welcoming event.

We may return to Maurice Scève's *Délie* to observe the classical male lyric tradition with which Louise Labé is playing. In Scève's dizain 168, which accompanies the emblem of Actaeon—"Fortune par les miens me chasse" (Fate hunts me down with my own)—the image of the poet as victim is strongly conveyed. The preponderance of past participles gives echo to this sorry state:

> Alors le Coeur, qui un tel bien compasse,
> Laisse le Corps prêt à être *enchâssé,*
> Et si bien a vers l'Ame *pourchassé*
> Que de soi-même et du corps il s'étrange.

Ainsi celui est des siens *déchassé*
A qui Fortune ou heur ou état change.

So does the heart, when considering such beauty,
Leave the Body open to be *trapped*
And is so *pushed* toward the Soul
That it becomes foreign to itself and its body.
    Thus is one *hunted down* by one's own
Whose luck or state is changed by Fate. (ll. 5–10)[15]

So it is that men as the poet/hunters are metamorphosed and brought
face to face with their innermost selves. As Leonard Barkan posits, "what
Actaeon sees in the mirror after his transformation is for the first time a
sense of his own identity" (322). Therefore, not only does the Diana-
Actaeon myth serve as a rich reference for the unattainability of the perfect
lover, but it also, as in the case of Scève, describes the male poet's confrontation with himself. Besieged and transformed at the hands of his own
craft, the poet/hunter trembles forever in the crucial balance of living and
dying at his own hands. Just as the myth describes him, so will it destroy
him.

Louise Labé's wayward nymph is clearly not so threatened by Diana,
though her story remains no less compelling. If the Ovidian myth provides
the male Petrarchan poet with the powerful, oxymoronic tension between
attraction and repulsion, ecstasy and obliteration, its pertinence for a
woman poet such as Labé is quite different. Rather than informing a poetics of confrontation and abandonment, the story as retold in a woman's
voice and perspective, speaks to the privilege of female community and its
power as exemplified in the goddess Diana. Admittedly, the sonnet is by
no means deliriously celebratory; in the tercets, the nymph recounts her
defeat, and the poem closes on her despair. Yet the curious exit from this
story is ultimately, perhaps, testimony to a more positive and restorative
aspect of the depicted events.

The dramatic conclusion of Ovid's tale is the startling metamorphosis
and gruesome ravaging of the unfortunate Actaeon:

ille fugit per quae fuerat loca saepe secutus,
heu! famulos fugit ipse suos. Clamare libebat:
"Actaeon ego sum: dominum cognoscite vestrum!"

He flees over the very ground where he has oft-times pursued; he flees (the
pity of it!) his own faithful hounds. He longs to cry out: "I am Actaeon! Recognize your own master!"(ll. 228–230)

Actaeon's plight, as illustrated so forcefully by Scève, is that of being
hunted down, unrecognized by his old companions. Humphries's translation depicts Actaeon in this way, "Actaeon . . . once pursuer . . . is now

pursued, / Fleeing his old companions"(63). On the contrary, Labé's "Nynfe estonnée" is recognized, welcomed, and attended to. "Qu'as tu trouvé, *o compagne*" (What did you come across, my *friend*), she utters, in stark contrast to the address given to Actaeon. Labé subverts the Ovidian metamorphosis with a poignant transformation of her own. Actaeon, or the Actaeon figure in the story as she has told it, undergoes an intratextual metamorphosis from Actaeon to Nymph. As with Pernette Du Guillet's rendition of the myth, a major figure in the story (this time Actaeon) has been radically rewritten. Again the question is begged, To what end? How does this feminization of Actaeon and the concomitant redirection of the original tension of the transformational act speak to Louise Labé's differing poetic agenda? The conclusion of sonnet XIX offers a response.

The drama of the Diana-Actaeon encounter is accomplished within the quatrains of the sonnet. The last line of the second quatrain, "Et me voyant sans arc et sans carquois" (And seeing me with neither bow nor quiver), sets up the tercets that comprise a dialogue between the two reunited Nymphs. The narrator's friend interrogates her as to her sorry, beleaguered state, and she responds with the sad tale of an unsuccessful hunt. The description of her desperate, pathetic state—having shot all her arrows and thrown her bow in panic—contrasts sharply with Diana, relaxing, "Apres avoir mainte beste assenée." Her humiliating defeat at the hands of her own arrows further echoes the cruel demise of Actaeon, devoured by his own dogs. As witnessed in Scève's emblem "Fortune par les miens me chasse," this poet/hunteress's Fate as well attacks from within. Rather than read this "within," however, as indicative of what Barkan described as the perennial contention with the "holy" or "beastly form of [her]self as a hunter," or with her "psyche"(322), we propose a confrontation that takes place "within" Louise Labé's social and literary milieu.

Indeed, Louise Labé's sonnet XIX is surrounded by ample evidence to suggest that Diana and her community of nymphs may, in an important way, be read as emblematic of the author's desired, and often directly summoned, community of Lyonnaise women contemporaries: the "Dames Lionnoizes." Although it is undeniable that Louise Labé was in close contact with the famous, *male* literary figures of her city—witness the entirely male-authored set of homages at the end of her *Euvres*—the constituency that she cultivates most explicitly within her own writing is female.

Her work is dedicated to her friend, "Clémence de Bourges, Lionnoize" whom she encourages in her dedicatory letter to "mettre en lumiere un autre qui soit mieux limé et de meilleure grace" (bring to light another which might certainly be more polished and eloquent). The first elegy includes the supplication "Dames, qui les lirez, / De mes regrets avec moy soupirez" (Ladies, who read this, / Mourn with me over my unhappiness)—a group of women later qualified in the third elegy: "Quand vous lirez, ô Dames *Lionnoises,* / Ces miens escrits pleins d'amoureuses noises

. . . Ne veuillez pas condamner ma simplesse" (When you read, o ladies *of Lyon*, / These my writings filled with love's trials . . . Please don't condemn my simplicity). Further on in this same elegy, Labé names herself within this group as she passes the narrative voice to Amour who says to her: "Tu penses donq, ô Lionnoise Dame, / Pouvoir fuir par ce moyen ma flame" (You think, o lady of Lyon, / That you will be able thus to avoid my flame). Having opened the *Euvres* with an address to her dearest Lyonnaise contemporary, Labé closes, in her twenty-fourth sonnet, with a final address to their female coterie: "Ne reprenez, Dames, si j'ay aymé: / Si j'ay senti mile torches ardentes" (ll. 1–2) (Don't condemn me, ladies, if I have loved: / If I have felt the flame of a thousand burning torches). Given such a highly constructed frame of reference to this female community, the sorority of Diana and her nymphs as depicted in sonnet XIX may provide further intertextual resonance to Labé's desire for her women contemporaries' sympathy and companionship.

Lament is the mode common to both the dialogue between the nymphs in sonnet XIX and to the plea for dialogue demonstrated in Labé's repeated evocations of the "Dames Lionnoises" throughout her entire work. As is evident from the context of the various inscriptions of the "Dames Lionnoises," Labé's preoccupation during these addresses is the question of censure and acceptance given her audacious foray into the public, literary arena. She continually demands pardon, having exposed the "ennuis, despits et larmes" (suffering, disappointments and tears) of the "jeune erreur de ma fole jeunesse" (naive misfortunes of my youthful folly) (Elegy III, ll. 3, 6). As François Rigolot convincingly demonstrates, however, Louise Labé's *Euvres* as a whole work to unite rather than oppose the author and her presumed lady censors. Having quoted Labé's opening to her epistle to Clémence de Bourges, François Rigolot states,

> A la censure fictive qu'imposaient les "Dames" à l'intérieur du texte fait place un autre type de sanction sociale. Les "severes loix des hommes" ont remplacé les non moins sévères lois des femmes qui jugeaient la *persona* de Louise au tribunal des bonnes moeurs. La revendication de l'"honneste liberté" de se cultiver *contre* les préjugés masculins permet d'unir les "Dames Lionnoises" entre elles et de présenter un front commun au-delà de leurs divisions intestines.[16]

> The fictive censorship wielded by the "Dames" within the text gives way to another type of social sanction. The "severes loix des hommes" (harsh laws of men) have replaced the no less harsh laws of the women who judged the persona of Louise in the court of proper conduct. The revindication of the "honneste liberté" (proper right) to express oneself *despite* men's prejudices serves to unite the "Dames Lionnoises" amongst themselves so as to present a common front which might rise above their internal disagreements.

Whereas the "Dames Lionnoises" may well be feared by Labé as the moral arbiters of her unrestrained poetry, there exists a higher, harsher judge of her (and of her friends') actions: male authority. As Rigolot rightly leads us to surmise, these repeated references to the ladies of Lyon may ultimately serve as a unifying gesture that helps to define an oppositional community.

In such a view then, the battle-worn nymph of sonnet XIX speaks as a woman besieged by more than the resistant and overpowering "passant." As Actaeon was devoured by his own hounds, and as the nymph is wounded by her own arrows, so might Labé be "hounded" and beset in her pursuit of a place within male, literary society. So, at the peaceful and fiercely protected pool of Diana, does she find a respite from this confrontation. Her companion reaches out, listens, comforts, and encourages in much the same way that Labé asks her female contemporaries not to judge, but to encourage; not to remain silent, but to join her; she pleads the "vertueuses Dames" to "eslever un peu leurs esprits par-dessus leurs quenoilles et fuseaus" (lift their minds a bit above their distaffs and spindles).[17] The sonnet's opening tableau of Diana surrounded by her friendly nymphs, thus becomes a utopian vision of retreat for Labé's female compatriots. Diana, the all-powerful deity who begins the sonnet described in such confidence and splendor, presides over this potential, literary gynaeceum.

———

Such a positive reading of Labé's sonnet XIX, an admittedly mournful lament, is best qualified perhaps in two interconnected ways. First, the women's dialogue that Labé privileges in her sonnet and mirrors throughout her text in the "Dames Lyonnoises" topos is clearly *potential*. As much as the reputation of the learned ladies of Lyon thrived in the early part of the sixteenth century, no all-female *salon*, or indeed a great deal of women's publishing, can be shown to have existed. Thus, our characterization of Labé's community-building strategies is presented as strictly textual, utopian, visionary. The case of Pernette Du Guillet should serve to remind us, however, that such a lack of community did not entirely impede women's unpublished literary engagement. As Du Guillet's writing desk full of poetry attests, women of Lyon, perhaps more than the few we know of, developed the lyric craft and remained very much engaged in the creative, scholarly debates of their day. In this way, Pernette Du Guillet's conciliatory Diana represents the quiet, yet fruitful exchange between male and female poets of her society. Redescribing Diana as a goddess of compromise, Pernette Du Guillet relates a personal story of a private, demure, yet unquestionably productive life of letters.

Second, Louise Labé's *Euvres* in general, and her sonnet XIX in particular, show an indebtedness to, perhaps even dependence upon, the publication of Pernette Du Guillet's *Rymes*. In fact, Antoine Du Moulin's prefatory work "Aux Dames Lyonnoizes" informs much of the community-building rhetoric upon which Louise Labé relies. His epistle to the ladies of Du Guillet's great, learned city is a virtual paean to the intelligence and literary potential of her compatriots. He encourages them to follow in her example.

> . . . les Cieux nous enviantz tel heur la nous ravirent, ô Dames Lyonnoises, pour vous laisser achever ce qu'elle avoit si heureusement commencé: c'est à sçavoir de vous exerciter, comme elle, à la vertu: et tellement, que, si par ce sien petit passetemps elle vous a monstré le chemin à bien, vous la puissiez si glorieusement ensuyvre . . . (2–3)

> . . . and Heaven, so envious of our great fortune, took her from us, o ladies of Lyon, in order that you might finish that which she so beautifully began: that is to say, to encourage you, as she, to great virtue: so that if by this the product of her leisure hours she has shown you the true path, you may then just as gloriously follow in her steps . . .

Antoine Du Moulin's incitement only builds as he speaks of the perfect conditions, both intellectual and climatic, in which these ladies live for creating poetry. He praises "la vivacité des bons espritz, qu'en tous artz ce Climat Lyonnois a tousjours produict en *tous sexes*" (the liveliness of spirit that this Lyonnaise climate has produced for all the arts in *both sexes*) (3, my emphasis). Du Moulin concludes his lengthy epistle with a long defense of the virtuousness of his audience and counsels the ladies of Lyon to dismiss their critics who are but "asses chewing thistles"(4).[18]

Louise Labé's dedicatory epistle to the *Euvres* only reinforces this incitement through the example of Clémence de Bourges whom she encourages in like manner to better her own, personal efforts. So do her multiple evocations of the "Dames" mirror Du Moulin's persistent address while at the same time attending to the sensitive issues of censureship and cooperation. Yet, as is obvious from Labé's decision to publish, her poetry transcends the private realm of a concealed, literary correspondence and takes on the polemics and the risks of a woman's public voice. For this, she must offer defense, encouragement, and, as our reading of sonnet XIX suggests, a vision of how this might be possible. Whether or not the mythologically inspired community exists or will exist for her, its textual inscription is of high importance. Thus, from a woman lyricist's privileged perspective, her huntress, though hunted, need not fear annihilation. Her feminized Actaeon may well be on the verge of metamorphosis, but it will be a welcome transformation of a lonely and threatened life into a supportive, nourishing companionship.

NOTES

1. Maurice Scève, *Délie*, ed. Françoise Charpentier (Paris: Gallimard, 1984) 22, ll. 3–4, 7–10. The dizain presents a comparative study of two faces of the goddess beginning with Hecate ("Comme Hecaté tu me feras errer"), known as the "Artemis of the crossroads." This malevolent association is countered by the more positive, though no less riveting, invocation of Diana herself. Translations throughout this essay are my own.

2. Gisèle Mathieu-Castellani has done important work on the use of the Diana figure by male writers of the sixteenth century and later. See in particular "La Figure mythique de Diane dans *L'Hécatombe* de d'Aubigné," *Revue d'Histoire Littéraire de la France* 78, no. 1 (1978): 3–18; "Le Nombre et la lettre; pour une lecture du sonnet XCVI de *L'Hécatombe à Diane* de d'Aubigné," *Revue des Sciences Humaines* 51, no. 179 (1980): 93–108; and "Lune, Femme: l'image de Diane chez Théophile et Tristan," *Onze Nouvelles Etudes sur l'image de la femme dans la littérature française du dix-septième siècle,* ed. W. Leiner (Tubingen: Narr, 1984), 39–44. In "Lune, Femme," Castellani argues convincingly of the triple heritage of Diana that informs all sixteenth-century readings of the goddess: the virgin (as pertaining to Actaeon), the unfaithful (as with Endymion), and the diabolical (Hecate, the sorceress). So it is that Scève can be seen playing with these associations, enhancing and deepening the spell cast by such a multivalent mythological figure.

3. Leonard Barkan, "Diana and Actaeon: The Myth as Synthesis," *English Literary Renaissance* 10 (1980): 317. See also his book-length study *The Gods Made Flesh: Metamorphosis and the Pursuit of Paganism* (New Haven: Yale University Press, 1986).

4. A number of current scholars of early modern women's writings have addressed the question of female writers' contention with societal proscription. See in particular the seminal works by Ann R. Jones, "Surprising Fame: Renaissance Gender Ideologies and Women's Lyric," in *The Poetics of Gender,* ed. Nancy K. Miller (New York: Columbia University Press, 1986), and Merry E. Wiesner, "Women's Defense of Their Public Role," in *Women in the Middle Ages and the Renaissance: Literary and Historical Perspectives,* ed. Mary Beth Rose (Syracuse: Syracuse University Press, 1986).

5. Citations of Pernette Du Guillet will be taken from her *Rymes,* ed. Victor Graham (Geneva: Droz, 1968). Translations are my own.

6. JoAnn DellaNeva, "Mutare/Mutatus: Pernette Du Guillet's Actaeon Myth and the Silencing of the Poetic Voice," in *Women in French Literature,* ed. Michel Guggenheim (Saratoga, Calif.: Anma Libri, 1988), 55.

7. In a similar vein, Gisèle Mathieu-Castellani's recent essay, "Parole d'Echo? Pernette au miroir des *Rymes*" (*L'Esprit Créateur* 30, no. 4 [1990]: 61–71), tends toward this more redemptive reading of Du Guillet's elegy. She states: "En dépit de la censure qui dicte une fin conventionnelle au roman de libération, le rêve de maîtrise élaboré sous le couvert d'une fantaisie continue à dire le souci qu'a la rêveuse de naître à elle-même, à l'écart des discours et des mythes aliénants" (68) (In spite of a censure that dictates a conventional ending to the novel of liberation, the dream of a control elaborated beneath the cover of fantasy conveys the concern the dreamer has of being born to her self, apart from alienating discourses and myths).

8. Elégie III, "La Nuict," ll. 184–189. Victor Graham enumerates the multiple references of Scève as "Jour" beginning with Epigramme II: "commençay louer à voix haultaine / Celuy qui feit pour moy ce Jour au Monde" (I began praising aloud / He who was for me the Light of the World) (cf. ed. Graham 9, n.4).

9. In a line of argument not to be pursued within this context, it might be suggested that abandonning, or at least weakening, Diana's fiercely enforced code of chastity was far more transgressive than even presuming to take on her name in the first place.

10. Again, with respect to Du Guillet's role in the student-mentor relationship that informs the playfulness of this description, Mathieu-Castellani tends toward an interpretation of the Diana figure as being much more self-serving, even sadistic ("Parole d'Echo?" 67).

11. "Antoine Du Moulin Aux Dames Lionnoizes," *Rymes,* 1–4.

12. Louise Labé, *Oeuvres Complètes,* ed. François Rigolot (Paris: Flammarion, 1986), 41. All further citations from Labé will refer to this edition. A full translation of Louise Labé's epistle can be found appended to my essay, "Louise Labé in Search of Time Past: Prefatory Strategies and Rhetorical Transformations," *Critical Matrix* 5 (1990): 63–88.

13. Ovid, *Metamorphoses,* ed. and trans. F. Miller (Cambridge: Harvard University Press, 1977), Book III, ll. 155–158, 163–168. All citations and translations conform to this edition unless otherwise noted.

14. Ovid, *Metamorphoses,* trans. Rolfe Humphries (Bloomington: Indiana University Press, 1955), 62.

15. Scève, *Délie,* 145, my emphasis. The original text is clearly crucial to my interpretation here given the common root, "chasser." The emblem depicts Actaeon, with just his head transformed, surrounded by his angry dogs.

16. François Rigolot, "Louise Labé et les 'Dames Lionnoises': les ambiguïtés de la censure," in *Le Signe et le Texte: Etudes sur l'écriture au XVIᵉ siècle en France,* ed. Lawrence Kritzman (Lexington, Ky.: French Forum, 1990) 23.

17. Dedicatory epistle, 42.

18. "Qu'il fault necessairement que les Asnes voisent tousjours à leurs chardons."

Catherine Des Roches's
Le Ravissement de Proserpine
A Humanist/Feminist Translation

℘

Tilde Sankovitch

In late 1585 or early 1586 Catherine des Roches writes from Poitiers to her publisher, Abel L'Angelier, in Paris, to excuse herself for being late with a promised manuscript, namely the translation—obviously discussed and arranged between them sometime before—of Claudian's *De Raptu Proserpinae* (*DRP*). Her letter, in the precious style typical of much of Catherine's correspondence, explains: "Monsieur, cette gentille Proserpine qui voit par vous le ciel français, désire de vous saluer, et peut-être se plaindre de moi, de ce qu'ayant, je ne sais comment, rendu plus étroite la belle robe blanche et noire qu'elle avait reçue de votre libérale courtoisie, je suis encore si tardive à l'en accoutrer" (Sir, that amiable Proserpina, who, thanks to you, will see the French sky, wishes to send you greetings, and maybe to complain about me, for, after having, I don't know just how, narrowed the beautiful black and white dress which your generous courtesy had awarded her, I have still delayed dressing her in it). Her excuse for the delay: "La maladie de ma mère m'a fait imaginer en telle crainte le règne ténébreux, que je n'ai su le décrire" (My mother's illness has caused me to imagine the dark underworld with such fear, that I was unable to describe it). However, now that her mother is better she has been able to return to work, and she gives a progress report (no preciosity here!): "J'ai transcrit les deux premiers livres de Claudian, espérant d'achever bientôt le troisième tout d'un fil" (I have transcribed the first two books of Claudian, and I hope to finish the third at one stretch). In her next letter to L'Angelier she announces: "La fille de Ceres s'en va en espérance de vous trouver, et vous suppliant humblement la recevoir, je n'ose vous recommander d'en avoir soin,

55

craignant montrer une défiance de vous en qui chacun se doit fier. Je ne puis aussi ne vous la recommander point, vue l'affection que je lui porte" (The daughter of Ceres has gone forth in the hope of finding you, and begging you humbly to receive her, I dare not recommend her to your care, fearing to show a lack of trust in you, in whom everyone must trust. But I am also unable not to recommend her, since I feel such great affection for her). She goes on to discuss the other pieces, besides the translation, which will make up the forthcoming volume, and its title. She leaves it to L'Angelier, as "godfather" of the book, to choose a name, but she suggests "Missives ou lettres ou Epistres" because indeed letters by herself and her mother compose well over a third of the book; Catherine believes that such a title might pique the curiosity of the public and maybe encourage sales. Because this will be the first collection of letters by women to be published in French, she might well be right. In any case, the book appears in March or April of 1586 with the title: *Les Missives de Mes-dames des Roches de Poitiers, mère et fille. Avec le Ravissement de Proserpine prins du Latin de Clodian. Et autres Imitations et meslanges poëtiques.*[1]

What had prompted Catherine to translate that particular text? Composed in the late fourth century, Claudian's poem was largely ignored from the seventh through the eleventh centuries, but a renewal of interest and enthusiasm occurred in the twelfth century and continued for a long time. In the fourteenth century Chaucer and Petrarch, among others, knew *DRP* well, and, from the beginning of printing on, editions are plentiful.[2]

Catherine des Roches would thus have encountered no problem in obtaining a good, usable, Latin text for this, the first French translation, and I have not been able to determine just which edition she used. It is tempting to speculate that she discussed her project with Joseph-Juste Scaliger, who, in 1574, came to live in the Poitou and became a frequent visitor "in the pleasant Poitevin salon of Madame and Mademoiselle des Roches."[3] He had great respect for the two women and translated in Greek Catherine's "Stances au Roy"—a translation that was published with the original in the 1579 *Oeuvres de Mes-dames des Roches de Poitiers, mère et fille. Seconde édition,* also published by L'Angelier, and prefaced by Scaliger's remark that the original is the work of the "eruditissima puella ac Poetrïa, Catherine des Roches." In 1603, Scaliger publishes an edition of *DRP* in Leiden.[4] Who sparked whose interest in the text? The translator in the editor, or vice versa? We may see here one of these not so rare coincidences of humanist interests focused on the same subject. *DRP* was well known by the Italian Humanists, such as Poliziano, whose writings were familiar to the Dames, as well as by the French Humanists.[5]

But beyond that erudite recognition of a fashionable Latin text and the humanist desire to engage in the enterprise of translation, the myth of Ceres and Proserpina is of particular interest to Madeleine and Catherine des Roches. It is clear they hear in it echoes of a theme that rings constantly throughout their own works, as it forms the justification and structure of their poetic undertaking: the mother-daughter bond seen as a guarantee of creative life.[6] The Dames des Roches saw very clearly the problems that the desire for poetic creativity and the need for interaction with predecessor-poets pose, especially for women, notably the problem of intellectual access to the Greek and Latin texts. Constance Jordan has pointed out that "the profession of letters was legally open to women in the sixteenth century, however difficult of access it was in practice," and she, after describing some of these difficulties, concludes that the lives most women led presented "real obstacles to any authorship to which they might aspire."[7] It is therefore no wonder that Madeleine and Catherine des Roches feel that women are not meant to study and to write (inseparable activities for all would-be humanist authors); moreover, Madeleine protests several times through her work against what she sees as an unjust prohibition imposed by the conventions of a society that destines women for domestic rather than intellectual and artistic work.

The male poets of the French Renaissance see themselves as the legitimate heirs to a long and exalted poetic tradition, both mythological (Apollo, Orpheus) and actual, namely "les poëtes antiques, / Ces grands Démons humains" as Jodelle calls the classical models.[8] This conviction of belonging to a prestigious tradition, and to the no less prestigious institution of French contemporary poetry, confers on these poets considerable self-confidence and creative assurance. For women writers, those attributes are not so easily acquired.

The Dames des Roches develop several stratagems to establish poetic self-confidence, and the main one, the one that concerns us here, is the valorization of the intimate bond between themselves. To penetrate into the almost exclusively male sphere of humanist learning and writing is no small undertaking for women, and only by dint of their constant cooperation and reciprocal encouragement are Madeleine and Catherine des Roches able to initiate and continue the work they see as the core of their lives: poetry is made possible for them as a mother-daughter activity. All their volumes include an "Epistre à ma Fille" and an "Epistre à ma Mère," letters to each other in which they reaffirm their creative inseparability and interdependence. In these letters, and throughout their work, they write their own "mother/daughter plot" (to use Marianne Hirsch's expression),[9] and structure it as a continuation of their primary connection, that of birthing and of giving birth, of giving and receiving life. That connection, both biological and intellectual/creative, runs in an unbroken flow between them. Their poetic creativity is made possible by their inseparability, which nothing or nobody is to interrupt or disrupt. They maintain, in their life as in their work, an exceptional—pre-Oedipal—mother/daughter closeness that a strong male presence could only disturb. Catherine is the only surviving child of Madeleine's first marriage, and her father died when she was five years old. Madeleine remarried, but her second husband seems not to have come, in any way, between mother and daughter; nor was there the distraction of another child. Catherine steadfastly refused to marry in order not to be separated from her mother, and they die the same day, October 11, 1587, of the plague that ravaged Poitiers.

The Ceres-Proserpina myth appeals to Catherine because she sees in it the indispensable closeness that has made her a poet. At the same time, she is able to escape from the myth's anxiety because no male intervention has ever separated her from her mother, as Proserpina was forcefully separated from Ceres. In Catherine's life no loss occurs such as tears the goddess from her child, and no "compromise solution" is needed,[10] such as the one that allows Proserpina to spend part of her time with her mother.

That the Dames des Roches's closeness was not a fact applauded by their contemporaries is demonstrated by Etienne Pasquier, a friend and frequent visitor to the Dames, who, no doubt expresses a generally held opinion when he comments disfavourably on Catherine's decision to remain unwed: "Il n'y a qu'une chose qui me déplaise en cette maison, qu'étant la fille belle en perfection, tant de corps que d'esprit, riche de biens, comme celle qui doit être unique héritière de sa mère, requise en mariage par une infinité de personnages d'honneur, toutefois elle met toutes ces requêtes sous pieds: résolue de vivre et mourir avec sa mère"[11] (There is but one thing which displeases me in that house, and that is the fact that the daughter, perfectly beautiful in body and mind as she is, rich in property, since she is her mother's only heir, has been asked for her hand in marriage by a great number of highly placed men, yet has refused all these proposals, determined to live and die with her mother).

In refusing marriage Catherine refuses the exigencies of the myth that prescribe mother/daughter separation, as well as the demands of the biological/economic circulation that allows society—"la société productrice-reproductrice" as Kristeva calls it—to perpetuate itself.[12] By their determined and exclusive togetherness the Dames des Roches are able to salvage the narrative of their life from the "patriarchal reality"[13] in which the story of Ceres and Proserpina remains inscribed through the force of the ravisher's intervention. Yet the Dames have been made to feel the pressure of tradition and of "normalcy," in favor of Catherine's marriage. The possibility of separation, existing as it did in their society's expectations, was constantly held before them as the "normal" and therefore desirable way of being. In translating *DRP* Catherine writes the nightmare from which she and her mother escape: the nightmare of a sundering all the more complete because Claudian's text stops with the rapt and does not relate the partial restoration of Proserpina to her mother. As a potential victim of the "normal" mother/daughter separation—a potentiality that, in her case, remains unfulfilled—Catherine is aware of the danger, which she defines as creative death, and of her own escape.

Man-as-intruder and the connected woman-as-victim emerge as themes: these themes also define the structure of the Ceres-Proserpina myth, and it is therefore no wonder that *DRP* appealed deeply to Catherine. This text, out of the canon accepted by the Humanists, must have spoken to Catherine with the familiarity of her own voice, her own fear, her own refusal.

Let's explore now how Catherine des Roches treats Claudian's poem and in effect makes it her own invention. As she started on her translation project, she was certainly aware of the fact that the subject and problem of translation were among the foremost preoccupations of her contemporaries, as various and often opposing attitudes toward the philosophy of "interpretation linguarum" were formulated by humanist scholars. Two main bodies of thought—one trying to define translation in terms of method and code, the other acknowledging the interpretative/creative aspects of the translating act—dominate the debates that, not surprisingly, touch upon urgent questions concerning the nature of language, the interaction between cultures, and the humanistic enterprise as a whole. Madeleine and Catherine des Roches must have been familiar with these debates, as they took an evident interest in the intellectual and literary life of their period, and as two of the most active participants, Etienne Pasquier and Jacques Peletier, were among their intimates. Both Peletier (in his *Art poëtique*) and Pasquier (in his letters and *Recherches de la France*) theorize about translation as a many-faceted experience.[14] It lies outside the scope of this paper to recapitulate in depth the complexities of humanist translation theory and practice as Glen P. Norton has explored them.[15] Let it suffice to sketch a brief context for Catherine's project.

For Peletier the notion of fidelity to the original author/text is very important: "Car un Traducteur, comment saurait-il mieux faire son devoir, sinon en approchant toujours le plus près qu'il serait possible de l'Auteur auquel il est sujet?" (111) (How could a translator better fulfill his duty than to be always as close as possible to the author in whose service he is?). Although an absolutely faithful, word-for-word reproduction of a text in another language is impossible—"pour raison que deux langues ne sont jamais uniformes en phrases" (110)[16] (because two languages are never phrasally uniform)—Peletier wants the translator to strive for as complete a fidelity as possible and to remain strictly faithful to what he calls "le sens de l'auteur" (105) (the meaning of the author), which Norton defines as "the expressive autonomy of the source" (302).

For Etienne Pasquier a greater fluidity of meaning is unavoidable because he, as the historian he is first and foremost, is very aware of the profound differences between the sociopolitical and cultural institutions of different eras and civilizations, differences reflected in their respective linguistic equipments. In several of his letters he points out the great difficulty of a strict translation, which assigns to the translator the ungrateful task of rendering "les belles et nobles conceptions des étrangers, sans qu'il y aille grandement du nôtre" (the beautiful and noble conceptions of strangers, without any great input of our own) as he complains in a letter to Jacob Cujas,[17] adding that "il n'y a que les inventeurs qui se perpétuent" (only inventors perpetuate themselves). The solution for the creative Humanist seems to lie in the combination of translation (i.e., service rendered to an "other"—"étranger"—text) and invention (i.e., valorization of one's own creativity).

Theoreticians like Pasquier and others, such as Abel Mathieu and Henri Estienne, view meaning "almost by definition as unstable,"[18] a notion that allows a translator like Catherine des Roches a certain amount of creative leeway vis-à-vis Claudian's text. Her fidelity is, in any case, less to Claudian than to the Ceres-Proserpina story that evokes her emotional response.

Though Catherine's verse-rendering of *DRP* is rather close, there is obviously no attempt to bring about a word-for-word version. She calls her work an "imitation"—compare the title of the volume. As Thomas Greene points out, the distinctions made by humanist scholars between *translatio, paraphrasis, imitatio, allusio,* in actual poetic practice "are likely to seem arbitrary; parts of many imitations might well be regarded as translations, while most Renaissance 'translations' are already interpretations" (51). Greene also remarks that "the tribute of variation includes rejection" (195). By her variations—elaborations, digressions, contractions, and so on—Catherine des Roches rejects *DRP* as an indifferent text and turns it into a text expressive of her own and her mother's difference, of their needs, of their creative and unique ideology. Their "difference" is of course situated first in their gender, which separates them from most of the contemporary poets and Humanists; second, within their sex, in their strange-seeming closeness; and third, in their application of that closeness to the process of literary work. By making *DRP* into an expression of that difference, Catherine appropriates the text to her—to their—experience.

I will not reproduce here my line-by-line comparison of the two texts, but rather I will indicate the four main categories of changes that Catherine imposes on Claudian's poem and give a few examples.

1. Catherine stresses the closeness of Ceres and Proserpina, and the mother's protectiveness toward her daughter. These motifs are regularly either inserted into or elaborated upon when they are present in the Latin text. For example, where the Latin illustrates Ceres' protectiveness with the image of the cow following her calf, the French version amplifies that notion by expanding the Latin "sequitur" into an evocation of the body and its shadow, the same image, but reversed, Catherine uses in her 1583 "Epistre" to describe her closeness to her mother: "je vous suis partout

comme l'ombre le corps" (I follow you everywhere as the shadow follows the body).[19] As part of this group we must see the motif, stressed also in Claudian, of Proserpina as *only* daughter of Ceres. But, while Claudian attributes this to the fact that, after Proserpina's birth, Ceres became unfruitful, Catherine des Roches explains it by stressing that Proserpina could never be surpassed and that her birth should *therefore* not be followed by another one. Here we have an exaltation of Proserpina and a choice of uniqueness, similar to Catherine's uniqueness in her relationship with her mother, rather than Claudian's mention of Ceres' exhausted womb.[20] On the contrary, Catherine stresses the fruitfulness of Ceres by consistently adding adjectives such as "blétière" (grain-bearing) or "jaune" (yellow), indicative of ripening wheat, to the goddess's name, where the Latin often has simply that proper name and no more.

2. A second category, closely related to the first, concerns the expression of Ceres' grief when she discovers her daughter missing. Although this motif is of course important in Latin and often treated by Claudian very touchingly, Catherine elaborates upon it every time it appears. This emphasis on the grief a parent feels for a child extends even beyond the Ceres-Proserpina duo. So, for instance, when Claudian evokes, in a simile, the inundation of Thessaly by the river Peneus, Catherine amplifies the unimportant mention of the river's name by evoking the "father in despair because of love for his daughter, [who] wanted to render Thessalia's fields infertile," a reference to the loving and grieving Peneus, father of the unhappy nymph Daphne.[21] The seemingly gratuitous elaboration upon Peneus' name gains significance in the Dames de Roches's context. The most striking example of this elaboration upon the motif of parental sorrow occurs in Ceres' dream-vision, when the goddess has a premonitory dream of evil come upon her daughter. While the essential elements of the Latin text (*DRP* III, 67–110) are repeated in French, they are greatly amplified, into sixty-one lines, and new details are added. So, at the beginning of the disquieting vision, Ceres in her sleep reaches out for her daughter: "sa forte main s'allonge / Pensant prendre sa fille, et serre bien souvent / La mousse verdissante, ou le fuiable vent" (Her strong hand reaches out / intending to grasp her child, but instead clutches / at the green moss or at the insubstantial wind). This gesture of need and the sign of loss are new additions to *DRP.*

3. A third category stresses the outrage of the *raptus* and presents man as an aggressor. All the words of the family *ravir—ravisseur, ravi, ravissement*—are used much more frequently than the Latin's *raptus,* and the ravishment is clearly presented—as it is not markably in Latin—as a crime. It is called "a fraud," "a shameful incest," an infraction of "the holy laws"—all connotations absent from Claudian's version. In the description of the rapt itself, we note on the one hand an abbreviation of the fully picturesque

detailed description of the advent of Pluto's chariot, but on the other hand, an elaboration of the act itself and its devastating effect on both Proserpina's attendants and Proserpina herself. These motifs, barely evoked in Latin, are here rendered with a wealth of graphic, evocative details. We see Proserpina "half-dead," we see her held by force against the ravisher's breast, trying in vain to free herself from his unwelcome embrace with her delicate hands, we hear her crying for help "in a pitiful voice."

4. A fourth, last, category deals less with the stressing, or adding, of certain motifs, but rather with style. Catherine des Roches tends consistently to render the catastrophe more immediate and more personal than is the case in Claudian's text. Many of her deletions as well as her amplifications may be explained that way. For instance, while she incorporates the *Praefatio* to the work as a whole—an evocation of poetic challenge and endeavor—she deletes the *Praefatio* to Book II. This last preface consists in an elaborate comparison between Hercules, whose exploits caused Orpheus to take up his lyre again after a period of silence, and Florentinus, the city prefect of Rome (mid 395–end 397) who had functioned as a second Hercules to Claudian by encouraging him to write. Thus the preface falls outside the sphere and preoccupations of Catherine and Madeleine and in fact delays the unfolding of the drama; hence it is absent from Catherine's work. In the same way, some of Claudian's long, purely descriptive passages—of the flowery flanks of Mount Etna, for instance—are either omitted or minimized, while important (in the Dames's context) passages—such as the lamentation of Proserpina after the rapt—are amplified. In the latter passages, the language is often made more simple and more directly touching by eliminating "superfluous" and distancing features such as many mythological references. Other alterations brought to the Latin contribute to the immediacy effect. So, for instance in the beginning of Book I, where the Latin, setting the scene, uses *ecce* (see, look) (*DRP* I, 15), Catherine des Roches, depicting herself as a witness, repeats twice *je vois* (I see), bringing to the scene the empathy of the first person observer. In the plaint of Proserpina the Latin says: "Tantas quo crimine movimus iras?" (By what crime do we cause such anger?) (*DRP* II, 254); the plural *movimus* probably refers to an evil deed committed by mankind. In French we read the much more direct, more pathetic, "Qu'ay-je fait pauvrette . . . / Quels crimes ont commis mes innocentes mains?" (What have I, poor little one, done . . . / What crimes have my innocent hands committed?). When Proserpina's nurse recounts to Ceres what happened when the mysterious charioteer appeared (*DRP* III, 244), she evokes the essential fact in the following simple statement: when the light of day returns after the passage of the chariot, "Proserpina nusquam"—Proserpina is nowhere to be seen. In French: "Il ravit Proserpine, et detournant la bride / Les pieds-de-corne vont où son desir les guide" (He ravishes Proserpina, and, turning the bridle around / Makes his hard-hoofed steeds go where his desire guides

them). A committed and clearly assigned crime in French versus a merely puzzling disappearance in Latin.

To quote Greene again: "Any creative variation contains an element of refusal" (195). Through her variations, Catherine des Roches refuses Claudian's *DRP* as an epic of grave cosmic necessity and majesty, structured and motivated by the chtonic god's justified desire for a wife. She displaces the emphasis from the awesome and impersonal universality of the Latin epic to the depiction of a violation, of a forcible and traumatic intrusion.

In the first lines of Book I (1–3) Claudian announces his subject. He writes that he intends to sing "inferni raptoris equos adflataque curru / sidera Taenaerio caligantesque profundae / Iunonis thalamos . . ." (the horses of the infernal ravisher and the stars darkened by the chariot from the underworld, and the gloomy bridal chambers of the underworld Iuno). Catherine announces her subject in a different way. She says that she intends to evoke

> le char et les chevaux de ce grand ravisseur
> Qui laissant de l'Enfer les richesses avares
> Devins enamouré de nos Trésors plus rares.
> *Donc* je veu chanter la profonde Iunon,
> Que le lit nuptial a fait changer de nom

> the chariot and the horses of that great ravisher,
> Who, leaving behind the underworld's scanty riches
> Became enamored of our more precious treasures.
> *Therefore* I intend to sing the infernal Iuno,
> Whose name was changed by the bridal bed.[22]

We notice the impersonality of the Latin: the accent is on the ominous presence of the chariot and the horses and on the somber chambers Proserpina is to occupy in the underworld. A decor is evoked of power and violence on the one hand, of gloom and darkness on the other—an impressive setting for the chtonic, cosmic, drama that will be enacted. Catherine on the contrary underlines the contrast between the deprived but powerful ravisher from the realm of darkness and the preciousness as well as the vulnerability of his victim, the treasure from the realm of light. She posits the figure of the victim, of the prey. When she writes "*therefore* I intend to sing" her emphasis is all on the "infernal Iuno," and she calls special attention to the notion, absent from the Latin, of the imposed change of name. Catherine's work is indeed about the forcible, enforced alteration that occurs when Proserpina is changed against her will from daughter of Ceres and carefree maiden, into a violated, submitted creature, a secondary being, designated now by a name that evokes a parallel but inferior function (she will now be an infernal, not a heavenly Iuno) rather than her own substance, connections, and identity. The bond between mother and daughter is painfully destroyed, and, by the same token, for Catherine des Roches bonds of harmony and order within the natural world are also sundered. In the beginning of Book I she writes—a notation present but more tentative and impersonal in Claudian—that Pluto, in his anger about being unwed "Ebranla tellement cette ronde machine, / Que l'on pensait la terre et le ciel en ruine" (so shook the universe that heaven and earth seemed destined for ruin).

The violent breaking of fruitful, harmonious bonds: there is Catherine's subject as it is the focus of her and her mother's deepest fears. In another work, her long narrative poem "L'Agnodice" (1579), she writes about the tragedy that occurs when the bonds between women are forcibly broken: excluded from each other they are also excluded from both poetic creativity and learning, and they are condemned to ailing lives, changed into faceless, nameless, feeble creatures. Only female solidarity, effected by the protagonist, Agnodice, can rescue women and restore them to creative health (Sankovitch, chap. 2). In her adaptation of *DRP* Catherine stresses or rather introduces these preoccupations, her own and her mother's, that form the keystone of their feminist poetic strategy.[23]

Norton notes "the organic dependency of translation on the ebb and flow of society at large" (323). While Catherine's translation seems to depend less on the evolution and condition of society than on the microcosm of her particular relationship with her mother, it also expresses their shared need for participation in the dominant intellectual and poetic sphere, a need that echoes the need of other actual and prospective women authors and thus becomes expressive of a cultural reality comprising but exceeding their own.[24]

In her "imitation" of *DRP* Catherine des Roches accomplishes two goals at the same time: first, she penetrates into the sphere of the Latin texts, where her male contemporaries find nourishment and reassurance, not only as a passive reader, but also as an active interlocutor, student, and critic of such a text. In other words, by bridging the gap between cultures, she is able to "mitigate historical solitude,"[25] thus establishing herself as a humanist poet. Second, in choosing this particular text for translation, she imbues it with her own ideology of mother/daughter closeness and, by extension, the need for female solidarity: she forcefully bridges the gap between herself and the dominant culture by imposing on that culture her own seal; she is able to mitigate gender-originated solitude, thus establishing herself as a specifically female—feminist—poet. She marks the alien and painfully conquered sphere of learning and poetry with an imprint unlike that of any other humanist poet: it is the imprint of her creative fear as well as her creative power, and it corresponds to the possibility of and the need for a new institution—that of women poets.

NOTES

1. The Dames des Roches, a mother, Madeleine (c. 1520–1587), and a daughter, Catherine (1542–1587), from Poitiers, wrote and published a substantial body of work, consisting of poems, prose dialogues of a philosophical nature, translations of Latin texts, letters, and even a tragi-comedy. For an introduction to their life and work and a list of the early editions, see George E. Diller, *Les Dames des Roches: Etude sur la vie littéraire à Poitiers dans la deuxième moitié du XVIe siècle* (Paris: Droz, 1936). A modern edition is not yet available, but Anne R. Larsen is currently preparing such an edition. All quotes in this essay are taken from the 1586 edition. In transcribing them, I have modernized letters and added accents. The translations are mine.

2. For a history of the transmission and a discussion of the successive editions of Claudian's poem, see J. B. Hall's study preceding his edition, *Claudian. De Raptu Proserpinae* (Cambridge: Cambridge University Press, 1969). All quotes are taken from the latter. For a study of Claudian's work, including *DRP*, see also Alan Cameron, *Claudian, Poetry and Propaganda at the Court of Honorius* (Oxford: Clarendon Press, 1970).

3. Anthony Grafton, *Joseph Scaliger: A Study in the History of Classical Scholarship* (Oxford: Clarendon Press, 1983), 226.

4. See Hall, *Claudian*, 85–86. Scaliger used the 1602 Claverius edition, and also the 1534 Isengrin edition (Hall, 86). It is therefore possible, and even probable, that Catherine also used the Isengrin as her base text.

5. Thomas Greene, *The Light in Troy: Imitation and Discovery in Renaissance Poetry* (New Haven: Yale University Press, 1982), 157–158.

6. Tilde Sankovitch, *French Women Writers and the Book: Myths of Access and Desire* (Syracuse: Syracuse University Press, 1988), chap. 2.

7. Constance Jordan, *Renaissance Feminism: Literary Texts and Political Models* (Ithaca: Cornell University Press, 1990), 173.

8. Etienne Jodelle, *Oeuvres complètes*, ed. Enéa Balmas, 2 vols. (Paris: Gallimard, 1965) 1: 181.

9. Marianne Hirsch, *The Mother/Daughter Plot. Narrative, Psychoanalysis, Feminism* (Bloomington: Indiana University Press, 1989).

10. Hirsch, *Mother/Daugher Plot*, 5.

11. Etienne Pasquier, *Oeuvres Complètes*, 2 vols. (Geneva: Slatkine Reprints, 1971) 2: 166.

12. Julia Kristeva, *La Révolution du langage poétique* (Paris: Seuil, 1974), 10. On the issue of women as a circulating exchange value within patriarchy, see Gayle Rubin's classic essay on this subject, "The Traffic in Women: Notes on the 'Political Economy' of Sex," in *Toward the Anthropology of Women*, ed. Rayna R. Reiter (New York: Monthly Review Press, 1975), 157–210. Ian Maclean stresses repeatedly the fact that, during the Renaissance, in all domains, "the female sex is considered in the context of the paradigm of marriage," *The Renaissance Notion of Woman* (Cambridge: Cambridge University Press, 1980), 66. Catherine's refusal of what, in effect is seen as a natural law, "inseparable from the notion of woman" (Maclean, 75) constitutes therefore an act of considerable originality and daring. See also Ruth Kelso, *Doctrine for the Lady of the Renaissance* (Urbana: University of Illinois Press, 1956), chap. 7.

13. Hirsch, *Mother/Daughter Plot*, 6.

14. Jacques Peletier du Mans, *L'Art poëtique*, ed. André Boulanger (Paris: Belles lettres, 1930).

15. Glen P. Norton, *The Ideology and Language of Translation in Renaissance France, and their Humanist Antecedents* (Geneva: Droz, 1984).

16. For the implications of the term and notion of "phrase" in this context, see Norton, *Ideology*, 333.

17. Pasquier, *Oeuvres*, 2: 37.

18. Norton *Ideology*, 330.

19. Latin: "Hanc fovet, hanc sequitur; vitulam non blandius ambit / torva parens" (*DRP* 1: 127, 128). French: "Le corps n'est jamais veu plustot suivy de l'ombre, / Que sa Mère la suit de pensers et de pas, / S'accommodant pour elle aux enfantins esbats. / Ainsi voit on souvent la petite genice / De sa mère froncée attirer la blandice" (The body is never seen without being followed by the shadow, for her mother follows her with her thoughts and with her steps, adjusting her gait, for her child's sake, to childish frolics. Thus one often sees a little heifer, attracting the blandishments of its frowning mother).

20. Latin: "fessaque post primos haeserunt viscera partus" (*DRP* I: 124). French: "un autre enfantement / Ne devoit point suivir ce divin ornement: / Proserpine en valeurs surpassant un grand nombre" (Another birth was not to follow that divine ornament, since Proserpina surpassed, by her qualities, a great number).

21. Latin: "Sic, cum Thassaliam scopulis inclusa teneret / Peneo stagnante palus et merso negaret / arva coli" (*DRP* II: 179–181). French: "Pené au désespoir pour l'amour de sa Fille, / Enfermant les rochers voulut rendre stérile / Le champ Thessalien" (Peneus in despair because of love for his daughter, by enclosing the rocks intended to render Thessalia's fields infertile).

22. The emphasis is mine.

23. Among contemporary feminists, Mary Daly regrets "the fundamental lost bonding . . . the bond between mothers and daughters" (*Gyn/Ecology: The Metaethics of Radical Feminism* [Boston: Beacon Press, 1978], 346), and Adrienne Rich calls "the cathexis between mother and daughter . . . the great unwritten story" (*Of Woman Born* [New York: Norton, 1976], 225). Gayatri Spivak writes that "the restoration of a continuous bond between mother and daughter even *after* the 'facts' of gestation, birthing and suckling, is indeed of great importance as a persistent effort against the sexism of millennia" ("French Feminism in an International Frame," in *Feminist Readings: French Texts/American Contexts*, ed. Colette Gaudin et al., *Yale French Studies* 62 (1981): 183), but she warns that the mother-daughter connection may be coopted by the patriarchy. The Dames avoid that danger by making the bond between them not an end in itself, but the very basis of their creative project, and by extending that bond, in works such as the "Agnodice," to other women.

24. Authors such as Pernette du Guillet, Louise Labé, Hélisenne de Crenne, Marie de Romieu also express the need to participate in the humanist culture of their time, both implicitly by their work, and explicitly by encouraging other women to write.

25. Greene, *Light in Troy*, 191.

MARGUERITE DE VALOIS AND THE PROBLEMATICS OF FEMALE SELF-REPRESENTATION

ℰ℈

Patricia Francis Cholakian

It is sometimes said that women lack the literary imagination to write about anything but themselves; and this would seem to be corroborated by the number of memoirs produced by Frenchwomen during the *ancien régime.* Does it necessarily follow, however, that these women found it easy to write about themselves? The autobiographical "I" is a fictional construction, the subject of an invented narrative. When the "I" was also a woman in a society that saw the woman as *object,* how could she speak as *subject* of her own narrative? To do so, she would have to deny her objectification by the masculine gaze. In other words, to represent herself in a first-person account of her life, a woman had to usurp the status of subject, to which a man, as the master of the gaze, acceded by birthright.

In addition, a woman was faced with the scarcity of literary models on which to base her text. The figures and tropes of all writing are determined, to a great extent, by the figures and tropes of one's literary predecessors. Before one can write, one must have read. When a sixteenth-century woman wanted to tell her story, few if any women writers had attempted such a project. As a result, she was forced to imitate, consciously or unconsciously, models whose "I," while deeming itself universal, was in reality masculine, and whose narratives recounted the experiences, anxieties, and values of a man's world.

There is a great difference between writing *like* a man and writing *as* a man. In studying the problematics of early female self-representation, it is important to look closely at this gap between the woman writer's assumption that she must imitate her male predecessors and her ability to do

Portrait of Marguerite de Valois. Anonymous. Sixteenth century (courtesy of Musée des Beaux-Arts de
la ville de Blois).

so.[1] I address this question here by examining one of the first autobiographical works known to have been written by a woman[2]—the *Mémoires*
of Marguerite de Valois (1552–1615), composed around 1600 and published in 1628.[3]

Most early memorialists saw themselves as historiographers and limited themselves to narrating public events, usually connected with war or
politics.[4] Marguerite's library contained the writings of many of these
sixteenth-century chroniclers.[5] And it is probable that when she decided
to compose her own memoirs she had them in mind. A brief glance at
Monluc's *Commentaires,* one of the better known of these works, reveals
the distance separating her text from the conventional sixteenth-century
memoir. Monluc, who had been accused of misappropriating the spoils of

war, wrote an account of his fifty-five years of loyal service to the crown. His book, modeled on Caesar's *Gallic Wars,* was intended for military officers.

Marguerite had no such career to vindicate. Indeed, if anything, she had to justify her lack of achievement. Daughter, wife, and sister of kings, she had been a bystander rather than a participant in the events around her. Yet she did not intend her memoirs to be an account of what others had done. As she stated in her preface, she wanted to write about her own fortunes, the subject on which she alone was qualified to testify. To do this, however, she had to find a way to represent herself at the center of a life lived on the margins of history. She was faced with a dilemma—either to adapt the conventional memoir (the record of public achievement) to her story or to adapt her story to the conventions of the genre. In fact, she ended up doing both, thus producing a text in which the tension between form and content reflects the tension of writing as a woman.[6]

When men like Monluc portrayed themselves in their memoirs, they could follow in the footsteps of a Julius Caesar, who had already written about public life lived as a man. They also had other powerful prose models, like Plutarch's *Lives,* that demonstrated how a man's life story should look. For Marguerite, however, there existed no such writings about the female experience.[7] Literary images of women in the late Middle Ages and Renaissance were usually stereotypes—the idealized lady of "courtly" literature or the oversexed trickster of the *fabliaux* and *nouvelles.* Representations of historical women were limited to the stories of "good" and "bad" women compiled by participants in the "Querelle des Femmes." This meant that women had almost no viable literary models for narrating their experiences as women and that their self-perceptions relied, at least in part, on an androcentric ideology of femininity.

With no representational tradition on which to model her text, the woman memorialist found herself in a double bind, forced to position herself either inside or outside a discourse inscribing woman as men's fantasy of the other. To place herself inside this discourse was to accept the role of object and lose her own voice; to place herself outside it was to be exiled from the very territory she was trying to enter—the world of letters. Marguerite de Valois's narrative inscribes her attempt to find a way out of this dilemma.

Her text covers the years 1558 to 1582. In it she treats her early childhood, her marriage and its bloody sequel the St. Bartholomew's Day Massacres (August 23–24, 1572), the court intrigues spawned by the rivalry between Catholics and Protestants, the events preceding her estrangement from her husband, and her imprisonment in the château of Usson (1586–1605).

The essential facts of her life can be summed up by listing the kings to whom she was related. She was the granddaughter of François I, the daughter of Henri II, the sister of François II, Charles IX, and Henri III, and the wife (eventually divorced) of Henri IV de Navarre. One must not forget, however, that she was also the daughter of a powerful woman, the formidable Catherine de Médicis.

To those familiar only with her legend,[8] it will come as some surprise that "La Reine Margot," popularly believed to be one of the most promiscuous women in French history, portrays herself as completely asexual. Yet as Mariéjol comments, she is one of the most chaste writers of the sixteenth century.[9] She characterizes her relations with her husband as "sisterly," repeatedly drawing attention to the fact that for most of their married life they slept in separate beds. She never alludes to the famous love affairs. Most historians assume that her *Mémoires* repress the truth about her love life and that she really was the nymphomaniac her legend makes her out to be. There is reason to believe, however, that her enemies exaggerated her licentiousness for religious and political reasons. It is surely no coincidence, for instance, that a Protestant poet, Agrippa d'Aubigné, was one of the Catholic princess's most outspoken detractors. It is also important to remember that at Renaissance courts it was considered normal for a married lady to have one or more "servitors." I shall not concern myself here with establishing the "facts" about Marguerite's sex life. Instead I shall discuss the far more important issue of how and why she represented herself as she did.

Marguerite de Valois begins her *Mémoires* by affirming that she is different from other women. In her preface addressed to Brantôme (35–37), she writes, "Je louerois davantage vostre oeuvre si elle ne me louoit tant. . . . C'est un commun vice aux femmes de se plaire aux louanges, bien que non meritées. Je blasme mon sexe en cela, et n'en voudrois tenir cette condition" (I would praise your work more, if it did not praise me so much. . . . It is a vice common in women to take pleasure in praise, even when it is undeserved. I blame my sex for this and do not want to be part of this condition). At first glance this appears to be merely a graceful acknowledgment of the *Discours* he wrote in her honor. It is much more, however. By establishing a direct link between Brantôme's text and hers, Marguerite enters and interrupts a long conversation between men about women. The work Brantôme called simply "Des Dames," and which his editors called *Les Dames illustres,* was itself the response to an earlier text, Boccaccio's *De mulieribus claris,* which in its turn was a commentary on Plutarch's *Mulierum virtutes,* which was a discussion of Aristotle's remarks about women in the *Politics.*[10] Marguerite's preface is imbricated, therefore, in a series of intertexts treating the question of woman's Nature.

Her disavowal goes to the heart of the matter by questioning the conventional way of representating women. Like the other male "feminists" in the "Querelle des Femmes," Brantôme was countering the argument claiming that women were mentally defective and morally depraved. His work was original in its praise of the virtuous women of his own century. Indeed he went much further by contending that the women he described were as able as their male contemporaries. Marguerite, he argued, was as worthy to reign as any king. Despite his evident admiration for Marguerite, Brantôme's argument is not really convincing, however. When he compares a public address by her to Cicero's *Orations*, he does not mention what she said; nor does he give evidence of her statemanship, tact, or political acumen to support his claim. Instead, he devotes nearly half of his text to describing her physical appearance. He calls her a miracle of God, graced with perfect features, a beautiful body, a superb figure, and the carriage of a goddess. He also cites the ecstatic comments of other men who were transfixed by her charms. The princess he describes is a precious work of art, richly garbed, covered with jewels, narcissistically absorbed in enhancing her appearance, and above all sensually exciting. Although there is no doubt that he is sincere in his "feminist" zeal for Marguerite's cause, Brantôme's essay turns her into a fetish. It is the product of masculine desire.

In her preface, Marguerite refuses to take narcissistic pleasure in his encomium and "blames" those of her sex who enjoy such flattery. What Brantôme has produced is art, she argues, not truth. Even as she praises his skill, therefore, she is discrediting the validity of what he has written and, by implication, the clichés and conventions of female representation. The woman writing her *Mémoires* in 1600 is not, she says, the woman Brantôme praises so lavishly. "Si j'ay eu quelques parties de celles que vous m'attribuez, les ennuis les effaçans de l'exterieur, en ont aussi effacé la souvenance de ma memoire" (If I once had some part of the charms you attribute to me, the hardships that erased them on the outside have also erased them from my memory). Her emphasis on time's erasure of beauty underlines the essential difference between her project and his. In his portrait she is frozen in time, whereas the life story she is writing must deal with process and change.

The problem of self-representation is linked to the problem of self-recognition. Reading Brantôme's words, she finds it impossible to recognize herself. "De sorte que, me remirant en vostre discours, je ferois volontiers comme la vieille madame de Rendan, qui, ayant demeuré depuis la mort de son mary sans voir son miroir, rencontrant par fortune son visage dans le miroir d'un autre, demanda qui estoit celle-là" (Thus seeing myself reflected in your *discours*, I would gladly do as did the elderly Madame de Rendan, who having lived since her husband's death without looking in her mirror, happened to see her face in another's and asked who was the woman she saw).

Marguerite's reaction to Brantôme's portrait inscribes the predicament of women trapped in a masculine sign system. To represent herself, she must deny what she sees in the portrait/mirror—the object frozen in time.

She must find instead a way to portray herself from inside the female body. When she calls attention to the ravages wrought by time and misfortune, she is in effect stepping out of the frame in which his *discours* has transfixed her and asserting the right to construct herself as subject.

Assertion, however, is not proof, and telling the truth turns out to be far from easy for the reasons discussed above. Although Marguerite announces as her grand theme the disparity between nature and fortune, her text turns out to be "comme les petits ours, en masse lourde et difforme . . . un chaos" (like bear cubs, a heavy shapeless mass . . . a chaos). Uncertainty about the shape of her narrative becomes more and more apparent in the *Mémoires*. At first, she self-consciously imitates Plutarch, who began his biographies with paradigmatic anecdotes of childhood that prefigured his heroes' futures. She searches her memory for "enfantines actions . . . d'aussi dignes d'estre ecrites que celle de l'enfance de Themistocles et d'Alexandre" (childish acts . . . as worthy of being written down as those of Themistocles [actually Alcibiades] and Alexandre).[11] She cites two such incidents from her childhood. In the first (37–38), she tells how her father took her on his lap and teased her to choose a little boy as her "servitor." She chose not the good-looking duc de Guise, but the marquis de Beaupréau because he was "plus sage," whereas Guise was constantly hurting his playmates and always wanted to be the boss—"Augure certain de ce que nous avons veu depuis" (Certainly an omen of what we have since witnessed). Of course, as she wrote, she knew perfectly well that the little boy she had disliked because he was mean and bossy would one day instigate the St. Bartholomew's Day Massacres and plot to overthrow the king.

The second anecdote (38–39) concerns a brief period when Protestantism "infected" the French court. Among those temporarily won over was her brother, the future Henri III, who tormented her with his zeal for the new faith, throwing her prayer books into the fire and threatening her with beating if she didn't convert. The young Marguerite refused to be intimidated. Although only seven or eight at the time, she vowed she would be whipped or even killed rather than see herself damned. Her trial ended when their mother forced Henri to return immediately to the religion of his fathers. A Catholic all her life, Marguerite evidently relates this incident to demonstrate her steadfast adherence to the religion from which she never departed, even during her years as the wife of a Protestant. She is also concerned, however, with proving that she, like Plutarch's heroes, was endowed with the stuff of which heroes are made; thus, she gives evidence that even as a child she displayed the moral fortitude required of a ruler.

These anecdotes are meant to project the image of a child destined for great things, but they also inscribe the daughter's position in the royal family. The first, when her father takes her on his lap, evokes the way patriarchally constructed sexuality will determine her future. The second shows her at the mercy of a bullying older brother, who will eventually accede to the throne, by dint of having been born male. Although she displays remarkable force of character in opposing him, she can be saved only by the intervention of her all-powerful mother, whose main concern seems to be her son's error and not her daughter's virtue.

Although Marguerite begins by imitating Plutarch, it becomes more and more apparent that she cannot make her story conform to the heroic mold. A glorious future did not lay in store for the sister of four brothers, all in direct line for the throne. Nor was Marguerite destined to follow in her mother's footsteps as widowed regent. For her, as for most women of her time, "nature" had little control over "fortune." As a result there is a constant disparity in her *Mémoires* between the events of her life and the importance she assigns to them.

This becomes evident when she narrates the experience that initiated her into adulthood (43–49). Soon after her brother Henri's victories over the Protestants in 1569, he takes his sister aside and offers to make her his ally. He has been observing her, he says, and has concluded that she is intelligent, perceptive, and loyal, qualities that fit her to represent his interests to their mother, who, he fears may favor the king, their older brother Charles IX. When she agrees, he informs Catherine of their pact and urges her to treat Marguerite as his equal.

His proposal, producing an immediate change in Marguerite, reveals a hitherto unsuspected aspect of her character. Until then, she writes, she had been a carefree child, interested only in dancing and hunting, not even caring how she looked or what she wore. This emphasis on a childish lack of self-awareness preceding the discovery of a goal or mission is typical of the "loss of innocence" narrative. Henri's request took her so completely by surprise, she says, that she felt like Moses when he saw the burning bush and almost replied, as had he, that she was unworthy. Although likening herself to the founder of occidental monotheism may seem both pathetic and ludicrous, for the young princess, an invitation to participate in the family intrigues is a glimpse of the promised land. She awakens to a new sense of self: "Toutesfois trouvant en moy ce que je ne pensois pas qui y fust, . . . me sembla à l'instant que j'estois transformée, et que j'estois devenue quelque chose de plus que je n'avois esté jusques alors. Tellement que je commençay à prendre confiance de moy-mesme" (45) (Yet finding in myself what I did not think was there, . . . it seemed to me that in an instant I was transformed and that I became something more than I had been before. So much so that I began to feel self-confident). The task with which Marguerite was entrusted may not be comparable to Moses'; however, one should not underestimate its importance in an environment where personal relations were the unique path to power. Not only is Henri next in line for the throne, but his offer also allows her to establish close ties with the power behind the throne whom until now Marguerite had hardly dared approach—her mother, Catherine de Médicis. When Marguerite agrees to become her brother's go-between, her mother promises to speak to her with as much pleasure as if she were her favorite son. Marguerite leaves no doubt that this was a high point in her existence: "Ces parolles firent ressentir à mon ame ce qu'elle n'avoit jamais ressenti" (46) (These words made me feel in my soul what I had never felt before).

Her dreams of glory are short-lived, and "envieuse fortune" enters the picture. Suddenly, Henri instructs Catherine to break off all relations with Marguerite. His sister has grown beautiful, he says, and he has secret information that she is being courted by her former playmate, the ambitious duc de Guise, and may betray their secrets to him. Marguerite's disgrace is instantaneous. Furious with her brother and shaken by her mother's rejection, she falls gravely ill and nearly dies. Only after the duke is safely married to someone else is she exonerated of Henri's charge.

Becoming a woman puts an end to Marguerite's hopes. Henri's decision reflects the widely held assumption that female desire and political credibility are mutually exclusive. Although she probably did not understand the full significance of this episode, this passage demonstrates how her second-class status within the royal family was determined by fear of her sexuality. Moreover, Catherine's lack of sympathy for her daughter's predicament reveals the extent to which daughters (and women in general) were devalued in this milieu. Catherine wastes no time getting her beautiful, strong-minded daughter safely out of the way. She negotiates her daughter's betrothal to the Protestant leader, Henri de Navarre, despite Marguerite's reminder that she is a devout Catholic.

At this point her narrative wanders farther and farther from the Plutarchan model and becomes a text in search of a subject. Her failure to retain her brother's confidence makes it impossible for her to go on pretending that she is telling a hero's story. Writing of the "triomphe" and "magnificence" of her wedding, she seems to become the beautiful object portrayed by Brantôme. She describes her royal garments, complete with ermine, jeweled crown, and a train so long it had to be carried by three princesses. Fully conscious of what she is doing, she addresses Brantôme directly, remarking that this is the kind of writing at which he excelled.

In her preface, she rejected Brantôme's image of her, and in the first pages of her memoirs, by saying that in her youth she had no interest in how she looked, she emphasized the courage, intelligence, and ambition she possessed as a young girl. In this passage, which marks the formal end of her girlhood, she represents herself for the first and only time as the opulently garbed mannequin depicted by Brantôme. Her queenly garments created the illusion of power, but in fact they robbed her of it.

Her marriage, which so exacerbated tensions between Protestants and Catholics that it was immediately followed by the massacre of thousands of Huguenots, destroyed Marguerite's hopes for a significant public role.

As a daughter who could not inherit the crown, she had not been taken seriously by a mother concerned only with preserving the succession for her sons. As the Catholic wife of a Protestant leader, she became an outsider in both camps. Whereas the first pages portray her as resolute and perceptive, she is now seen as passive and voiceless, totally dependent on the will of others.

Her marginalization is apparent in her celebrated account of what happened in the Louvre on the night of the massacres. She describes her terror and bewilderment as she grows increasingly aware that something ominous is about to take place. Forced by her mother to leave the room lest she overhear their plans, Marguerite goes to bed "toute transsie et esperdue, sans me pouvoir imaginer ce que j'avois à craindre" (57) (very frightened and confused, yet unable to imagine what I had to fear). In the middle of the night, a crowd of her husband's allies, all strangers to her, enter their bedroom to discuss the assassination of the Protestant leader Coligny. At dawn, her privacy is invaded again, this time by a wounded man pursued by four archers. For a moment, the frightened princess does not know whether she will be sexually assaulted by one or shot by the others. Seeking refuge in her sister's room, she is narrowly missed in the hallway by a halberd, while terrified Huguenots beg her to intercede in their behalf. This is the account of an ignorant and confused bystander, with no foreknowledge of or control over the gruesome events she witnessed.

Although these pages contain fascinating accounts of cape-and-dagger intrigue in the corridors of the Louvre, the reader is never sure where the narrator stands. Is she merely the chronicler of palace life, or is she a significant participant in the exciting events she describes? Likewise, it is difficult to discern in her actions a coherent and consistent line of conduct. At times she depicts herself as nobly disinterested, when for instance she refuses to divorce her Protestant husband because she suspects that his enemies want a pretext to kill him. A little later, however, she secretly informs the king that her husband and her younger brother François are about to defect to the Huguenots. Then after their arrest, she again switches sides and defends Henri in the *Mémoire justificatif.* Still later she agrees to spirit Henri and François out of the palace disguised as women. Yet even as she tells how she aided and abetted these enemies of the crown, she asserts her devotion to her brother King Charles. The result is a fragmented account in which there is no coherent sense of self. Although she clearly wants to narrate these events as if she were at their center, it is evident that she is only at their periphery. The men—her husband and brothers—are the real actors.

Marguerite has no control over her own movements and little influence on those around her. She tells how the king locked her up in her room to prevent her from communicating with her husband and brother, both of whom have at last managed to escape from the Louvre, the former without even informing her of his departure. After having been traded to Henri de Navarre in marriage, Marguerite becomes in effect a hostage to his return. It is true that in an absolute monarchy freedom is severely limited, but the men, managing spectacular escapes and joining the rebel forces, are able to exercise considerable control over their destinies. Such actions never seem to be an option for Marguerite. She does not even have the right to join the husband she was forced to marry. She must wait many months before obtaining the king's permission to journey to his headquarters in the south of France, and then she is allowed to leave only in her mother's company. Whether she is conscious of doing so, the image Marguerite projects of herself is that of woman as victim. The "envieuse fortune" of which she complains is in reality the patriarchal structure that denies her autonomy.

Nevertheless, Marguerite struggles to infuse her narrative with epic significance. For instance, speaking of the death of Charles IX and the detested Henri III's accession to the throne, she inserts a long digression on premonitions, concluding with an allusion to Brutus's dream—also found in Plutarch. She goes into great detail about her mother's extrasensory experiences and then asserts that she herself has always had forewarning of important events, a gift she attributes to her royal blood. The daughter's desire to assimilate her mother's power to herself is evident in her lengthy account of Catherine's portentous dreams. All of this leads up to the revelation that when she came face to face with the new king, she was seized with violent chills and trembling, despite the heat of the day.

Just as she overdramatizes this relatively banal event, she also exaggerates the slender parts she played on the stage of history. To make it appear that her presence was essential, she alters the chronology surrounding the peace treaty between her brothers, Henri III and François.[12] Likewise, she devotes many pages to a trip to Flanders, where she tried to convince the Flemish noblemen to accept her younger brother as their leader. As I suggested above, all early memorialists were caught between historiography and autobiography. In Marguerite's *Mémoires,* however, the conflict between the two genres was exacerbated by her gender. Whereas for a man like Monluc the private and the public merged in a life lived as a soldier, for a woman the private was central, and the public was peripheral. Marguerite's royal birth *seemed* to make her an exception to this rule, but in fact she, like most women, had no access to political power.

But Marguerite never resigned herself to merely recording what she had witnessed. Her struggle to occupy the center of her *Mémoires* eventually moves them away from historiography and toward the introspection that characterizes autobiography. This shift is discernable in the passage telling how, during her emprisonment in the Louvre, she discovered the pleasures of reading and the consolations of religious devotion. Reading and religion not only helped her overcome the loneliness and boredom of her confinement, but they also taught her to evaluate her life on the basis of spiritual and intellectual criteria, rather than political achievements. When at last her brother the king decides to free her, the princess claims that she bore him no grudge, "ayant passé le temps de ma captivité au plaisir de la lecture" (89) (having spent the time of my captivity in pleasurable reading).

Marguerite's reaction to her captivity corroborates Heilbrun's perception that philosophical resignation to suffering is a recurrent theme in women's autobiographies. Heilbrun writes that women tend "to find beauty even in pain and to transform rage into spiritual acceptance" because "what has been forbidden to women is anger, together with the open admission of the desire for power and control over one's life."[13] Without friends, abandoned by her husband and condemned by her mother and brother, Marguerite seeks consolation in the life of the mind, a habit that will stand her in good stead during the long years of isolation in Usson.

But if this intellectual and spiritual resignation is the feminine equivalent of heroic action in Marguerite's case, the reading from which it sprang was also the necessary prelude to writing about herself. Undoubtedly, Marguerite's reflections on her own life originated in her meditations on the works she read, as did her desire to interpret her existence in terms of the heroic values they inscribed. Naïvely identifying with the male authors in her library, she learned to imagine herself as the subject of a first-person narrative.

Her feminine propensity to stifle anger and appear morally superior also manifests itself in her relationship with her husband. She represents herself as disinterested and loyal, motivated only by a firm commitment to duty. She rejects her mother's suggestion that she obtain an annulment by swearing that Henri is "not a man." She tells of devotedly nursing him through serious illnesses, some of which, she asserts, were brought on by his sexual excesses. When he peremptorily dismisses her favorite lady-in-waiting, she explains that he was only obeying the king's orders and hastens to add that breaking off relations with him over this incident was imprudent. Although Henri escaped from the Louvre without informing her of his departure, when he writes a letter begging her to keep him informed of what is going on at court, she complies with alacrity. She seeks permission to join him in Gascony, while arguing that it is her duty to be with her husband. Later when the Huguenots decide to go to war with the Catholics, she continues to put Henri's interests above her religious affiliation. She contends that she supported him faithfully in all his endeavors and that his jealous mistresses succeeded in alienating him.

Even when she seems at her most abject, her dependence on Henri is political, however, rather than emotional. She wants his friendship because with it she can assume her rightful place as his queen—furthering his interests, counseling him wisely, and presiding over his court. In fact, the virtues she attributes to herself as wife are those characteristic of the male hero: unselfishness, high-mindedness, loyalty.

It is clear, however, that she is not motivated solely by the desire to portray herself as a dutiful wife. Her position vis-à-vis her husband was precarious, and his good opinion was especially desirable at the time she was writing. Bauschatz believes that Marguerite composed these memoirs to convince Henri of her devotion and loyalty. Nor is it impossible that she hoped they would dispose her former husband to release her from Usson. The young princess who dreamed of becoming another Moses or Alexander was now desperately intent on staying in her husband's good graces; she dreaded not his infidelity but his hatred.

Thus she looks back with nostalgia on the years she spent with him in Gascony, where in fact, she seems to fulfill her childhood promise and act with "judgment and resolution." In Pau, where Catholicism is outlawed, and her coreligionists are arrested and beaten after attending mass in her chapel, she demands that Henri dismiss the man responsible for this outrage and vows never to set foot again in this city. Likewise, she demonstrates her wisdom by advising the Huguenots not to wage war with the crown, advice they do not follow, to their regret.

Nevertheless, she hardly draws a flattering portrait of the "vert galant." Although she completely suppresses all reference to her own sexuality, she does not refrain from speaking freely of his. She portrays the future Henri IV as a lovesick puppy, childishly dependent on his wife's sympathy and advice, easily taken in by jealous mistresses, and fainting from exhaustion, caused in her opinion by his sexual excesses. Furthermore, she makes it clear that he often treated her unjustly. Although she repeatedly asserts that his adulterous flirtations did not bother her and that she was never jealous, when Henri impregnates a lady-in-waiting named Fossette, even the infinitely tolerant Marguerite comes to the end of her patience, for this situation calls her status into question and robs her of the respect due Henri's wife and queen. No doubt realizing that this time he has gone too far, Henri tries to conceal the truth, pretending that his mistress is suffering from "stomach trouble." Only when Fossette is on the point of giving birth, does he confess the truth and beg for his wife's help. Marguerite's reply conforms to the image she has drawn of herself as devoted and dutiful wife, "Je luy dis que je l'honorois trop pour m'offenser de chose qui vînt de luy; que je m'y en allois, et y ferois comme si c'estoit ma fille" (168) (I told him that I honored him too much to be offended by anything of his doing and that I would go to her immediately and treat her as if she were my daughter). Marguerite calls in her own doctor, and personally assists at the birth. The child, a daughter, is born dead. When, however, Henri, who has gone hunting, returns and orders his exhausted wife to pay a call on Fossette, she allows her resentment to spill over: "Il se fascha fort contre moy, et, ce qui me despleust beaucoup, il me sembla que je ne meritois pas cette recompense de ce que j'avois fait le matin" (168) (He was very angry with me, and what displeased me the most was that it seemed to me I did not deserve this reward for what I had done that morning). This is almost the only instance in the *Mémoires* when Marguerite does not think better of criticizing Henri or excuse his ingratitude.

As a result of the Fossette affair, Marguerite makes the fatal mistake of returning to court, and her *Mémoires* break off as she is explaining this decision. It is not known whether she ever finished them. If she did not, it may have been because she found it too painful to speak of the years that followed. Her separation from her husband precipitated the scandal and disgrace that eventually resulted in her confinement at Usson. In 1582, her brother Henri III accused her of adultery and banned her from his court. He then had her arrested at Palaiseau and tried to force her servants to testify against her. Although he later retracted his charges for lack of evidence, Marguerite found herself alone and bereft of support in the middle of a war-torn country, wandering from place to place until she reached Usson in November 1586. If she had written about these events, could she have continued to suppress the truth about either her marginality or her sexuality? Even as a practical matter, would it have been politically expedient to describe how the rift with her husband deepened and how he refused to protect her from her enemies? Throughout the *Mémoires*, her desire to invent a heroic persona for herself forced her to practice what Mariéjol calls her "raccourcis chronologiques qui ne disent qu'une partie de la vérité"[14] (chronological shortcuts that tell only part of the truth). Did the last Valois princess lay down her pen because she could no longer write about herself as if she were a man?

Like most autobiographers, Marguerite de Valois's aim was to justify and make sense out of her existence. As she neared fifty, she found herself alone and powerless—never having played a major role in public affairs, cheated of becoming France's queen. The meaning of such a life could only be found in claiming superior qualities of the mind and heart. Even as she recalled the blows dealt her by "envieuse fortune," therefore, she persisted in representing herself as more noble than those around her. The persona she constructed for herself is thus a genderless incarnation of heroic virtue. To the modern reader, it is clear, however, that in this text self-representation intersects with the politics of gender.

Paradoxically, the fact that Marguerite de Valois was a woman was what motivated her to write as if she were a man. The oppressions and constraints of her existence were the consequence of having been born female. But to convince her husband, her reader, and herself of her moral worth, she tries to construct herself as different from other women. As Hélène

Cixous insists, the story of female sexuality is the story that is not told.[15] Yet the very conspicuousness of its absence makes it present, for, from the moment her father takes her on his knee, the threat of female desire pervades Marguerite's story.

Attempting to construct a subject that conforms to the literary models of her reading, Marguerite de Valois minimizes her femininity; she refuses to identify herself with Brantôme's representation of a beautiful woman or to acknowledge her sexuality. As a result the highly problematic text leaves the reader with many questions and few answers. Nevertheless, this early attempt by a woman to tell her story departs from the masculine memoir in the way it narrates the writer's private experience as daughter and wife, foregrounds her vulnerability and powerlessness within the royal family, and privileges intellectual and spiritual development over political action. The woman who represents herself as not a woman in order to represent herself as a hero cannot conceal the facts of an existence that is anything but heroic. Her text's inability to come to terms with what she is, becomes, in the last analysis, the sign that marks it indelibly as feminine.

NOTES

1. Sidonie Smith, in *A Poetics of Women's Autobiography: Marginality and the Fictions of Self-Representation* (Bloomington: Indiana University Press, 1987), studies the emergence of autobiography at the end of the Middle Ages and the problematics of female self-representation in that historical context. She argues that the autobiographical genre emanating from the "new notion of man" in the Renaissance "construes the autobiographical subject as always male and thereby ignores the interdependences of the ideology of gender and the ideology of individualism that spawned the new discursive form" (26). Smith's textual analyses deal only with works in English. More recently, Faith Beasley has produced a ground-breaking study of Frenchwomen's *Mémoires* composed between 1660 and 1680. She focuses on how women changed the definition of history by chronicling the "particular." See her *Revising Memory: Women's Fiction and Memoirs in Seventeenth-Century France* (New Brunswick: Rutgers University Press, 1990).

2. I am using the word "autobiographical" in its broadest sense—a text whose author, narrator, and protagonist are the same (historical) person. There do not seem to be any published book-length autobiographies by Frenchwomen before Marguerite de Valois's *Mémoires,* but Liselotte Dieckmann's claim in her translation *Memoirs of Marguerite de Valois* (Paris: Papers on French 17th Century Literature, 1984) that Marguerite was "the first woman known in history to have written her autobiography" is overstated (10). Christine de Pisan wrote the story of her life in *La Vision Christine.* Louise de Savoie also produced a brief journal, although her subject was more her son, François I, than herself. Sidonie Smith claims that *The Book of Margery Kempe* (1436) is the first extant woman's autobiography in English.

3. All references are from *Mémoires et autres écrits de Marguerite de Valois, La Reine Margot,* ed. Yves Cazaux (Paris: Mercure de France, 1971). The translations are mine. A translation in English by Liselotte Dieckmann is available. The most reliable biography is Jean H. Mariéjol's *La Vie de Marguerite de Valois, Reine de Navarre et de France (1553–1615)* (Paris, 1928; reprint, Geneva: Slatkine, 1970). Cathleen Bauschatz's excellent essay "'Plaisir et proffict' in the Reading and Writing of Marguerite de Valois," *Tulsa Studies in Women's Literature* 7, no. 1 (1988): 27–48, is the best literary analysis of the *Mémoires.*

4. For theoretical definitions of early *Mémoires,* see especially Philippe Ariès, "Pourquoi

écrit-on des mémoires?" in *Les Valeurs chez les mémorialistes français du XVIIe siècle avant la Fronde,* ed. Naomi Hepp and Jacques Hennequin. Actes et Colloques 22 (Paris: Klincksieck, 1979), 13–20; Bernard Beugnot, "Livre de raison, livre de retraite: Interférences des points de vue chez les mémorialistes," in *Les Valeurs chez les mémorialistes,* 47–64; Marc Fumaroli, "Les Mémoires du XVIIe siècle avant la Fronde," *XVIIe Siècle* 94–95 (1971): 5–37 and "Mémoires et histoire: le dilemne de l'historiographe humaniste au XVIIe siècle," in *Les Valeurs chez les mémorialistes,* 21–45; Marie Thérèse Hipp, *Mythes et réalités: enquête sur le roman et les mémoires (1660–1700)* (Paris: Klincksieck, 1976); and Derek A. Watts, "Self-Portrayal in Seventeenth-Century French Memoirs," *Australian Journal of French Studies* 12 (1975): 264–285 and "Seventeenth-Century French Memoirs: New Perspectives," *Journal of European Studies* 10 (1980): 126–144. According to Georges May, the word *mémoires* may apply to the narrative of external events in which the author was an active participant, the narrative of external events in which the author was a passive observer, and the narrative of the author's life in its most personal aspects. Modern usage, he observes, tends to define the first two as "mémoires" and the third as "autobiographie." See Georges May, *Autobiographie* (Paris: Presses Universitaires de France, 1979 and 1984), 122–123.

5. See Mariéjol, *La Vie,* 318.

6. Smith sees this tension as characteristic of women's autobiography: "Struggling with conflicting purposes and postures, she slides from one fiction of self-representation to another . . . the story of man is not exactly her story; and so her relationship to the empowering figure of male selfhood is inevitably problematic"; see *A Poetics of Women's Autobiography,* 50.

7. Writing as late as 1988, Carolyn Heilbrun could remark, "There still exists little organized sense of what a woman's biography or autobiography should look like," *Writing a Woman's Life* (New York: Norton, 1988). Later she adds, "I have read many moving lives of women, but they are painful, the price is high, the anxiety is intense, because there is no script to follow" (39).

8. See for instance Alexandre Dumas's *La Reine Margot* (Paris: Calmann Lévy, 1887).

9. Mariéjol, *La Vie,* 159.

10. See Constance Jordan, "Boccaccio's In-Famous Women: Gender and Civic Virtue in the *De mulieribus claris,*" in *Ambiguous Realities: Women in the Middle Ages and Renaissance,* ed. Carole Levin and Jeanie Watson (Detroit: Wayne State University Press, 1987), 25–47.

11. See Cazaux's note in the *Mémoires,* 279.

12. See Cazaux's note in the *Mémoires,* 301.

13. Heilbrun, *Writing a Women's Life,* 12, 13.

14. Mariéjol, *La Vie,* 14.

15. Hélène Cixous, "The Laugh of the Medusa," trans. Keith Cohen and Paula Cohen, *Signs* 1 (1976): 875–893.

*PART
TWO*
உ

WRITING THE BODY
AND
THE POETICS
OF
FEMININE DESIRE

LOUISE LABÉ
The Mysterious Case of the
Body in the Text
ৡৰ

Paula Sommers

French feminists have recently urged women to write the body feminine and inscribe in their works experiences that challenge an androcentric literary canon.[1] In striving to develop gynocentric discourse they are responding to social and historical conditions that are in many ways unique to the twentieth century, and their project cannot be reflected back in time without incurring the dangers of anachronism. Women in early modern Europe might subvert traditional literary strategies to express themselves, but they could not invent a radically new language that would expose the female body and exalt its biological functions.[2] Profiting from the intellectual freedom of the Renaissance and the relatively liberal society of Lyons, Louise Labé, nevertheless, included in her *Euvres* a refined expression of feminine desire, and a number of critics believe that the body, which is the focus or site of this desire, is the key to understanding her poetry. Gérard Guillot gives this theory its most extreme statement:

> Louise Labé elle, et plus qu'aucune autre de ces poétesses, assume son corps et son sexe, la totalité de son être. C'est en cela que nous disons qu'elle est femme. Elle a bâti son existence et la destinée de sa poétique sur le mode de l'humaine féminité. Savoir comment ce corps est assumé reste donc, pour l'oeuvre de la Belle Cordière, la question essentielle.[3]

It is Louise Labé more than any other of these women poets who assumes her body and her sex, the totality of her being. It is because of this that we say she is a woman. She has built her existence and the destiny of her poetic practice

85

Pierre Woériot, Portrait of Louise Labé, 1555 (courtesy of Bibl. Nationale, Paris).

on the mode of human femininity. Knowing how the body is assumed, therefore, is the essential question for the work of the "Belle Cordière."[4]

Françoise Charpentier also acknowledges Labé's sophisticated rendering of
the body and its sensations: "La souffrance se dit à l'état pur, et le corps
se trouve comme décanté, lavé, de tout alibi spiritualiste"[5] (She expresses
suffering in its purest state, and the body appears as though decanted or

purified of any spiritual excuses). Charpentier, however, recognizes some peculiarities in Labé's representation of the body, for she mentions "une indistinction voulue de son corps et du corps de l'autre" (29)[6]—a deliberate blending of her body and that of the other. This observation, reaffirmed by François Rigolot, Peggy Kamuf, and Ann R. Jones, immediately raises a question.[7] To what extent does Labé really claim her body?

Close reading of the prefatory letter and the elegies suggests that there is no simple answer to this question, but it is clear that Labé has less affinity with the confident assumption of the body by Cixous and other French feminists than she does with Adrienne Rich in the following passage from *Of Women Born:*[8] "I know of no woman . . . virgin, mother, lesbian, married, celibate, for whom her body is not a fundamental problem." Labé's problem results partly from a social order that assigns women secondary status, partly from traditional mind-body dualism, and partly from the difficulties inherent in the literary representation of the body. In her preface she recognizes that, for women, the body defines both gender and subordination:

> Estant le tems venu, Madamoiselle, que les severes loix des hommes n'empeschent plus les femmes de s'apliquer aus sciences et disciplines: il me semble que celles qui ont la commodité, doivent employer cette honneste liberté que notre sexe ha autre fois tant desirée, à icelles aprendre. (41)

> Since the time has come, Mademoiselle, that the severe laws of men no longer prevent women from applying themselves to the sciences and disciplines, it seems to me that those who can do so must use the noble liberty that our sex so desired in former times, to learn them.

The tension between *hommes/lois* and *femmes/obeissance* in this passage is mitigated by the opposition between *autrefois* and *tems venus,* but subsequent paragraphs demonstrate that the educational liberalism of the Renaissance has not altered women's ancillary status. They may aspire to intellectual equality with men, but not to political power. They may form a sisterhood to encourage one another, but they may not go out into the streets unaccompanied. Access to the humanistic disciplines offers a vital, if partial, liberation because it can give women the power to change the perception of themselves and their bodies. This key factor in Labé's thinking emerges in the following paragraph where humanistic learning is linked with the production of texts and textual production evokes metaphors based on clothing:

> Et si quelcune parvient en tel degré, que de pouvoir mettre ses concepcions par escrit, le faire songneusement et non dédaigner la gloire, et s'en parer plustot que de chaines, anneaus, et somptueus habits: lesquels ne pouvons vrayement estimer notres, que par usage. (41)

And if anyone succeeds to such a degree that she can record her thoughts in writing, she should do so carefully and not disdain glory, and adorn herself with this rather than chains, rings and sumptuous garments: for we cannot say that these things are truly ours, save by custom.

Learning, glory, writing—the products of thought that expresses an inner, authentic self—contrast here with that which is "notres . . . par usage," the adornments of the body. Adornments are both alien and alienating. Chains are signs of wealth but also of servility and bondage. Rings evoke the promises, but also the obligations of matrimony. Fine clothing indicates status, ceremony, the prerogatives and the duties of social position. Collectively, they recall the reified woman whose body is not her own, but the object of the masculine gaze and an item of exchange in the formation of social alliances through marriage.[9] Labé proposes a process of substitution in which text replaces apparel. Because clothing in the Renaissance clearly distinguished gender, her metaphor is consistent with the feminist tone of the letter. By focusing on adornment or cover, however, she is less provocative than Montaigne in his prefatory remarks to the reader:

> Je veus qu'on m'y voie en ma façon simple, naturelle et ordinaire, sans contantion et artifice: car c'est moy que je peins . . . Que si j'eusse esté entre ces nations qu'on dict vivre encore sous la douce liberté des premieres loix de nature, je t'asseure que je m'y fusse très-volontiers peint tout entier, et tout nud.

> I want to be seen here in my simple, natural, ordinary fashion, without straining or artifice; for it is myself that I portray. . . . Had I been placed among those nations which are said to live still in the sweet freedom of nature's first laws, I assure you I should very gladly have portrayed myself here entire and wholly naked.[10]

The essayist playfully offers to expose what propriety requires that he conceal, while Labé takes pains to show that she has no intention of exposing an individualized or unprotected body to the public gaze. Any reference to nakedness, however facetious, in a preface intended to present writing to women as a respectable activity with potentially great rewards would be out of place. Instead Labé argues that the text with which the woman writer is to clothe herself functions as *écrit* or *science* and not as intimate revelation. Like the real garment, it can display artistic skill or beauty while screening what the wearer chooses to conceal.

Assuming the body in the prefatory letter is, then, far from simple. The site of gender, the object of social regulation, it is intimately associated with adornment, yet adornment draws attention in its own right and reflects upon itself, while shielding the body of the wearer. Because the textual garment draws attention to the mind and to artifice, Labé quite logically evokes a conventional humanistic topos that opposes transient material possessions and the lasting glory achieved through learning: "Mais l'honneur que la science nous procurera, sera entierement notre: et ne nous pourra estre oté, ne par finesse de larron, ne force d'ennemis, ne longueur du tems" (41) (But the honor that learning will obtain for us will be entirely ours and cannot be taken from us by the cunning of thieves, the strength of enemies or the length of time). As matter, the body is on the negative side of this polarity so that the preface ultimately situates it as inferior to the mind and as an object that is clothed/concealed and subjected to social constraint. In both instances there is tension between the woman's inner self and her body.

While the preface is concerned with the role of the woman writer, Labé's perception of the body in the elegies is mediated by Petrarchan tradition.[11] The first elegy demonstrates her ability to manipulate the conventional vocabulary:

> Au tems qu'Amour, d'hommes et Dieus vainqueur,
> Faisoit bruler de sa flamme mon coeur,
> En embrasant de sa cruelle rage
> Mon sang, mes os, mon esprit et courage . . . (I:1–4)

> In the days when love, conqueror of men and gods,
> Burned my heart with his fire,
> Enflaming with his cruel rage
> My blood, my bones, my spirit and courage . . .

The conventions are such that what appears in these verses is not so much a recognizable body as parts of a Petrarchan corpus or discourse. As Claude Reichler notes,[12] "Toute fiction interprétative aliène le corps comme tel; celui-ci reste sans doute disponible, mais aussi toujours rebelle, irréductible à sa représentation" (All interpretative fiction alienates the body as such; the latter remains doubtless available, but also always rebellious, irreducible to its representation). The Petrarchan persona constructs the body from within as a site of conflict between pain and pleasure, frustration and desire. The body of the beloved is fragmented, fetishized, and subjected to metaphorical metamorphoses that showcase rhetorical dexterity. As Reichler reminds us, drawing upon modern psychology, in a very profound sense there can be no body in the text: "Le corps, le vrai nous apparaît lié à l'archaïque, à l'oubli, à la dimension de la perte, dont la psychanalyse a si fortement revivifié le sentiment" (3)[13] (The body, the real one appears to us as linked to the archaic, to the forgotten, to the dimension of *loss* for which psychoanalysis has so strongly renewed our feeling).

Not surprisingly, representation of the body in the elegies consists of a series of exempla that express alienation, continuing and enhancing the strategies of the prologue with its focus on a female inner self versus an adorned body, and mind versus body. Thematically, they reveal a distinct frame-and-center pattern with elegies I and III addressed to the ladies of Lyons and dominated by the figure of the Amazon. Elegy II expresses the persona's lack of confidence in mere physical beauty as a means of attracting the beloved. In each text the female body, in keeping with Petrarchan convention, is vulnerable to the power of love. But this vulnerability is all the more impressive because it must overcome determined resistance, and this resistance can symbolize a feminist desire for independence rather than mere acquiescence in Petrarchan tradition. This is particularly clear in Labé's exploitation of Amazon figures.

The first of these, Semiramis, occurs in elegy I. The cultivated Renaissance reader would be familiar with this story and with the larger tradition that included figures like Hippolyta, Penthesilea, and Camilla in classical literature and more contemporary Amazons from the works of Ariosto or the many volumes of the *Amadis*.[14] Although there are cultural variations in the depiction of Amazons, they function in androcentric literature as transgressive figures. Daughters of Ares and Aphrodite, they combine conventionally male attributes of warlike vigor, courage, and dominance with an exotic feminine beauty. Because the Amazon resists or refuses marriage, achieves control of her own reproductive processes, and according to some legends, sacrifices one of her breasts to achieve greater military efficiency, her body is the instrument of her own will. For the male writer she is, therefore, a figure who must be overcome by the hero.[15] Theseus slays Hippolyta. Achilles looks with amorous passion at Penthesilea only after she is dead. Negative Amazons in the *Fairy Queen* (Radigund) must be overcome by heroines whose prowess in battle (Britomart) can be identified with Christian ideology.

As Monique Wittig's *Les Guérillères* demonstrates, the woman writer may view the Amazon as a positive figure precisely because of the independence and strength she symbolizes. Because this independence is precluded by the Petrarchan code that governs the elegies, Labé's Amazons are humbled and defeated by love. Their transgressive character is softened, if not eliminated, and the persona portrays the active, resourceful lives they lead prior to the *innamoramento* with the utmost sympathy. Semiramis appears initially, not as a transgressive or threatening woman, but as a Queen who successfully leads her nation:

> Semiramis, Royne tant renommée,
> Qui mit en route avecques son armée
> Les noirs squadrons des Ethiopiens,
> Et en montrant louable exemple aus siens
> Faisoit couler de son furieus branc
> Des ennemis les plus braves le sang . . . (I: 61–66)

> Semiramis, Queen so reknowned,
> Who defeats with her army

The dark squadrons of Ethiopians,
And, giving praiseworthy example,
Made flow with her furious spear
The blood of the bravest enemies . . .

The following narrative slowly strips her of external signs of prowess—
military accoutrements that place her in the public and political realm—
and reveals a weak female body:

Qu'est devenu ce fer et cet escu,
Dont tu rendois le plus brave veincu?
Ou as tu mis la Marciale creste,
Qui obombroit le blond or de ta teste?
Ou est l'espée, ou est cette cuirasse,
Dont tu rompois des ennemis l'audace? (I: 75–80)

What has become of the spear and shield
With which you overcame the bravest?
Where have you put the Martial helmet
That concealed the gold of your hair?
Where is the sword, where the armor
With which you broke the spirit of the enemy?

Loss of armor and exposure of the hair portrays a sudden descent from the
realm of Athena—the helmeted goddess par excellence—to that of Venus,
and passion triumphs over reason.[16] The emergence of a lustful self, a weak
female body characterized by sensuous languor and a will that no longer
responds to the commands of the superego leaves Semiramis defenseless
and so confused that she no longer recognizes herself—"Ainsi Amour de
toy t'a estrangée" (I: 89).

The Semiramis episode continues and radicalizes the metaphorical
opposition between inner and outer established in the preface. She is a
tragic figure because hubris leads her to identify with her public persona
and its military adornment—helmet and breastplate—while ignoring the
inner realm of sexuality. In the third elegy Labé again resorts to the Amazon figure, this time associating it with her own persona. While the persona
shares with Semiramis the fall from a state of androgynous harmony and
self-control to alienating passion—"Tant que ne peu moymesme me con-
noitre" (III: 72)—there are significant differences. The persona's "military" exploits are limited to displays of horsemanship and athletic prowess
before an admiring audience and do not entail the shedding of blood. Because Mars is allied with *sçavoir*, needlework and music, the Amazon of
the third elegy is a figure whose civilized, if not ultracivilized aspect, is
diametrically opposed to the vaguely disturbing image of the pagan
Queen. Were it not for love, in effect, Labé's persona would have maintained an ideal "Renaissance" balance between mind and body. She is

defeated, but not stripped of her armor and compelled to lie silently and helplessly "sur une couche" in the position of Semiramis. Her identification with Ariosto's Bradamante and Marphise immediately reflects upon Labé's role as writer. Indeed, both before and after the *innamoramento* her persona is actively engaged in transforming life into a work of art. When the intellectual and physical balance that she cultivated before the lover's fatal glance escape her, she turns to poetry, portraying herself as a sister of Sappho and disciple of Apollo. Exaltation of the voice and the textual fabric it creates replaces the metaphorical stripping of Semiramis and recalls the message of the prefatory letter. Through her writing, Labé's persona retains something of the Amazon's strength and vigor.

In the second elegy Labé abandons the Amazon pattern. Concern with the body now becomes more immediate as the persona, confronted with an absent and possibly unfaithful beloved, struggles to define herself in opposition to an unknown rival:

> Si say je bien que t'amie nouvelle
> A peine aura le renom d'estre telle,
> Soit en beauté, vertu, grace et faconde,
> Comme plusieurs gens savans par le monde
> M'ont fait à tort, ce croy je, estre estimée. (II: 55–59)
>
> . . . .
>
> Je ne dy pas qu'elle ne soit plus belle:
> Mais que jamais femme ne t'aymera,
> Ne plus que moy d'honneur te portera. (II: 72–74)

> I know well that your new friend
> Can scarcely be so esteemed
> Be it for beauty, virtue, grace and eloquence
> As several learned, well-traveled men
> Have convinced me, wrongly perhaps, I am.
>
> . . . .
>
> I do not say that she is not more beautiful
> But that no woman will ever love you more
> Or bring you greater honor than I.

In her preface Labé seemingly accepts without question the female obligation to be beautiful, for she is content to combine women's competition with men "en beauté"—their traditional role and the one that usually gave them superiority—with other areas of rivalry—"science et vertu." In these verses from the second elegy the theme of physical attractiveness is again combined with "science" so that bodily appearance, while important, is not in itself sufficient.[17] The persona begins her self-assessment by referring to her fame, recalling the agenda set forth for women writers in the letter to Clémence de Bourges. Fame derives from qualities listed in a single, emphatic verse—"Soit en beauté, vertu, grace et faconde." Viewed in terms of Neoplatonic philosophy, these interrelated characteristics display themselves through the body.[18] The appearance of the body reflects the state of the soul. Speech similarly validates character and complements the impression made by physical beauty. The structure of Labé's enumerative verse emphasizes both *beauté* and *faconde,* although the placing of *faconde* with its sonorous nasal vowel at the end of the line gives slightly greater importance to eloquence and suggests that beauty and virtue naturally culminate in speech. Indeed, the fact that her fame exists especially among the learned men suggests that *faconde* may eclipse rather than merely complement physical beauty in the creation of fame.

The suggestion is confirmed in the second quotation as the persona, who seemed so confident of her beauty in verse 57, suddenly expresses doubts. Rather than compete with another woman in the realm of mere physical appearance that, in spite of Neoplatonic theory, implies subjective, relative values over which she has no control, the persona reminds her beloved of the unique distinction that he can gain from the devotion of such a famous and eloquent woman. She thus accomplishes a transition from body to mind, from an appearance that may or may not satisfy the beholder to character, intelligence, and especially *faconde.*

Before the reader begins the sonnets, Labé's letter to Clémence de Bourges and the three elegies already define a complex relationship between the female poet/persona and the body. This relationship is generally characterized by insecurity and tension because of an enduring split that places the body outside where it can be defined by the gaze of the other and the self inside struggling for a more authentic means of recognition and validation. Viewed from without and in the context of the love poetry, the body, which is required to be beautiful, competes with the bodies of other females for the attention of the beloved. Anxiety ensues because there can be no guarantee that the persona will win this competition. Viewed from within, the persona's body conforms to Petrarchan convention as a center of perception, memory and suffering. Suffering is particularly acute and particularly feminine when physical passion suddenly challenges an amazonian condition characterized by joyous independence and dominant reason. It creates a state of confusion in which the persona no longer recognizes herself, one in which the body appears as obstacle to, rather than agent of, the will.

To some degree the sonnets continue the tension expressed in the elegies and the prefatory letter. Labé's persona is still unsure of her physical beauty:

> Las! que me sert, que si parfaitement
> Louas jadis et ma tresse dorée,
> Et de mes yeus la beauté comparée
> A deus Soleils . . .
>
> . . . . .
>
> Donques c'estoit le but de ta malice
> De m'asservir sous ombre de service? (XXIII: 1–4, 9–10)

Alas! What does it serve me if
You once praised perfectly my golden tresses,
And compared the beauty of my eyes
To two suns . . .
. . . . . .
Was it, then, your malicious goal
To enslave me by feigning love service?

There is no necessary connection in these verses between signifier and signified, no reason to assume that the persona's body conforms to the Petrarchan ideal or that the lover's language is other than misleading rhetoric.
The persona has, in effect, no reliable image of her physical appearance in
either her own mind or the discourse of the other.

In other sonnets the relationship between the persona and her body
can attain a complexity that the elegies and the letter to Clémence de
Bourges scarcely anticipate:

On voit mourir toute chose animée,
Lors que du corps l'ame sutile part:
Je suis le corps, toy la meilleure part:
Ou es tu donq, o ame bien aymée?
Ne me laissez pas si long temps pamée,
Pour me sauver apres viendrois trop tard.
Las, ne mets point ton corps en ce hazart:
Rens lui sa part et moitié estimée. (VII: 1–8)

We see that all living things die
When the subtle soul leaves the body:
I am the body, you the nobler part:
Where are you, then, o well-beloved soul?
Don't leave me fainting for so long,
After, you would come too late to save me.
Alas, don't put your body in such danger:
Give back its part and esteemed half.

Three distinct modes of discourse concerning the body intersect in these
verses.[19] The Christian view that defines the human condition in terms of
the body-soul unity dominates the first quatrain. In the second quatrain
reference to *moitié* introduces the concept of the Neoplatonic androgyne
that establishes lovers as parts of a single entity in which male and female
are perfectly balanced. Finally, Labé recognizes a third perspective, derived
from the physiological understanding of sexual differentiation and assuming that the female is passive, cold, moist, life-sustaining and the male active, dry, warm, life-giving. Manifest in the association of the female persona with passivity and the lover with life and energy, the third code tends
to be subverted by the larger context. Because the persona has a voice as
well as a body and dares to address the beloved her "passivity" is a literary

construct, a reprisal of the Petrarchan positioning of love-struck poet and inaccessible or unresponsive beloved. The mingling of substantives throughout these quatrains—feminine persona designated by the masculine *corps*, masculine beloved by the feminine *âme* and *moitié*—further emphasizes the androgyne theme and, therefore, disrupts the rigid gender differentiation evoked by the third code.[20] The sonnet thus fails to provide an independent, specifically feminine body, although it confirms the erotic, unitive pattern that Charpentier, Rigolot, and others have noted.

Sonnet thirteen also exemplifies mutuality or "indistinction voulue."[21] Here the persona's assumption of a sensuous, feminine body is expressed by words that carry the rime—"ravie," "amie" and finally, "heureuse." The body, however, remains more than ever a problem. The hoped for unity with the beloved can occur only in fantasy because flesh cannot achieve the enduring embrace of ivy:

> Oh si j'estois en ce beau sein ravie
> De celui là pour lequel vois mourant:
> Si avec lui vivre le demeurant
> De mes cours jours ne m'empeschoit envie:
> Si m'acollant me disoit, chere Amie,
> Contentons nous l'un l'autre, s'asseurant
> Que ja tempeste, Euripe, ne Courant,
> Ne nous pourra desjoindre en notre vie:
> Si de mes bras le tenant acollé,
> Comme du Lierre est l'arbre encercelé,
> La mort venoit, de mon aise envieuse:
> Lors que soeuf plus il me baiseroit,
> Et mon esprit sur ses levres fuiroit,
> Bien je mourrois, plus que vivante, heureuse.

> Oh, if I were borne away into that fine breast
> Of him for whom I die with longing,
> If I were not prevented from living the rest
> Of my short days with him by envy.
> If, embracing me he said, dear friend
> Let us be content one with another
> Knowing that no tempest, Euripus or current
> Will separate us in this life:
> If, holding him closely in my arms
> As ivy encircles a tree
> Death were to come, jealous of my pleasure:
> While he would be kissing me sweetly,
> And my soul would flee upon his lips,
> I would die gladly, content, more than in living.

Whether the last tercet is interpreted in modern terms as an expression of sexual climax or more traditionally as a Neoplatonic fusion of souls or an actual death, the persona's pleasure entails movement out of the body/ self into death/otherness. Assumption of the body in the sonnets is, rather paradoxically, linked with a complementary movement away from the body. This movement derives partly from the Petrarchan tradition where the intense sufferings of love may lead the poet to contemplate death and partly from the Neoplatonistic tendency toward transcendence, but it is given new significance because Labé is constantly aware of her need to move beyond the decorative role assigned to women and acquire a voice. Sonnet XVIII, another description of erotic fantasy, concludes with a tercet that illuminates the *Euvres* as a whole:

> Tousjours suis mal, vivant discrettement,
> Et ne me puis donner contentement,
> Si hors de moy ne fay quelque saillie. (12–14)

> I am always unhappy, living discretely,
> And I can find no contentment
> Unless I make some sally out of myself.

Satisfaction is, characteristically, not located in the body but in the written "saillie."[22] The sonnet recalls the preface:

> S'il y ha quelque chose recommandable apres la gloire et l'honneur, le plaisir que l'estude des lettres ha acoutumé donner nous y doit chacune inciter: qui est autre que les autres recreations: desquelles quand on en ha pris tant que lon veut, on ne se peut vanter d'autre chose, que d'avoir passé le tems. Mais celle de l'estude laisse un contentement de soy, qui nous demeure plus longue-ment. (42)

> If there is something to recommend after glory and honor, the pleasure that the study of letters customarily gives us should incite us to learn: this is differ-ent from other recreations, for when you have enjoyed them as much as you want, you can boast only of having passed the time. But study leaves an inner contentment that lasts longer.

Labé assumes the body as a given, as a problem, an outer self not often consistent with the inner perception of self, object of the other's gaze, lo-cus of desire and frustration, but also, and most important, subject of liter-ature and, therefore, of one's own creation, potential link with an enlight-ened sisterhood and an even broader community that can provide the glory she is seeking. To return to Gérard Guillot Labé assumes a body only to dress it in poetic texts. Femininity lies not in the body alone but in the combination of body with discourse that articulates and transcends the body.

NOTES

1. Their attitudes are, of course, changing as time progresses so that writing the body can assume a number of interpretations. I have in mind here the theories of Luce Irigaray in

Speculum de l'autre femme (Paris: Editions de Minuit, 1974) and *Ce Sexe qui n'en est pas un* (Paris: Editions de Minuit, 1977); and Hélène Cixous, *Souffles* (Paris: des femmes, 1975). For a general selection of texts on French feminism, the Marks-Courtivron anthology *New French Feminisms* (Amherst: University of Massachusetts Press, 1980) is helpful, and so is Helena Michie's *The Flesh Made Word: Female Figures and Women's Bodies* (New York: Oxford University Press, 1987). See also articles by Ann Rosalind Jones, "Writing the Body: Toward an Understanding of 'l'écriture féminine,'" *Feminist Studies* 7 (1981): 247–263; Elaine Marks, "Women and Literature in France," *Signs* 3 (1978): 832–855; Robert Scholes, "Uncoding Mama: The Female Body as Text," in *Semiotics and Interpretation* (New Haven: Yale University Press, 1982) 127–142; and Susan Suleiman, ed., *The Female Body in Western Culture* (Cambridge: Harvard University Press, 1985).

2. Ruth Kelso's *Doctrine for the Lady of the Renaissance* (Urbana: University of Illinois Press, 1956) provides the most convenient introduction to the cultural attitudes that governed women of the time. See also Kathleen Ashley, "Medieval Courtesy Literature and Dramatic Mirrors of Female Conduct," in *The Ideology of Conduct,* ed., Nancy Armstrong and Leonard Tennenhouse (New York: Methuen, 1987), 25–37; Peter Stallybrass, "Patriarchal Territories: The Body Enclosed," in *Rewriting the Renaissance,* ed. Margaret Ferguson et al. (Chicago: University of Chicago Press, 1986), 123–142; and Ann Rosalind Jones, "Nets and Bridles," in *The Ideology of Conduct,* ed. Nancy Armstrong and Leonard Tennenhouse, 39–72.

3. Gérard Guillot, *Louise Labé* (Paris: Seghers, 1962), 88.

4. Unless otherwise indicated, all translations are mine.

5. Françoise Charpentier, *Oeuvres de Louise Labé précédées des Rymes de Pernette du Guillet* (Paris: Gallimard, 1983), 28.

6. Charpentier's analysis occurs in the introduction to her edition of Louise Labé's *Euvres.* Quotations of Labé in this article, however, are based upon François Rigolot's edition of Labé's *Oeuvres Complètes* (Paris: Flammarion, 1986).

7. See Ann R. Jones, *The Currency of Eros* (Bloomington: Indiana University Press, 1990), 155–178; Peggy Kamuf, "A Double Life (Feminism II)," in *Men in Feminism,* ed. Alice Jardine and Paul Smith (New York: Methuen, 1987), 93–98 and François Rigolot, "Gender vs. Sex Difference in Louise Labé's Grammar of Love," *Rewriting the Renaissance,* ed. Ferguson et al., 287–298. Sources for a broader discussion of Labé would include Karine Berriot, *Louise Labé. La Belle Rebelle et le François nouveau, suivi des Oeuvres complètes* (Paris: Seuil, 1985); Enzo Giudici, *Louise Labé e l'"Ecole lyonnaise": Studi e ricerche con documenti inediti* (Naples: Liguore, 1964); Lawrence Harvey, *The Aesthetics of the Renaissance Love Sonnet* (Geneva: Droz, 1962); Dorothy O'Connor, *Louise Labé, sa vie et son oeuvre* (Paris: Les Presses françaises, 1926); Elisabeth Schulze-Witzenrath, *Die Originalität der Louise Labé. Studien zum weiblichen Petrarkismus* (Munich: Fink, 1974); and Chiara Sibona, *Le Sens qui résonne* (Ravenna: Longo, 1984).

8. Adrienne Rich, *Of Woman Born* (New York: Norton, 1976). I have excluded the *Débat de Folie et d'Amour* from this article because of the plurality of voices. I want to concentrate on the relationship between the first-person, feminine persona and the female body as Labé describes or experiences it. For further discussion of the dedicatory letter, see Kazimierz Kupisz, "L'Epître dédicatoire de Louise Labé à Mlle de Bourges," *Le Lingue straniere* 13 (1964): 17–28.

9. For further analysis of Labé in reference to bourgeois conventions or attitudes, see Jones, *Currency of Eros,* 155–178.

10. Michel de Montaigne, *The Complete Essays,* trans. Donald M. Frame (Stanford: Stanford University Press, 1957), 2.

11. A number of scholars have shown interest in Labé's adaptation of Petrarchan conventions to a feminine point of view. Among the more interesting works are those by Andrea Chan, "Petrarchism and Neoplatonism in Louise Labé's Concept of Happiness," *Australian Journal of French Studies* 14 (1977): 213–232, and "The Function of the Beloved in the Poetry of Louise Labé," *Australian Journal of French Studies* 17 (1980): 46–57; Gillian

Jondorf, "Petrarchan Variations in Pernette du Guillet and Louise Labé," *Modern Language Review* 71 (1976): 766–778; Gisèle Mathieu-Castellani, "Les Marques du féminin dans la parole amoureuse de Louise Labé," in *Louise Labé: les voix du lyrisme,* ed. Guy Demerson (Saint-Etienne: Institut Claude Longeon, 1990), 189–205; Elisabeth Schulze-Wittzenrath, *Die Originalität der Louise Labé;* Karen Wiley, "Louise Labé's Deceptive Petrarchism," *Modern Language Studies* 9 (1981): 51–60; and Dudley Wilson, "La Poésie amoureuse de Louise Labé et la tradition poétique de son temps," in *Les voix du lyrisme,* 17–34. With regard to Renaissance feminism in general, consult Constance Jordan, *Renaissance Feminism: Literary Texts and Political Models* (Ithaca: Cornell University Press, 1990). For suffering as a major theme in the sonnets, see M. J. Baker, "The Sonnets of Louise Labé: A Reappraisal," *Neophilologus* 60 (1976): 20–30.

12. Claude Reichler, *Le Corps et ses fictions* (Paris: Minuit, 1983), 2.

13. Whether one chooses to cite contemporary poetic tradition and the fragmentation or dismemberment of the body (see Nancy Vickers, "Diana Described: Scattered Woman and Scattered Rhyme," *Critical Inquiry* 8, no. 2 [1981]: 265–279) or cite the Lacanian explanation of a totalized body as being physically inaccessible (Michie, *Flesh Made Word*, 149), Labé never attempts a complete description of the body.

14. For further background on the Amazon, see Abbey Wettan Kleinbaum, *The War Against the Amazons* (New York: McGraw-Hill, 1983), and Donald Sobol, *The Amazons in Greek Mythology* (New York: A. S. Barnes and Co., 1972).

15. Blake Tyrell provides the most thorough analysis of the Amazons as an inversion of patriarchal culture in the context of classical literature, *Amazons: A Study in Mythmaking* (Baltimore: Johns Hopkins University Press, 1984).

16. Margaret Miles in *Carnal Knowing: Female Nakedness and Religious Meaning in The Christian West* (Boston: Beacon Press, 1990), 48–53, provides an in-depth discussion of the link between hair and lust.

17. As Jones points out in "City Women and Their Audiences: Louise Labé and Veronica Franco," in *Rewriting the Renaissance,* Labé never attempts a description of her own beauty: "To do so would mean facing a possibly unsurmountable contradiction: to praise herself as seen from without, to speak as desired object and desiring subject at the same time" (306). Jones notes in the same article (304) that Labé's writing is also shaped by the "constant presence of men as the ultimate critics . . . of women's beauty, of their merit as poets."

18. For further discussion, consult Marsilio Ficino's commentary on Plato's *Banquet:* Discourse I: 4; Discourse II: 3; V: 1–4; VI: 2.

19. Guillot cites this sonnet as exemplifying a carnal orientation toward the body (89). Andrea Chan ("Function of the Beloved") reports a more spiritual interpretation, arguing that the sonnet presents "a composite being, whose forces are concentrated in its spiritual parts" (54). For other readings, see Lawrence Harvey, *The Aesthetics of the Renaissance Love Sonnet* (Geneva: Droz, 1962), and Chiara Sibona.

20. See François Rigolot, "Gender vs. Sex Difference," for discussion of gendered language in Labé.

21. See the discussion of mutuality and a summary of attitudes toward it in Jones, *Currency of Eros,* 165–167.

22. Labé's "saillie" and sonnet XVIII have provoked considerable commentary, most recently from Rigolot, "Gender vs. Sex Difference"; Kamuf, "A Double Life"; and Jones in *Currency of Eros,* 172–173.

"Trop en Corps"
Marguerite de Navarre and
the Transgressive Body

ʕə

Colette H. Winn

The body has a great part in our being, it holds a high rank in it;
so its structure and composition are well worth consideration.
Those who want to split up our two principal parts and sequester them
from each other are wrong. On the contrary, we must couple and join
them together again. We must order the soul not to draw aside
and entertain itself apart, not to scorn and abandon the body
(nor can it do so except by some counterfeit monkey trick), but to rally
to the body, embrace it, cherish it, assist it, control it, advise it, set it
right and bring it back when it goes astray; in short, to marry it and be
a husband to it, so that their actions may appear not different and
contrary, but harmonious and uniform.

—Montaigne, "Of Presumption"

The Renaissance understood the physical body in relation to its nobler counterpart, the soul. As a consequence, the relationship of Same and of Other was not without its problems. Parlamente's well-known definition of the "parfaictz amans" (perfect lovers) following novella XIX of Marguerite de Navarre's *Heptameron* points to the problematic rapport between body and soul as dualistic metaphysics conceives of it:

> L'ame, qui n'est creée que pour retourner à son souverain bien, ne faict, tant qu'elle est dedans ce corps, que desirer d'y parvenir. Mais, à cause que les sens, par lesquelz elle en peut avoir nouvelles, sont obscurs et charnelz par le peché du premier pere, ne luy peuvent monstrer que les choses visibles plus approchantes de la parfection, après quoy l'ame court, cuydans trouver, en une beaulté exterieure, en une grace visible et aux vertuz morales, la souveraine beaulté, grace et vertu.[1]

The soul, which was created solely that it might return to its Sovereign Good, ceaselessly desires to achieve this end while it is still within the body. But the senses, by means of which the soul is able to have intelligence of its Sovereign Good, are dim and carnal because of the sins of our forefather Adam and

99

Title page of Marguerite de Navarre's *Heptaméron,*
Paris, 1560 (courtesy of the Newberry Library,
Chicago).

consequently can reveal to the soul only those things which are visible and
have some nearer approximation to perfection. The soul runs after these
things, vainly thinking that in some external beauty, in some visible grace and
in the moral virtues it will find the sovereign beauty, the sovereign grace and
the sovereign virtue.

We have here two *topoi* popularized in Renaissance France by Ficino's commentaries: the motif of the soul imprisoned in the body and eager to break free to return to its celestial origin, and the notion that by means of the senses the soul first awakens to Beauty. But in suggesting that physical beauty is deceptive, Marguerite de Navarre departs from Ficino: "*cuydans trouver, en une beauté exterieure . . . la souveraine beaulté*."[2] For her, paradoxically, the physical body is both the origin, the starting point of the ascension process, and the obstacle (either as prison or mere hindrance) between man and God.[3] If man is to continue his journey upward, he must first reject the Flesh.

Thus, the passage from human to divine, from a carnal to a spiritual existence, implies a radical leap. As a result there is a pervasive tension in Marguerite's work. This tension is generated, on the one hand, by her consciousness of her physical being and its exigencies—her sense of belonging to this world—and, on the other hand, by the will to transcend the Flesh in order to reach the state of "nothingness" (dépouillement) necessary to divine ascension.[4] Marguerite's spiritual meditation begins with an attempt to define her position toward the physical body and eventually leads to reconciliation with the self. In exploring the ways in which human beings experience their corporeality, she strives to resolve her internal conflict and comprehend/embrace the physical aspect of being.

"De l'ensemble de son oeuvre, il apparaît qu'au plus profond de son angoisse fut toujours une crainte, celle de ne pas encore aimer Dieu d'un amour assez fort, d'un amour total. Celle de garder en somme, dans les formes mêmes de la foi, des vestiges de mondanité," observes V.-L. Saulnier. (In her work overall, it seems that at the deepest point of her anguish there exists a fear, the fear of failing to love God with the greatest possible love, total love—the fear of harboring, in the very form of her faith, the remains of worldliness).[5] The inadequacy Marguerite attributes to her love for God is due to her "charnelle sensualité" (carnal sensuality),[6] to her sense of being "trop en corps" (too embodied), a fact that she deplores in a letter written in late November 1522 to her spiritual father, Guillaume Briçonnet.[7] Marguerite here condemns the physical body whose nature is to go astray, thereby endangering that perfect union of opposites, the soul and the body, of which we are composed. By its insatiable appetites, its illnesses and miseries, and its egotistical love, the transgressive body continually diverts us from that which is essential.

To explore the Queen's changing attitude toward the physical body, I examine here two types of representations of the transgressive body in Marguerite de Navarre's works, the erotic body and the mourning body.

Without denying the Fall, Ficino maintains a certain optimism in his vision of man. Marguerite de Navarre, however, has no illusions.[8] The vision of fallen man permeates her work. "[Il] n'est rien si bestial que la personne destituée de l'esperit de Dieu" (*Heptameron* 322) (Nothing more resembles a brute than a person deprived of the spirit of God) (421), concludes Oisille after the story of a woman "qui preferoit son plaisir à tout l'honneur du monde" (321) (who preferred her pleasure to all the honor in the world) (421). The body is the driving force of sin, the archetype of corruption.

In the *Heptameron*, the chaste body contrasts sharply, by its nature and its rarity, with the elemental body, ruled by instinct and passion. The undisciplined body transgresses its own limits. Novella II tells the story of a manservant who is driven by irrational sexual desire to attack the muleteer's wife. When she resists, he stabs her repeatedly with his sword and rapes her as she lies dying.

"Bestialle amour" (animal lust) reveals the dark side of humanity.[9] For it corrupts that which is good in us: reason.[10] As Nicole Cazauran puts it, "alors même qu'il semble suivre sa nature, l'homme se dénature" (Even when he appears to follow his nature, man is corrupt).[11] And the mind soon becomes as corrupt as the body. In the grip of passion, the prior of Saint-Martin-des-Champs became "ung homme furieux et non seullement hors de conscience, mais de raison naturelle" (179) (not only was he apparently without conscience, he was also completely bereft of his natural reason) (258). Saint-Aignan's wife in the first story "aimoit si fort qu'elle en estoit demye enragée" (12) (became half demented with love) (71). And the foolish lady from Pamplona, observes Saffredent, lived "en telle volupté, que raison, conscience, ordre ne mesure n'avoient plus de lieu en elle" (213) (so sensuous an existence that reason, conscience, order, and moderation no longer had any place in her) (297). One can find as many examples showing that "fureur" (fury) has the power to conquer men and women, the humble and the great alike, causing them to forget the law of God (our "conscience") and the law of men ("la renommée").

"Vilaine follye" (ugly folly) strikes where one would least expect, surprising those who are least inclined to love "par mal" (115) (for bad reasons) (187).[12] The longer it is repressed the more violently it is likely to erupt. As she lies next to her son, "the devout woman" forgets that she is a mother (novella XXX). Another "devout woman" (novella XXXV) is consumed by desire at the sight of her handsome priest. In this case though, the fire of the flesh assumes a spiritual form that in the end turns out to be the most insidious of carnal deceits:

> Ainsy ce feu, soubz tiltre de spirituel, fut si charnel, que le cueur qui en fut si embrasé brusla tout le corps de ceste pauvre dame; et, tout ainsy qu'elle estoit

tardive à sentyr ceste flamme, ainsy elle fut prompte à enflamber, et sentyt plus tost le contentement de sa passion, qu'elle ne congneut estre passionnée. (255–256)

> The fire of her passion beneath its spiritual guise was carnal to such a degree that the flames raging in the poor lady's heart spread throughout the whole of her body. Being slow to feel the heat, she caught fire all the more quickly and experienced the pleasure of passion before she had even realized that it was passion that had her in its grip. (346–347)

Even the noblest of women can fall prey to burning passion. In novella XX, the Seigneur de Riant finds the widow who refuses to give herself to him "couchée dessus l'herbe entre les bras d'un palefronier de sa maison, aussy laid, ord et infame que de Riant estoit beau, fort, honneste et aimable" (154) (lying on the grass in the arms of one of her stable-boys! A stable-boy as dirty, common, and ugly as de Riant was handsome, gallant, and refined!) (232).[13]

Marguerite proceeds to describe the effects of erotic passion on the human body, a subject that fascinated her contemporaries, both literary and scientific.[14] The physiological manifestations vary from one subject to another: paleness, loss of appetite and rest, weight loss for some (novella IX); healthy appearance and stoutness for others (novella XXXV, XXII). The entire body is transfigured by "lovesickness," especially the face, which is often hardly recognizable. Under the influence of erotic desire, the features become distorted, the complexion turns crimson, and the gaze suddenly lights up in a furious blaze:

> Quant Floride veit [le] visaige [d'Amadour] et ses oeilz tant alterez, que le plus beau tainct du monde estoit rouge comme feu, et le plus doulx et plaisant regard si orrible et furieux qu'il sembloit que ung feu très ardant estincellast dans son cueur et son visaige; et en ceste fureur, d'une de ses fortes et puissantes mains, print les deux delicates et foibles de Floride. (78)

> His whole expression, his face, his eyes, had changed as he spoke. The fair complexion was flushed with fiery red. The kind, gentle face was contorted with a terrifying violence, as if there was some raging inferno belching fire in his heart and behind his eyes. One powerful fist roughly seized hold of her two weak and delicate hands. (147)

Elsewhere in the *Heptameron* one can find other examples in which appearance speaks the body's transgressions.[15] The undisciplined body, as we have seen, is often unhealthy. In novella XXVI, the emaciated, fleshless body of the young Seigneur d'Avannes returning from his "pellerinaige" to see the woman "qui avoit en son cueur ce grand prophete Amour" (210) (in whose heart was lodged that great prophet Love) (294), does not deceive the virtuous lady:

Mais, quant elle le veit si maigre et descoloré, ne se peut tenir de luy dire: "Je ne sçay, Monseigneur, comme il vat de vostre conscience, mais vostre corps n'a point amendé de ce pellerinaige." (213)

But when she saw how thin and wan he was, she could not help saying to him: "Monsieur, I cannot guess what state your conscience is in, but you do not look as if your body has benefited from your pilgrimage." (297)

Elsewhere, the body reveals its true nature by wounds and oddities. In novella IV, the face of the gentleman "tout sanglant d'esgratineures et morsures" (30) (streaming with blood from the bites and scratches) (92) betrays his wicked intentions while proclaiming the chastity of the lady who escaped him. In novella XXXII, the "teste toute tondue" (completely shaved head) of Bernage's young spouse exposes woman's sin. "L'arraiement des cheveulx n'apartient à l'adultaire" (244) (the crowning glory of woman no more becomes an adulteress than the veil becomes a harlot) (333), the husband explains. The lover's skeleton hanging in the lady's chamber and his skull, from which her husband forces her to drink, serve to remind the adulteress of her "faulte" and the evil that she has caused. In novella XLIII, the female body known to her lover only in the secrecy of the dark chamber is finally singled out by a chalk mark and covered with shame when Jambicque's "folly" is made public. Finally, in novella XLIX, the chained bodies of the three companions who seek to humiliate their unfaithful lady mirror the body of the same lady, captive of its sensual appetites.

Rebellious by nature, the body must be subjected to constant surveillance. Self-control begins with disciplining the body. For sixteenth-century man, *concupiscencia* and *garrulitàs* went hand-in-hand;[16] to silence the body one must silence the tongue as well.

In the *Heptameron,* sexuality is omnipresent but silenced by the conventions of the day.[17] For women, any attempt to satisfy sexual desire or even express it is severely censured. Feminine honor requires sweet gentleness, patience, obedience, modesty, and, above all, chastity.[18] Man, however, acquires honor by courage, magnanimity, and virility.[19] Thus, when Parlamente condemns the wickedness of the tapestry-maker from Tours who deceives both his wife and his mistress, Hircan reprimands her and continues praising the remarkable virility of the old chap as "ung grand acte de vertu, tant au corps que à l'esperit, de sçavoir dire et faire chose qui rend deux contraires contens" (307–308) (The point is that the man satisfied them both in one morning! *I* think that he showed great prowess, both mentally and physically, considering that he managed to act in such a way as to satisfy conflicting interests) (404).

The distrust of the body and the distrust of speech melded perhaps because, as psychoanalysis teaches us, "words are often a substitute for action."[20] In novella IV, the lady-in-waiting cautions the princess against seeking vengeance and making her attempted rape public. Silence is essential, she explains, not only because woman's honor is at stake but because she may find herself "ramentevant choses qui sont si plaisantes à la chair" (33) (remembering things that are so pleasing to the flesh). Many have escaped from danger the first time, only to succumb the second. Novella LXII describes the tragic consequences of speech. For the amusement of "a certain lady of royal blood," a young woman tells a story that she swears is true. It purports to concern the rape of someone else, but, at the crucial point, she gives herself away. When the chambermaid came in, she recalls, the aggressor snagged the sheet with his spur. Then, she exclaims: "Jamais femme ne fust si estonnée que moy, quant je me trouvay toute nue" (378) (Never was a woman more distressed than I was when I found myself completely naked). The freudian slip amounts to a confession.[21] "Quand on a prins grand desplaisir à l'euvre," Parlamente concludes, "l'on en prent aussi à la memoire, pour laquelle effacer Lucresse se tua" (379) (when one experiences distress at some action, one also experiences distress at the memory of it. That is why Lucretia killed herself) (487).

Generally, Marguerite speaks the body through the voice of the Masculine Other. The male discussants speak willingly of sex and sexuality; the women shy away from it. When conversation shifts to sex, the ladies remain silent even though they may be directly implicated. When for example, in the prologue, Hircan suggests that they occupy themselves with "quelque passetemps qui soit plaisant au corps" (8) (some pastime which will be agreeable to the body), Parlamente blushes and, scolding her husband, recommends that they choose instead a pastime in which everyone can join, such as storytelling. As Patricia Cholakian puts it, "The female rejects the sex act in favor of the speech act and substitutes dis-course for inter-course. But although female desire will become one of the principal subjects of this discourse, it will continue to be encoded as problematic and ambiguous, the mysterious question for which no answer is provided, the gap over which (like the bridge across the raging river) the woman's text must be constructed."[22] Likewise, when Hircan suggestively admits "ma femme et moi, nous sommes enfans d'Adam et d'Eve" (my wife and I are the children of Adam and Eve), Parlamente withdraws into a silence that simultaneously reveals and conceals the truth. Finally, when, on the morning of the fourth day, Hircan and Parlamente arrive late for Oisille's lesson, Hircan excuses himself by saying "j'ay une femme, je n'y puis aller si tost" (236) (I have a wife, and therefore I could not come so early!) (324); but Parlamente accuses herself of sinful idleness:

> J'estois marrye d'avoir esté paresseuse quand je suis arrivée icy; mais puisque ma faulte est occasion de vous avoir faict si bien parler à moy, ma paresse m'a doublement proffité, car j'ay eu repos de corps à dormir davantaige et d'esperit à vous oyr si bien dire. (236)

> I was angry with myself for being lazy when I arrived, but as my failing has led you to speak so excellently, my laziness has yielded twice the profit—I have

rested my body by sleeping longer, and given repose to my mind by listening
to your excellent words. (324)

Silence is often woman's way of saving appearances. When confronted by
her lover, Jambicque denies their secret rendezvous (novella XLIII). Her
silence reaffirms, albeit only temporarily, her chastity. But silence may also
be the only way to combat the flesh. What a woman keeps from others
by her silence may well be what she conceals from herself, "le plaisir trop
abominable" (the too abominable pleasure) that she avoids confronting.
In novella X, the nascent desire of Floride for Amadour is depicted as
"quelque chose plus qu'elle n'avoit accoustumé" (65) (something more
than she had previously experienced), as the "unspeakable" that woman
refuses to explore. Lawrence Kritzman notes the following in regard to this
novella: "Marguerite's text thus translates the enigma of female desire as
an exiled signifier which no longer has a proper signified. The representation of desire as a nameless thing (quelque chose) characterizes female sexuality as something elusive yet always present; it is, in fact, an obscure object of perception which no consciousness can ever completely master."[23]
Overall, sex and sexuality are spoken by detour, allusion, or metaphor as if
the author were trying to strip language of its "physicality."[24] In Freud's
terms, such linguistic deceits betray repressed desire. I would not go that
far, but it is true that indirection effects a certain distance that, in this case,
seems to indicate Marguerite's attempt to distance herself from the body—
a body that is experienced again and again as "trop" (too much). The passage cited above concerning the sexual relations between Parlamente and
Hircan offers a solution to the problem of sexuality (sexuality in general
but, more specifically, female sexuality) by promoting not the chaste body
but instead a healthy, fulfilled body within a sacred union.

Indeed, in the *Heptameron,* the attempt to silence the body repeatedly
fails as if Marguerite became increasingly aware of the impossibility of such
attempts or, perhaps, their presumptuousness. Much like "amour vaine et
vicieuse" (vain and wicked love), repressed desire severs man from his natural disposition. As we observe in novella XIII, repressed love can affect the
functioning of the organs of the human body. As the captain is about to
say his farewells to the woman he loves, the body declares by its abnormal
behavior (uneven pulse, sudden perspiration, the disorders of excretion)
what the heart was concealing:

> Pour ne l'oser declarer [=sa passion], tomba quasi esvanouy, en luy disant
> adieu, en une si grande sueur universelle, que non ses oeilz seullement, mais
> tout le corps, jectoient larmes. (100)

> Not daring to declare his passion, he almost fell in a faint as he said his farewell.
> He broke out all over in a sweat—it was as if not only his eyes but his whole
> body were shedding tears.

Novella XXVI describes the ravages caused by forbidden passion. Abstinence affects the epigastric region (the lady suffers from an "opilation" [obstruction]) and engenders a depressive state ("melancholia") that finally provokes death:

> Elle tumba en une fievre continue, causée d'un humeur melencolicque, tellement que les extremitez du corps lui vindrent toutes froides, et au dedans brusloit incessamment. (217)

> Deprived of the consolation of being able to see and speak to the man who was life itself to her, she fell into a continuous fever due to a melancholic humour. Her extremities became quite cold and internally she burned incessantly.

In the *Heptameron,* virtuous love can fulfill itself, as M. F. Hans and G. Lapouge put it, only within "des corps de néant" (empty bodies).[25] Contrary to the erotic body that, once its desires are fulfilled, finds a certain peace within itself, the body that strives to purify itself or battles against the barbarous desire of the Other so as to preserve itself intact, is, as we have seen in the last example, a body that endures constant suffering—a body covered with wounds (Floride mutilates her face) or a body in agony, the body with which Christ redeemed sinners. We are here reminded of the redeeming death of the muleteer's wife; her last words echo Christ's words on the cross:

> À force de perdre son sang, [la mulletiere] senteit qu'elle approchoit de la mort; levant les oeilz au ciel et joingnant les mains, rendit graces à son Dieu . . . luy supplyant prendre en grey le sang qui, pour garder son commandement, estoit respendu en la reverence de celluy de son Filz, auquel elle croyoit fermement tous ses pechez estre lavez et effacez de la memoire de son ire. Et, en disant: "Seigneur, recepvez l'ame qui, par vostre bonté, a esté racheptée!" tumba en terre sur le visaige, où ce meschant lui donna plusieurs coups. (20)

> When at last she had lost so much blood that she felt death approaching, she raised her eyes to heaven and, joining her hands in prayer, gave thanks to her God.
>
> "Thou art my strength, my virtue, my suffering, and my chastity," she prayed, humbly beseeching that He would receive the blood, which, according to His commandment, was shed in veneration of the blood of His son. For she truly believed that through Him were all her sins cleansed and washed from the memory of His wrath. And as she sank with her face to the floor, she sighed, "Into thy hands I commend my spirit, my spirit that was redeemed by thy great goodness."
>
> Then the vicious brute stabbed her several times again. (80)

Cleansed of sin, the woman's body surrounded by women (yet another echo of the Crucifixion scene) purges the city of evil and reactivates faith:[26]

Toutes les femmes de bien de la ville ne faillirent à faire leur debvoir de l'honorer autant qu'il estoit possible. . . . Les folles et legieres, voyans l'honneur que l'on faisoit à ce corps, se delibererent de changer leur vye en mieulx. (21)

All the virtuous women of the town were present, as was their duty, to do all possible honour to her name. . . . For women of more wanton ways the sight of such respect being paid to her body made them resolve to amend their lives. (81)

In her last major play, the *Comédie au Mont-de-Marsan,* written in 1548, soon after the death of Francis I, Marguerite reexamines the problematics of the body through the confrontation between the fundamentally opposite philosophies of the "Mondainne" and the "Supersticieuse." The "Mondainne," as her name indicates, devotes herself exclusively to her body and earthly pleasures at the expense of her soul: "J'ayme mon corps . . . je le sens vivement" (I love my body . . . I feel it keenly). Contemptuous of the Flesh in which she sees nothing but "charogne" (carrion), the "Supersticieuse," to the contrary, mortifies her body and cultivates her soul "pour gaigner paradis" (to gain heaven). Then the "sage" comes in, and, in the name of Reason, she demonstrates that both the "Mondainne" and the "Supersticieuse" are wrong. We are made, she warns, of body and soul together. To glorify one at the cost of the other is necessarily to jeopardize the union of natures.

Car l'ame tant seullement
N'est l'homme; mais l'assemblement
Des deux, hommes lon doibt nommer.
Corps sans ames sont cadavers,
Charongnes pour nourrir les vers,
Qui de l'homme n'ont nul effect;
L'ame sans corps ne peult veoir
Et des euvres pert le pouvoir,
Dont elle n'est l'homme parfaict:
Mais l'ame au corps joincte et unie,
C'est l'homme . . . .

For the soul alone is not man; but the assemblage of the two is what one ought to call man. Bodies without souls are corpses, carcasses to feed worms, having none of the properties of man. The soul without the body cannot see and loses the power of works; thus it is not a perfect man. But the soul joined and linked to the body, that is man. (143)

Interestingly, the "Mondainne" is converted sooner than the "Supersticieuse." The "Sage," who is often perceived to be speaking for Marguerite, understands, and, soon after, the "Mondainne" too can see that, as a result of the Incarnation, the Flesh, rightly understood, is holy. For Marguerite, then, to love the Flesh is not as sinful as to condemn the Flesh—a lesson repeated in novella XXX. By constantly imposing restraints on her body, the stoic mother soon believes herself to be "impecable" (above sin). But she forgets that Flesh is weak and that we, therefore, should commend ourselves to God as Hircan cautions: "Mais le meilleur seroit, congnoissant sa foiblesse, ne jouster poinct contre tel ennemy, et se retirer au vray Amy et luy dire avecq le Psalmiste: 'Seigneur, je souffre force, respondez pour moy'" (233) (Better were it to recognize one's weakness, better not to try to do battle with such an enemy, but turning to the one true lover, to say with the Psalmist: "Lord, I am oppressed; answer thou for me") (321).

Perhaps the female experience—Marguerite's own experience as mother and lover as recounted in the *Dialogue en forme de vision nocturne* (1524), the *Navire* (1547), and the *Chansons spirituelles* (1549)—makes her realize the vanity of her attempt. She learns then that the grieving body cannot endure suffering in silence.

In these works, Marguerite laments the loss of her loved ones, her niece, Charlotte, and her brother, Francis, to whom she was deeply attached. In the latter case particularly, it is the physical absence of Francis, expressed here as the loss of "the unity of body" or the division of the brother-sister androgyne, that Marguerite laments most.

> Mais, hélas, mon corps est banny
> Du sien, auquel il feut uny
> Depuis le temps de nostre enfance (Chanson II)[27]

> But, alas, my body is banished
> From his, with which it had been joined
> Since the time of our childhood (my translation)

Deprived of its fundamental unity that the other provided, the female body feels mutilated, diminished, reduced to half. As a result, the nobler senses of sight and hearing (that is, insight) are tragically impaired ("je n'ois plus en terre ung tel langaige, / Je ne voys plus tel maistre et instructeur" (I can no longer hear such language on earth / I can no longer see such a master and teacher),[28] causing her eventually to wander further from God. "Tant de larmes jettent mes yeux / Qu'ils ne voyent terre ne cieux (Chanson II) (My eyes are so filled with tears / That they see neither earth nor heaven). In the *Navire* Marguerites focuses essentially on "charnelz recordz" (carnal recollections). In a series of "memory-paintings,"[29] she evokes the fifty-two years her late brother spent with her, seeking to render him physically present to the reader: "Je voy tousjours ton visage et beau taint, / Ton oeil joieulx" (I can still see your face and fine coloring / Your joyful eyes) (my translation). References to the body return persistently; they express Marguerite's desperate attempt (and her temptation in refusing to abandon carnal affections) to elaborate a text that would "contain" the beloved body. But human memory can only preserve parts of parts, "chair" (flesh), "visage," "face" (face), "bras" (arms), "pieds" (feet), "mains" (hands), "chef" (head), "oz" (bones), "voix" (voice), "yeux" (eyes), and so forth. Unable to reconstruct the whole, it "revives" instead the decomposed body, reminder of the lost unity; thus memory intensifies Marguerite's grief. Although for Marguerite, as Robert Cottrell notes, "language signals an ontological flaw" (196), she cannot remain silent: "Le taire me seroit louable, / S'il ne m'estoit tant inhumain" (It would be laudable for me to remain silent / If that did not seem to me to be so inhuman) (196). But when language fails to translate her sentiments, the body becomes the sole expression of her pain.[30] Tears, moans, and sighs constitute Marguerite's rhetoric.

> Mes larmes, mes souspirs, mes criz,
> Dont tant bien je sçay la pratique,
> Sont mon parler et mes escritz,
> Car je n'ay autre rhétorique. (Chanson I)

> My tears, my sighs, my cries,
> Of which I know so well the experience,
> Are my speech and my writing, for I have no other rhetoric. (197)

Thus, nonverbal, affective discourse speaks the body that, elsewhere, articulate language sought in vain to silence.

The Word is made Flesh: "plainct tant charnel" (plaint so fleshy, *Navire* vs. 242). And the Flesh no longer reduced to silence is finally made Word.

In sum, Marguerite condemns the transgressive body that causes us to be oblivious of our souls, only to realize that the body cannot be silenced and, more important, that to condemn the flesh is not in accord with the will of God. Those who mortify the Flesh, like the "Supersticieuse," are, in fact, still too much preoccupied with the self. Those who seek to overcome nothingness and negate the carnal, like the incestuous mother in novella XXX, deny the Fall and, at the same time, the mystery of the Incarnation. As Robert Cottrell rightly argues:

> [Marguerite] knew that the Christian cannot reject the world without rejecting Him. To deny the body is to deny what Christ redeemed when He became flesh. Even more scandalously, it is to deny Christ Himself, for His will operates through the flesh. Even in those texts in which [she] expresses a yearning for annihilation in Him, she creates a textual body, a fleshy form, that, embodying denial of the body, subverts her avowed rejection of matter and constitutes a redemption of corporeality mimetic of that effected by the Incarnation. (136–137)

Finally, those who deny the body, ruin "tout l'edifice," the perfect work of God.

Hence, in the end, Marguerite recognizes the ontological duality of man. In anticipation of Montaigne, she reconciles herself with the "char-nelle sensualité" while urging temperance (which results, as we have seen, in the rehabilitation of marriage) and "ferme foy" (a firm faith) (*Comédie de Mont-de-Marsan*, 307). More important, her failure to silence her body leads her to accept human nature as it is and recognize her own sinfulness, which corresponds to the experience of *mortificatio*,[31] the first step in the Christian's progress toward union with God (*scala perfectionis*). Her own suffering causes her eventually to be Christ's feminine counterpart and join God: "Pour estre bien vray Chrestien / Il fault à Christ estre semblable" (To be a true Christian, one must imitate Christ) (Chanson XXIX). Per-haps only then would she be able to break the silence imposed on woman and, like the shepherdess in the *Comédie au Mont-de-Marsan* who re-counts the joy of the *unio mystica*, to sing the body which, in its fusion/confusion with Other, recovers its power of "jouyssance":[32]

> Mon corps ne sens n'y n'ayme poinct,
> Car le sien où mon ceur est joinct
> Faict mettre le mien en oubly,
> Le sien de vertu anobly,
> Je le dy mien et le sens tel.

> I do not feel or love my body,
> For His with which my heart is joined
> Puts mine in oblivion
> His, enobled by its virtue,
> I call mine and feel as such. (my translation)

NOTES

1. Marguerite de Navarre, *L'Heptaméron*, ed. Michel François (Paris: Garnier, 1967), 151. All subsequent citations are from this edition. For the English translation, see P. A. Chilton, trans., *The Heptameron* (London: Penguin, 1984), 229. I am most grateful to Mela-nie Gregg, Anne R. Larsen, Robert McDowell, and Marian Rothstein who gave willingly of their time and expertise as I worked on the translation of this article.

2. In novella XXVI, when the Seigneur d'Avannes begins to praise the perfect body of the lady, which, he claims, reflects her perfect virtue, she cautions him against deceptive beauty: "je sçay très bien que je suis femme, non seullement comme une aultre, mais impar-faicte; et que la vertu feroit plus grand acte de me transformer en elle, que de prandre ma forme, sinon quant elle vouldroit estre incongneue en ce monde, car, soubz tel habit que le myen, ne pourroit la vertu estre conngneue telle qu'elle est" (215) (I know well that I am a woman, not only a woman like any other, but a woman so full of imperfections that Virtue would be performing a greater act in transforming me into herself than in taking on my form, unless she wished perchance to remain unknown to the world. For, hidden beneath such a garb as mine, Virtue could never be known as she truly is) (299).

On deceptive beauty, see Philippe de Lajarte, "*L'Heptaméron* et le ficinisme: rapports d'un texte et d'une idéologie," *Revue des Sciences Humaines* 37 (1972): 339–371.

3. Human love can lead man to divine perfection and a higher form of love, but it can also be a hindrance to the soul's progress. The prison of love motif or—and it amounts to the same thing—the sweetness of freedom motif appears in several of Marguerite's works: the

first Book of her longest poem, *Les Prisons* (1549), several novellas of the *Heptameron* (XXIV, LXIV, LXX among others), the *Navire* (1547), and the *Comédie des Quatre Femmes* (1542). In the latter, ironically, she who has not succumbed to love is the most captive of all.

4. On the influence of the Pseudo-Dionysius on Marguerite and the Neoplatonists, see Pierre Sage, "Le Platonisme de Marguerite de Navarre," *Travaux de Linguistique et de Littérature* 7, no. 2 (1969): 65–82; and Christine Martineau-Génieys, "Le Platonisme de Marguerite de Navarre?" *Réforme, Humanisme, Renaissance* 4 (1976): 12–35.

5. V.-L. Saulnier, "Marguerite de Navarre: art médiéval et pensée nouvelle," *Revue Universitaire* 63 (1954): 154–162; citation 161.

6. "Carnal sensuality" refers both to "l'amour terrienne qui esloigne l'homme de l'affection celeste" (418) (earthly love that draws man away from heavenly love) and, in general, to carnal values or material concerns.

7. See *Guillaume Briçonnet-Marguerite d'Angoulême Correspondance (1521–1524),* ed. Christine Martineau, Michel Veissière, and Henry Heller, 2 vols. (Geneva: Droz, I, 1975; II, 1979). On the influence of Briçonnet and the Reformers of Meaux, see Henry Heller, "Marguerite of Navarre and the Reformers of Meaux," *Bibliothèque d'Humanisme et Renaissance* 33 (1971): 271–310.

8. On these differences, Philippe de Lajarte, "*L'Heptaméron.*"

9. To remind man of his animal nature, in other words, to reduce the self to its true nature that is "Rien" (Nothing) is part of the *mortificatio* process. It corresponds to the first of the three steps of the *scala perfectionis* that symbolize for mystics the tripartite process of achieving union with God.

10. In the *Comédie jouée au Mont-de-Marsan* (1548) the "Sage" reminds the "Mondainne" and the "Supersticieuse" of the beautiful gift God gave man that, in terms of the hierarchy of being, places him at the center of the ladder: "Dieu a bien faict ung tresbeau don à l'homme / De luy donner raison, savez-vous comme? / Comme à ung ange . . . / Par la raison il diffère à la beste" (God gave a very beautiful gift to man / in giving him reason: do you know to what degree? / To that of an angel . . . / By reason man differs from the animals). See Marguerite de Navarre, *Théâtre profane,* ed. V.-L. Saulnier (Geneva: Droz; Paris: Minard, 1978), 280–281. Translations from the *Théâtre profane,* the *Navire,* and the *Chansons spirituelles* are by Robert Cottrell unless otherwise indicated. See *The Grammar of Silence: A Reading of Marguerite de Navarre's Poetry* (Washington, D.C.: Catholic University of America Press, 1986), 139.

11. Nicole Cazauran, *L'Heptaméron de Marguerite de Navarre* (Paris: CDU & SEDES, 1976), 226.

12. Marguerite's emphasis on the power of love as well as the vulnerable (naïve) side of woman tends to diminish female culpability.

13. On degrading love, see Michel Olsen, *Les Transformations du triangle érotique* (Copenhagen: Akademisk Forlag, 1976), 20, 48.

14. On the pathology of eros as it was understood by the medical philosophers of the time, on erotic frenzy, madness, and melancholia (discussed later), see Donald Beecher, "L'Amour et le corps: les maladies érotiques et la pathologie à la Renaissance," in *Le Corps à la Renaissance,* Actes du XXXe Colloque de Tours 1987, ed. Jean Céard, Marie-Madeleine Fontaine, and Jean-Claude Margolin (Paris: Aux Amateurs de Livres, 1990), 423–434; or the English version, "The Lover's Body: The Somatogenesis of Love in Renaissance Medical Treatises," *Renaissance and Reformation* 24, no. 1 (1988): 1–11. See also Marie-Madeleine Fontaine, "La Lignée des commentaires à la chanson de Guido Cavalcanti *Donna me prega:* évolution des relations entre philosophie, médecine et littérature dans le débat sur la nature d'Amour," *La Folie et le corps,* études réunies par Jean Céard avec la collaboration de Pierre Naudin et Michel Simonin (Paris: Presses de l'Ecole Normale Supérieure, 1985), 159–178.

15. Virtue does not always clothe itself in a perfect body (Rolandine, novella XXI, is not particularly beautiful), and, conversely, physical beauty does not always reflect the beauty of the soul.

16. Indeed, as Peter Stallybrass explains, "the connection between speaking and wan-

tonness was common to legal discourse and conduct books." See "Patriarchal Territories: The Body Enclosed," in *Rewriting the Renaissance—The Discourses of Sexual Difference in Early Modern Europe,* ed. Margaret W. Ferguson, Maureen Quilligan, and Nancy Vickers (Chicago: University of Chicago Press, 1986), 126. Humanist educators believed that woman should be guarded against two specifically female vices: garrulity and concupiscence.

17. See Colette H. Winn, "La Loi du silence dans *L'Heptaméron* de Marguerite de Navarre," *Romance Quarterly* 33, no. 2 (May 1986): 157–168.

18. "The supreme importance of chastity to a woman was most clearly shown in its linking with honor," notes Ruth Kelso. "Honor for both men and women was something external, a good name, for men a reputation for excellency in many things, for women in one thing, chastity." See *The Doctrine of the Lady of the Renaissance* (Urbana: University of Illinois Press, 1956), 98.

19. As Ian Maclean explains in *The Renaissance Notion of Woman—A Study in the Fortunes of Scholasticism and Medical Science In European Intellectual Life* (Cambridge: Cambridge University Press, 1980), "the dominant vice for each sex becomes the antithesis of the dominant virtue . . . and the most excusable vice the antithesis of the dominant virtue of the other sex" (62). In the patriarchal society of the Renaissance, woman is forced to accept the passive role to which man's aggressiveness reduces her: "Dieu a mis au cueur de l'homme l'amour et la hardiesse pour demander, et en celluy de la femme la crainte et la chasteté pour refuser" (279) (it was God who put love in men's breasts in the first place and gave them the boldness to do the asking, while He made women timid and chaste, so that they would do the refusing) (373).

20. "C'est dans le langage que l'homme trouve un substitut à l'acte." See Jean Laplanche and J.-B. Pontalis, *Vocabulaire de la psychanalyse* (Paris: Presses Universitaires de France, 1967), 33.

21. See Sigmund Freud, *Le Mot d'esprit et ses rapports avec l'inconscient* (Paris: Editions Gallimard, 1979), 157: "L'auteur du lapsus est soulagé de jeter le masque" (The person who utters the freudian slip is in fact relieved to reveal himself/herself).

22. Patricia Cholakian, *Rape and Writing in the Heptameron of Marguerite de Navarre,* "Ad Feminam" Series, (Carbondale: Southern Illinois University Press, 1991), 37.

23. Lawrence Kritzman, "Verba erotica: Marguerite de Navarre and the Rhetoric of Silence," in *The Rhetoric of Sexuality and the Literature of the French Renaissance* (Cambridge: Cambridge University Press, 1991), 51.

24. See Colette H. Winn, "Gastronomy and Sexuality: Table Language in the *Heptameron*," *Journal of the Rocky Mountain Medieval and Renaissance Association* 7 (1986): 209–218.

25. "L'amour courtois s'accomplit sur le néant des corps, ou bien avec des corps de néant. Il efface radicalement l'instinct, le plaisir, afin d'inaugurer le règne du désir. Il transfère l'acte amoureux dans la strate de la loi, du langage, au point que le terrain sexuel n'est plus qu'un lieu déshabité, un vide, un théâtre dans lequel jouent, en place des chairs, des règles de grammaire ou des règles juridiques" (Courtly love fulfills itself on the nothingness of flesh, or within empty bodies. It wipes out, radically, instinct, and pleasure so that desire may reign free. It relegates the love act to a legal and linguistic realm, to the extent that the sexual terrain is suddenly a disinhabited site, a void, much like a theatre in which grammatical and legal rules replace bodies). See M. F. Hans and G. Lapouge, *Les Femmes, la pornographie, l'érotisme* (Paris: Seuil, 1978), 384.

26. On the depiction of the body of Christ as female, see Caroline Walker Bynum, *Jesus as Mother: Studies in the Spirituality of the High Middle Ages* (Berkeley: University of California Press, 1982); and "The Body of Christ in the Later Middle Ages: A Reply to Leo Steinberg," *Renaissance Quarterly* 39, no. 3 (Autumn 1986): 399–440.

27. *Chansons spirituelles,* ed. Georges Dottin (Geneva: Droz; reprint Paris: Minard, 1971).

28. *La Navire, ou Consolation du roi François 1er à sa soeur Marguerite,* ed. Robert Marichal (Paris: Champion, 1956), 229–230.

29. The expression is from Paula Sommers, *Celestial Ladders: Readings in Marguerite de Navarre's Poetry of Spiritual Ascent,* Travaux d'Humanisme et Renaissance CCXXXIII (Geneva: Droz, 1989), 72. See also her reading of the *Navire,* 67–82.

30. On the untranslatability of the self, see Esham Ahmed, "Marguerite de Navarre's *Chansons spirituelles* and the Poet's Passion," *Bibliothèque d'Humanisme et Renaissance* 52, no. 1 (1990): 37–52.

31. As we have seen in novella XXX, the so-called "Cuyder," man's presumptuous pride in self, is the Christian's most cunning enemy. On the "Cuyder," see Raymond Lebègue, "Le Cuyder avant Montaigne et dans les *Essais,*" *Cahiers de l'Association Internationale des Etudes Françaises* 14 (1962): 275–284.

32. Once freed of the prison of language, voice recovers its preverbal harmony. On the symbolism of song, see Louis E. Auld, "Music as Dramatic Device in the Secular Theatre of Marguerite de Navarre," *Renaissance Drama* 7 (1976): 192–217. As to the character of the shepherdess, identified in the play as the "Ravie," and her songs that, for the most part, include refrains or couplets of popular songs, Saulnier notes: "Ce que la reine voulut montrer là, avec ce qui nous semble une sorte de hardiesse, c'est l'analogie profonde qui unit l'amour païen à l'amour divin, dans la confusion mystique des natures" (271) (what the Queen wanted to show by that, with what appears to us as a kind of boldness, is the profound analogy that unites profane and divine love in the mystical confusion of natures). On the affinities between mysticism and sensuality, see Jean-Noël Vuarnet, *Extases féminines* (Poitiers: Arthaud, 1980).

The French version of this article will appear in *Actes du Colloque International "Marguerite de Navarre" (1492–1549),* (Birmingham, Ala.: Summa Publications, 1994).

Carpe Diem, Poetic Immortality, and the Gendered Ideology of Time

ℒ

Cathy Yandell

"Comme la rose enfin devient un gratte-cu,
Et tout avec le temps par le temps est vaincu."
—French proverb

Just as an old rose is only good for scratching ass,
So everything, by time destroyed, in time will pass.[1]

Much of Renaissance lyric poetry reveals an obsession with time, both physical time with its menacing, ravaging powers and subjective time with its grounding in human imagination and experience. Poets, particularly, continually seek ways to beguile, deceive, tame, or conquer time, be it by magnifying the present moment or by securing their place in the future through writing. Social historian Lucien Febvre argues that an epoch that spent immeasurable hours on minute architectural and gastronomical details could not have considered time a precious commodity,[2] but in this assessment he clearly excludes the descendants of Petrarch—that is, all the humanist thinkers and poets who are the object of this inquiry.

Petrarch's formulations of time and its relationship to the thinking subject undoubtedly influenced the sixteenth-century humanist philosophy of time more than any other. Aristotle had conceived of time as a succession of instants based on the physical principle of movement, where each instant is the end of the before and the beginning of the after, where events follow each other without reference to past or future.[3] Augustine saw time as a more subjective phenomenon; he shifted the emphasis of time from the Aristotelian *moment* to the *present,* determined by an enunciating subject in relationship to whom both past and future are defined. For Augustine, time moves at the same inexorable speed for everyone, but time in Petrarch's conception, though equally merciless, can be shaped by individuals. This preexistentialist idea that human beings are ultimately responsible for their own time led to Petrarch's disquietude about his use of every hour of the day: he limited his sleep to six hours and worldly activities to two hours and devoted the remaining hours to study, reflection, and writing. In his writing, moreover, Petrarch seeks to effectuate victory over time through fame and idealized beauty.[4]

Echoing Petrarch's temporal obsession, French Renaissance male poets exploit two principal topoi, poetic immortality and carpe diem, both of which seek to inscribe the poet as a master of time. The desire for poetic immortality, embodied in the Horacian *exegi monumentum*, figures prominently in both Scève and the Pléiade. Carpe diem, the poet's exhortation to pluck the day, takes on multiple forms not only in the more celebrated Pléiade poets, but also in Marot, Scève, Saint Gelais, Des Périers, and Pasquier, to name only a few.

At the apogee of these motifs' popularity, two women poets, Pernette du Guillet in the 1540s and Catherine des Roches in the 1570s, formulate their versions of these temporal topoi, initiating a kind of poetic dialogue with their male colleagues. In the works of these women emerge subtly but decidedly different attitudes toward poetic immortality, carpe diem and the physical destruction of time.

Pernette du Guillet's *Rymes,* published by Antoine du Moulin in 1545, are framed by reflections on time, from the prefatory letter by the publisher to an epitaph by Maurice Scève following the *Rymes*. The attention accorded to fleeting time by these two men is not surprising, given that the poems were published shortly after Pernette's death at the age of about twenty-five.[5] Yet the scholarly editor's letter goes far beyond the predictable contemplations on death and the young poet's untimely demise. Indeed, the entire letter turns upon the axis of time, specifically Pernette's relationship to time, as both a woman and a poet.

In his preface addressed to the "Dames Lyonnoizes," Du Moulin situates Pernette's work as a perpetual reminder of absence or lack, where the present has meaning only insofar as it evokes the past and where the future consists only of unfulfilled promise. By using the verb "renouveller" twice in two adjacent sentences, he acknowledges that the publication of Pernette's poems will rekindle the women's regret. He further elicits, in a curious combination of sentimental and Neoplatonic terms, the temporal ambiguity of these poems, momentos of a promising future that was not to be: "la Mort . . . nous a privez de la consummation, que par cest heureux commancement la felicité de son celeste engin nous promettoit" (2). But while Du Moulin engages in these brief reflections on the abyss between Pernette's past and future, the editor reveals a greater interest in Pernette's use of time while she was alive:

> Veu le peu de temps, que les Cieux l'ont laissée entre nous, il est quasi incro-
> yable comme elle a peu avoir le loisir, je ne dy seulement de se rendre si par-

faitement asseurée en tous instrumenz musiquaulx, soit au Luth, Espinette, et autres, lesquelz de soy requierent une bien longue vie à se y rendre parfaictz, comme elle estoit. . . : mais encores à si bien dispencer le reste de ses bonnes heures, qu'elle l'aye employé à toutes bonnes lettres, par lesquelles elle avoit eu premierement entiere et familiere congnoissance des plus louables vulgaires (oultre le sien) comme du Thuscan, et Castillan . . . et apres avoit jà bien avant passé les Rudimentz de la langue Latine aspirant à la Grecque. (2)

Given the short time that the Heavens allowed her to stay among us, it is almost unbelievable that she could have the leisure not only to become such an accomplished player of all musical instruments, such as the lute, spinet, and others, which alone would require a long lifetime to reach perfection in them, as she did; but also that she could employ the rest of her hours so fruitfully in letters. She had complete and familiar knowledge of such vernacular languages (besides her own) as Italian and Spanish, and she had already learned the rudiments of Latin, aspiring also to learn Greek.

The structure of this praise uncovers significant information about Du Moulin's own attitudes toward what might be called "women's time" or perhaps about his understanding of what his audience would have expected or demanded in this regard. What is "quasi incroyable" is neither the quality of Pernette's musical genius nor her humanist endeavors, but rather the fact that she had the *loisir* to accomplish them and that she could make such good use of her time. Du Moulin exhorts the women of Lyons to follow Pernette's example, "et tellement, que, si par ce sien petit passetemps elle vous a monstré le chemin à bien, vous la puissiez si glorieusement ensuyvre" (3) (such that, if by this little pastime she showed you the path to goodness, you can gloriously follow her). But the two levels of Du Moulin's discourse here, as elsewhere in the preface, seem to contradict one another. At first glance, Du Moulin's respectfulness toward Pernette appears to dominate the text. His elevated exposition is continually undermined and challenged, however, by terms denoting the inconsequential nature of the *Rymes*. Scattered throughout the preface are such diminutive epithets for the *Rymes* as "ce petit amas de rymes," "ce peu de commencement," "ces petites, et louables jeunesses siennes" and, most significantly, "ce sien petit passetemps." Du Moulin's surprisingly apologetic apology of Pernette's *Rymes* ultimately reveals his conviction that while Pernette's work itself is not impressive, her consecration of time to music and letters has contributed to her "virtue" (he uses some form of this word six times during the preface) and that other "virtuous" women of Lyons should follow in her footsteps. Du Moulin thereby suggests that a woman's virtue is determined by her activities—in short, by the way she spends her time.[6]

Time is thus the driving force in Du Moulin's preface: time as a fleeting, irrecoverable entity, time as the motivator of regret, time that both promises and deceives, time as that phenomenon over which literature seeks to triumph, and finally time (particularly the way women spend it) as the principal determinant of virtue.

Pernette's poems reveal a radically different philosophy of time from that of Du Moulin's preface. Nowhere in her work does a hint of anxiety about the inexorable passage of time appear. Of course time in Pernette's poems is not physical time but rather amorous time—a time in which hope, desire, and deferral determine both the present and the future and in which memory circumscribes the past.[7] In her concept of amorous time, Pernette distinguishes herself from her male counterpart as well, in this case from her literary mentor Maurice Scève. Scève's response in Dizain 136 of the *Délie* to Pernette's Epigram XIII serves as a synecdoche of this difference. Using the rhetorical technique *contentio* or antithesis, both poets treat an identical theme: one soul, dying while living in sweet torment, in turn causes death in the other living soul. I. D. McFarlane, following Verdun Saulnier, holds that in Scève's response "we can see the poet trying to give greater clarity and balance to the themes initiated by Pernette."[8]

It seems to me, however, that by shifting the emphases in his response Scève significantly changes Pernette's poem. Both Scève and Pernette end their poems with an apostrophe to personified love:

> Dieu aveuglé, tu nous as faict avoir
> Du bien le mal en effect honnorable:
> Fais donc aussi, que nous puissions avoir
> En noz espritz contentement durable!
> (Pernette)

> Blind god, you have given to us
> The suffering in pleasure that leads on to honor;
> Make us, as well, able to preserve
> Long-lasting contentment, shared in our souls.[9]

> Dieu aveuglé tu nous as fait avoir
> Sans aultrement ensemble consentir,
> Et posseder, sans nous en repentir,
> Le bien du mal en effect desirable:
> Fais que puissions aussi long sentir
> Si doulx mourir en vie respirable.
> (Scève)

> Blind God, you have given to us
> Without any other agreement or consent,
> And let us possess, without any regret,
> The joy of suffering that leads to desire.
> Let us sense, for just as long,
> Such sweet death within the breath of life.[10]

In the final two verses, which form the *pointe* of both the epigram and the dizain, Pernette's grammatical insistence on the first person plural, "nous" and particularly "noz espritz," emphasizes the spiritual union of the lovers and not simply their common condition. The direct object of the poet's desire is "contentement durable" in Pernette's case and "doulx mourir" in Scève's. "Contentement," as a concordance of Pernette's poems would suggest, is the objective of her *contentio*. Some form of the word "content" figures nine times in the first fifteen epigrams, and with one exception it is used in conjunction with both the poet and her lover, systematically denoting reciprocity.[11] Pernette's notion of contentment seems further to draw from Leone Ebreo,[12] who defines contentment in opposition to greed, ambition, and exaggerated sexual appetite. In Epigram 9, for example, the "contentement" undercuts the initial antithesis ("Plus je desire, . . . Moins . . . puisse celuy veoir"), ending the poem with "luy content, je demeure contente." This contentment exists in suspended time, as does the "contentement durable" of Epigram 13. Though both poems are based on a parallel ("just as you, blind god, have made suffering respectable / desirable to us, so let us continue to have contentment / sweet death in life"), only Scève's establishes a temporal contingency: "Fais que puissions *aussi long* sentir." Scève's dizain thus shifts the emphasis of Pernette's epigram from spiritual union to common condition, from long-lasting contentment to sweet death, and from circular reciprocity to a more linear notion of contingency.

Suspended, amorous time also exists in Scève's *Délie,* of course, as the poet crafts timeless formulations of both precise moments such as the *innamoramento* and imprecise moments such as waking consciousness. But I would argue that Scève's temporal schema, while not entirely situated in linear, "cursive" time (as Nietsche called it),[13] projects nonetheless *Délie's* "vertu" and the poet's literary prowess squarely into the future.[14] The framing of dizain 136 corroborates this claim. At the end of dizain 135, as elsewhere in the *Délie,* Scève insists on death and Délie's power to transcend it through the immortality both of her "vertu" and of the poet's verses: "J'espereray en seure indamnité . . ./ En Terre nom, au Ciel eternité." (I shall expect with certitude . . . / glory on earth and in heaven, eternity). This conclusion evoking poetic immortality is significant because it not only casts a different light on the poet's references to death in dizain 136, but also represents Scève's only departure from the Vittoria Colonna sonnet of which dizain 135 is a translation. The departure underscores, moreover, the explicitness of Scève's poet's desire for poetic glory. Foreshadowing the famous "Tu me seras la Myrrhe incorruptible / Contre les vers de ma mortalité" of dizain 378, Scève posits the "nom," that is, "renom" or Petrarchan *fama,* as the key to triumphing over time. Pernette, in contrast, retains none of the projection into the future of her mentor. In the whole of Pernette's published work, never does she use the nouns "immortalité" or "éternité," and only twice does she use the adjective "immortel," both times simply to denote long-lasting "immortel souci" (Chanson 8) and "propos immortels" (Elégie 5). Pernettian temporal vocabulary includes instead terms inscribing a continuing present: "joye continuelle" (Elégie 5), "perseverence" (Epigrams 34 and 38; Elégie 5), "longue patience" (Elégie 5), "durable" (Epigrams 10, 13, and 43). Even Pernette's expression for the longest possible duration, "toute ma vie" (Epigrams 19 and 28), is inextricably linked with the present, carrying no connotation of the eternal.[15] In Epigram 19, for example, Pernette's poet offers a witty apology for not honoring last night's promise:

> Je te promis au soir, que pour ce jour
> Je m'en irois à ton instance grande
> Faire chés toy quelque peu de sejour:
> Mais je ne puis: parquoy me recommande,
> Te promectant m'acquicter pour l'amande,
> Non d'un seul jour, mais de toute ma vie.

> I promised you last night that today
> I would go, as you insisted,
> Visit you for a short while.
> But I cannot. So now I bid you farewell,
> promising you, to absolve this debt,
> not one day, but all of my life.

This clever "badinage" gives way to a more serious use of "toute ma vie" in Epigram 28, which ends with "vostre ardeur me convye . . . A demeurer vostre toute ma vie." The implication remains, however, an expansion of the present rather than a projection into the future.

Pernette's most subtle questioning of Scève's notion of poetic immortality can be found in Elegy 2. After disavowing her fantasy to transform Actaeon not into a "Cerf" [stag] but into her "serf" [servant], Pernette's poet concludes the elegy with a final wish:

> Laissez le aller les neuf Muses servir,
> Sans se vouloir dessoubz moy asservir,
> Soubz moy, qui suis sans grace, et sans merite.
> Laissez le aller, qu'Apollo je ne irrite,
> Le remplissant de Deité profonde,
> Pour contre moy susciter tout le Monde,
> Lequel un jour par ses escriptz s'attend
> D'estre avec moy et heureux, et content.

> Let him go, to serve the nine Muses,
> I must not insist on enslaving him to me,
> as I lack both grace and merit.
> Let him go; let me not anger Apollo,

filling him with powerful divinity
so that he stirs up the whole world against me,
which, one day, expects through my love's writing
to be, along with me, blessed and content.[16]

It is evident in these verses, as elsewhere, that Pernette's poet depre-
cates her own literary achievements while praising those of her Apollonian
mentor, and in this sense she willingly submits to Scève's literary superiority. But it seems to me that the ultimate desire of Pernette's poet is more
ambivalent, or at least more complex, than the one attributed to her by
several of her recent critics. Lance Donaldson-Evans writes, for example,
that "[Pernette's] submission to Scève is partial and voluntary and is accepted in the name of a higher purpose: the continuance of his poetic creativity" (95).[17] Certainly, Scève's continuing poetic production is at issue
in the poem, hence the elegiast's decision to allow Scève's return to serve
the Muses. But the inducement for Pernette's sacrifice is neither simply
Scève's poetic glory nor her own immortality in his verses. It is, rather,
through Scève's writing that the world and specifically the poet herself will
be "content," and as we have seen, "contentement" in the Pernettian sense
is defined not as satisfaction, but as a Neoplatonically reciprocal and dynamic state. Pernette's desire is thus once again formulated as an imminent
expectation for herself as Neoplatonic lover: "tout le Monde, / Lequel un
jour . . . s'attend / D'estre avec moy et heureux, et content" (Elégie II).
Although the desired state seems to be unattainable in the literal present
("un jour"), no future verb figures in the elegy, and the final impression is
one of impending plenitude perceived in the present.

Pernette's poet thus diverges from the temporal ideology of her mentor, replacing Scève's privileging of the immortal by the search for fulfillment in the present moment. It is tempting to see in Pernette's embrace
of the present a circular notion of time, anatomically female in its cyclical
repetition as distinguished from Scève's phallic, linear projections.[18] But
such a binary opposition of female and male attitudes toward time in
sixteenth-century French poets, while arguably applicable to Pernette and
her mentor, would be deceptively tidy in that it fails to account for other
women writers' very different arguments against the temporal ideology of
their male colleagues, as the work of Catherine des Roches illustrates.

Catherine des Roches, writing in Poitiers some thirty years after the
publication of Pernette's Rymes, like her predecessor from Lyon, charted
her own literary terrain to some degree in response to the male poets of
her intellectual circle. Young, graced with considerable "avantages exté-
rieurs" (as Michaud puts it),[19] charming, unattached, and resistant to all
advances, Catherine was in many ways the perfect addressee for the carpe
diem motif. And, judging from a series of forty-five poems entitled "Responces" in her Secondes Oeuvres, Catherine was indeed the recipient of

many such poems.[20] In these "Responces," Catherine explicitly rebuts the seductive poems of several unnamed admirers, among whom undoubtedly figures Estienne Pasquier, whose devotion is humorously immortalized in *La Puce de Madame des Roches* (1583).[21]

The ubiquitous motif carpe diem, or carpe florem, in depicting the vibrant bud metamorphosing into a withered rose, simultaneously signals an explicit confidence in the present moment and an implicit terror concerning the future. Privileging physical beauty, the prototypical carpe diem poem threatens the young woman addressee with the literal or implied portrait of her withered old age, which is presented as the alternative to her loving the poet now, while she is still beautiful.

Catherine formulates both philosophical and psychological objections to the temporal ideology inherent in the carpe diem motif, often within the context of rejecting the rhetorical aim of that motif (the woman's seduction). Her philosophical notions concerning the passage of time are less nostalgic than those of her predecessors of the Pléiade, reflecting rather traces of certain Greek and Roman writers in her stoic acceptance of time's relentless pace. In "Responce" 12, for example, Catherine's poet manifests a Heraclitean consciousness of time's power to change all things.[22] Establishing a parallel between aging and change in all of nature, the poet describes the passage of time as a succession, rendered circular by the reference both to waves and to the sun:

> Ainsi que l'onde pousse l'onde,
> Que la nuit va suivant le jour,
> Le Soleil, ornement du monde,
> Chasse les ombres à son tour.
>
> .   .   .   .
>
> Voions nous un plaisant visage
> Changer son vermeil en palleur?
> Nature bonne mere et sage
> En va metre un autre en valeur. 63v–64v

> As one wave sends off another,
> as night follows day,
> as the sun, the world's embellishment,
> chases away shadows in turn.
>
> .   .   .   .
>
> Do we now see a lovely face
> changing to pale from rose-red?
> Nature, good and wise Mother,
> will make another one beautiful in its stead.

The Senecan notion that all progresses according to a natural order, that one face should lose its beauty and pass it on to another, underlies these verses. Dismissing physical beauty as an ephemeral quality and there-

fore unworthy of lovers' attention, Catherine recommends instead the attraction of lovers by beauties found in the soul. Such an attraction, she
argues, is not only more enduring but also healthier in the largest sense of
the word:

> Il ne faut seulement represanter les faces.
> .   .   .   .
> Mais toutes les beautez demeurant en vostre ame
> Vous alumez aux cueurs une celeste flame,
> Et plus sain est celuy qui plus en est epris. (62r–62v)

> Do not (re)present only the faces.
> .   .   .   .
> but with all the beauties of your soul,
> you set fire to hearts with a celestial flame
> and happier is he who is taken with it.

Catherine further repudiates the carpe diem motif by directly rebuffing
her literary suitors, with varying psychological twists. Unlike Pernette,
whose female poet gladly participates as muse in the male poet's immortality if in so doing there results "contentement" for both parties, Catherine's
speaker refuses to be the object of the male poet's amorous fiction. In one
case she accomplishes this feat by outright rejection, chastising the male
poet for his incessant literary pursuit:

> Si est-ce que la Renommée
> Ne peut chanter vos vers tant dous,
> Que moy par leur Grace animée
> Ne vole au ciel avecques vous.
> Et plus vous me voiez indigne
> De tant de belles fictions,
> Et plus vostre Muse divine
> Est riche en ses inventions. ("Responce" 12, 64v)

> Fame can no more
> sing your sweet verses
> than I can fly to the heavens with you.
> And the more you see me indignant
> at such fancy fictions
> the more your divine muse
> is rich in her inventions.

In "Responce" 41, Catherine, adopting a quite different tactic, turns
the image of her own youthful beauty topsy-turvy and thereby throws the
ball back into the opponent's court. Flattering her flatterer, Catherine argues that it is not her face, a constantly declining entity, that should be
compared to a flower, but rather the poet's own soul:

Prenant pour argument une face fanie
Qui s'en va chécun jour declinant d'un degré.
Un Jardin plein de fleurs n'est pas si diapré,
Que vostre Ame paroit de Graces embellie . . . (77v)

Taking as proof a faded face
that declines a bit each day.
A garden filled with flowers is not as colorful
as your soul appears embellished by grace . . .

In addition to writing responses to carpe diem poems, Catherine also
includes an original carpe diem poem in her "Dialogue d'Iris et Pasithée"
(*Secondes Oeuvres*, 43v ff.). As if to distance herself more emphatically from
the fictional writer of the carpe diem poem, Catherine has the character
Iris read aloud the verses of her penultimate flame Nirée. The poem might
be called a "second-stage" carpe diem poem; its theme, as in Ronsard's
"Quand vous serez bien vieille," remains the centrality of the woman's
youthful beauty and its loss which is rhetorically linked to her spurning of
the male lover. But here the lover, weary of being enslaved to the lady,
proclaims his love to have been as evanescent as her youthful beauty:

Si j'ay fait autrefois
Cruel Amour à ton pouvoir hommage,
Or' je quite tes loix
M'afranchissant de ton fâcheux servage.

. . . .

A Dieu fleur de Printans
Qui commandiez à mes jeunes pensées,
Je voi au fil des ans,
Et vos beautez, et mes amours passées. (47v–48r)

If, Cruel Love, I praised your power long ago, now I am leaving your laws,
freeing myself from this tiresome slavery. . . . Farewell, spring flower, who
commanded my young thoughts. I see with the passing of the years, your
beauty, and my love, both vanished.

In the dialogue, Iris avows her distress at the thought of having lost
her beauty so quickly, but Pasithée assures her that either Nirée's eyes have
gone bad or he's lying ("il dement le veritable temoignage") (48r). In response to Iris's query about what she should do next, Pasithée, here a wise
mentor as distinguished from Tyard's wise acolyte, responds economically,
"vous devez lire." Study and research calm the spirit, chasing away vain
and frivolous thoughts, Pasithée assures her student. But because Pasithée
recognizes that Iris's principal desire is not to become a scholar but rather
to attract faithful lovers, the mentor concludes the dialogue by presenting
her message in terms Iris can understand: "Chécun veut aimer ce qui luy
ressemble . . . [23] Embellissez donc vostre ame, si vous desirez d'être

uniquement aimée par un Amy sage, accort, et sçavant" (49v) (Everyone seeks to love another who resembles him . . . Embellish, then, your soul, if you wish to be loved by a wise, clever, and knowledgeable friend). Thus according to Pasithée the young woman must reject not only the threat of lost beauty but also any suitor-poet who would formulate such a threat. And once again, the alternative proposed to fretting about lost physical beauty through the passage of time is simply to turn one's thoughts to the more enduring beauties of the soul. Here the poet Nirée's desire to dominate his young addressee by describing the lost beauty of her body is subverted by Pasithée's Neoplatonic championing of the soul, the human entity most immune to the vicissitudes of time.

The acquisition of wisdom through reading, writing, and study is far preferable to preoccupation with physical beauty, according to Catherine's poet, but the most long-lasting quality of all is "vertu." Pasithée ultimately sets up a clearly delineated hierarchy of the spiritual or mental and the physical, with "vertu" surpassing all spiritual qualities, and "la face," synecdoche of the aging body, representing the physical:

> Belle ne craignez point de tomber à mépris,
> Bien que plusieurs hivers vous ternissent la face,
> Decorez vostre Esprit de Vertus et de Grace,
> Car la Vertu retient ce que les yeux ont pris. (48v)

> Young beauty, do not fear becoming an object of contempt, even though several winters will tarnish your face, adorn your soul with virtues and grace, for virtue retains what the eyes have taken in.

The sense of the word "vertu" is predictably problematic. In reading "Responce" 34, one might conclude that virtue has assumed its modern meaning of righteousness, integrity and propriety:

> Si la Beauté, la richesse,
> Le sçavoir, la gentillesse,
> Decorent vostre Printans,
> Faites que la Vertu sage,
> Soit dedans vostre courage,
> Fleur de la Fleur de vos ans. (75v)

> If beauty, wealth, knowledge and kindness, adorn your spring, keep wise virtue in your heart, flower of the flower of your years.

But in "Responce" 12, "vertu" is also associated with "la parole" and by extension with the enterprise of writing:

> Ce n'est point le tans qui s'envole
> C'est la douce Fleur des beaux Ans,
> Mais par l'air de vostre parole
> La Vertu triomphe du Tans. (64v)

Time is not flying away, but rather the sweet flower of beautiful years, Yet by
the grace of your word Virtue triumphs over Time.

Thus for Catherine, as for the carpe diem poets, one of time's primary
characteristics is its physical destruction and specifically the toll it takes on
the human body. But she continually subverts the power both of bodily
deterioration itself and of the poets who use it as a threat by minimizing
the importance of physical beauty in comparison with the nobler quality
of "vertu," exemplified, as her character Pasithée explains, by the practice
of reading and writing.[24]

Although the examples of Pernette du Guillet and Catherine des
Roches are too limited to infer from them a consistent female ideology
of time in Renaissance France, the two poets do nonetheless effectuate a
significant departure from their male counterparts. The future, in the conception of these two poets, holds neither the inalterable promise of Scève's
"myhrre incorruptible," that is, the assurance of *exegi monumentum,* nor
the menacing terror of aging inherent in the carpe diem motif. Both Pernette's and Catherine's works, as distinguished from those of their male
colleagues, ultimately evince a temporal philosophy that seeks to acclaim
the enduring qualities of the present, be it through desiring amorous plenitude or through undermining the importance of time's power to destroy
the human body. This is not to say, of course, that these women humanists
disavow the future to such an extent that they have no ambitious designs
for a positive reception of their work and, in Catherine's case, for a readership that will continue well after her death. But both women poets reject
visionary versions of the future by preferring to conceive of it, whether
articulated in terms of Pernette's Neoplatonism or Catherine's stoicism, as
the continuing evolution of the present. Ironically, despite their avowed
inattention to poetic immortality,[25] both of these women, in contrast to
Ronsard's Hélène, have gained literary acclaim in their own right. And
their works, by challenging two of the commonplace sixteenth-century poetic topoi we thought we had fully understood, compel us to formulate
more nuanced readings of these topoi and to include questions of gender
in our inquiries into the temporal philosophy of early modern France.

NOTES

1. All translations are my own unless otherwise indicated.

2. Lucien Febvre, "Temps flottant, temps dormant," in *Le Problème de l'incroyance au
XVIe siècle* (Paris: Albin Michel, 1942), 365 and ff.

3. For an excellent and succinct description of the Aristotelian sense of time, see Paul
Ricoeur, *Le Temps raconté* (Paris: Seuil, 1985).

4. See Petrarch's *Triomphi* (Trionfi) in *Canzoniere e Triomphi* (Florence: Phil. di Giunta,
1544), 168r–181r, where fame conquers death, but time nonetheless conquers fame. The
letters from Petrarch explicitly reveal Petrarch's terror faced with time. See *Letters from Petrarch,* ed. Morris Bishop (Bloomington: Indiana University Press, 1966), 201. Alberti, too,
in Book 3 of *I Libri della famiglia* propagates the idea of time's preciousness by proclaiming

it, along with the body and the soul, as the most invaluable of human possessions. See Leone Battista Alberti, *Opuscoli morali,* trans. Cosimo Bartoli (Venice: F. Franceschi, 1568), 169; Ricardo Quinones, *The Renaissance Discovery of Time* (Cambridge: Harvard University Press, 1972), 190; Simona Cohen, *The Image of Time in Renaissance Depictions of Petrarch's 'Trionfo del tempo'* (Tel Aviv: S. Cohen, 1982), 89 ff. and 103 ff.

5. The year of Pernette's birth had been established as 1520, but because two of her poems were set to music and published in Paris in 1540, several scholars have questioned this late date. See V.-L. Saulnier, "Etude sur Pernette du Guillet," *Bibliothèque d'Humanisme et Renaissance* 4 (1944): 8, n.2; Pernette du Guillet, *Rymes,* ed. Victor Graham (Geneva: Droz, 1968), xv. All subsequent references are to this edition.

6. Several other sixteenth-century moral treatises evoke the equation between virtue and the way time is spent by women. The first moral quality to look for in a woman is diligence, writes Pierre Lesnauderie in *La Louange de mariage* (Paris: Pierre Sargent, 1523), fol. 2r. The 1523 edition (Paris: F. Regnault; B.N. in-4 Rés. 1046) is available but incomplete. For Juan Luis Vivès, "La dame vertueuse ne mange point son pain oyseuse." See Juan Luis Vivès, *Institution de la femme chrétienne,* n.d., trans. Pierre de Changy (Lyon: S. Sabon, [between 1541 and 1549]), 163. Thomas Artus maintains that the virtuous woman will emulate not Lucrecia but Cornelia, who spent her days in the company of good books and learned people. See his *Qu'il est bienséant que les filles soient sçavantes* (Paris: L. Breyel, 1600) in Ilana Zinguer, *Misères et grandeur de la femme au XVIe siècle* (Geneva: Slatkine, 1982), 80. The concept of "virtue" as it connects with time spent or "passetemps" in sixteenth-century France raises a number of gripping questions that I am currently pursuing but that are beyond the scope of the present essay.

7. On desire, hope, and the idea of the future, see Eugène Minkowski, *Le Temps vécu: études phénoménologiques et psychopathologiques* (Saint-Pierre de Salerne: G. Monfort, 1988), 86 and ff.

8. Maurice Scève, *Délie,* ed. I. D. McFarlane (Cambridge: Cambridge University Press, 1966), 411; V.-L. Saulnier, *Maurice Scève* (Paris: Klincksieck, 1948), 1: 260.

9. The translation is by Ann Rosalind Jones, "The Lyonnais Neoplatonist," in *Women Writers of the Renaissance and Reformation,* ed. Katharina Wilson (Athens: University of Georgia Press, 1987), 225.

10. This is Jones's translation (231, n.3) with the exception of the last two lines, which I have translated to reflect more explicitly the temporal reference present in the original.

11. In one case, "contentes" modifies the Graces, who because of Scève's virtue are contented to serve him (Epigram 3).

12. Léon Hébrieu, Léon Hébreu, Leo Hebraeus, *De L'Amour,* trans. Pontus de Tyard (Lyon: Jean de Tournes, 1551), 21–25.

13. For an interesting and provocative treatment of cursive time and monumental time in relationship to gender, see Julia Kristeva, "Women's Time," trans. Alice Jardine and Harry Blake, *Signs* 7 (1981): 13–18.

14. In his *Mesure de l'instant (Etudes sur le temps humain)* (Monaco: Editions du Rocher, 1977), 4: 11, Georges Poulet points out that Scève dreams of a time that would encompass all times, particularly times to come.

15. In his study of Pernette, Verdun Saulnier contends that Pernette avows to Scève "une fidelité éternelle" (62), yet the examples he cites, rather than evoking eternity, address enduring love in more immediate terms: "amour durable" (Epigram 10), "toute ma vie" (Epigrams 19 and 28), "ma ferme asseurance" (Elégie 1).

16. I have changed only line 3 from Jones's translation (230).

17. Lance Donaldson-Evans, "The Taming of the Muse: The Female Poetic Voice in Pernette du Guillet's 'Rymes,'" in *Pre-Pléiade Poetry,* ed. Jerry Nash (Lexington, Ky.: French Forum Publishers, 1985), 84–96. In "Pernette Du Guillet's 'Rymes': An Adventure in Ideal Love," *Bibliothèque d'Humanisme et Renaissance* 31 (1969): 570, Robert Cottrell writes that "[Pernette] abandons her dream of perfect terrestrial happiness for the sake of an oeuvre that will be admired long after she and Scève are gone," but he also acknowledges the "note of

self-confident serenity" concluding the poem. In "Mutare/Mutatus: Pernette Du Guillet's Actaeon Myth and the Silencing of the Poetic Voice," in *Women in French Literature,* ed. Michel Guggenheim (Saratoga, Calif.: Anma Libri), 55, JoAnn DellaNeva offers another reading: "That Du Guillet's elegy ends with this apparent failure is, of course, ironic, since the text itself bears witness to her obvious assumption of the poet's role." Lawrence Kritzman concludes, as I do, that Pernette's poet gains by her submissive stance, but for different reasons. "The illusion of subordination paradoxically allows Du Guillet to empower Scève and thus realize her own sense of autonomy through the recognition of his: a creative talent that will immortalize the object of his desire." See "Pernette Du Guillet and a Voice of One's Own," in his *Rhetoric of Sexuality and the Literature of the French Renaissance* (Cambridge: Cambridge University Press, 1991), 11–28.

18. See Gisèle Mathieu-Castellani, "Les Marques du féminin," in *Louise Labé: les voix du lyrisme,* ed. Guy Demerson (Saint-Etienne: Institut Claude Longeon; Paris: Editions du CNRS, 1990), 189–205. Without dissimulating the difficulty of her enterprise, she seeks out "les marques du féminin" in Louise Labé's sonnets. She warns against falling back into former stereotypes of female territory: "le fluide, le flou, le mou, l'humide, le flux incontrôlé, l'affectif" (190) (what is fluid, vague, soft, wet, uncontrollably changing, emotional).

19. M. Michaud, *Biographie universelle* (Paris: Madame C. Desplaces, 1843–1865), 10: 551.

20. Catherine des Roches, *Secondes Oeuvres* (Poictiers: Nicolas Courtoys, 1583).

21. For a reading of Catherine's contribution to this collection, see my "Of Lice and Women: Rhetoric and Gender in 'La Puce de Madame Des Roches,'" *The Journal of Medieval and Renaissance Studies* 21 (1990): 123–135. I argue that although it may first appear that Catherine has simply joined in the literary game of paradoxical encomia to the flea, her poem, by subverting Petrarchan and other commonplace rhetorical practices and by representing a feminized mythology, ultimately undermines the collection as a whole.

22. E.g., "no man steps into the same river twice." For similar thoughts expressed by Pythagoras and Epimarchus, see Quinones, *Renaissance Discovery of Time,* 209.

23. Socrates expresses this same sentiment in Plato's *Lysis:* "Toute chose, necessairement ayme son semblable." See Des Périers, *Recueil des oeuvres* (Lyon: Jean de Tournes, 1544), 22.

24. See Catherine's often-cited "A ma quenouille" in *Les Oeuvres de Mesdames Des Roches* (Paris: Abel L'Angelier, 1578), 122. On the spindle as subterfuge, see also Tilde Sankovitch, *French Women Writers and the Book: Myths of Access and Desire* (Syracuse: Syracuse University Press, 1987), 52–53; and Constance Jordan, *Renaissance Feminism: Literary Texts and Political Models* (Ithaca: Cornell University Press, 1990), 183.

25. Pernette constantly denigrates her own poetic powers, as we have seen. In "A mes escrits" Catherine argues, no doubt disingenuously, that her children-texts should not go out into the world as they are so poorly clothed (*Oeuvres,* 122–123). Certainly Madeleine des Roches argues explicitly for her daughter Catherine's future renown, but in terms not at all consonant with the "exegi monumentum" of either Scève or the Pléiade (*Les Oeuvres* a4r):

> Le Ciel te face avoir tant de desir
> Des sainctes moeurs le seul juste plaisir,
> Et le Daemon, qui l'oeuvre a commencée
> Guide si bien l'effect de ta pensée,
> Que tesmoignant à la posterité
> Combien d'honneur tu auras merité,
> Tu sois un jour, par vertu immortelle,
> Je t'ay tousjours souhaitée estre telle.

> May Heaven grant you such a desire
> For holy living, the only just source of pleasure,
> And the Daemon who began this work

Guide so well the issue of your thought
That as a witness to posterity
Of how much you will have merited,
You may become immortal someday through your virtue,
It is thus that I have always wished you to be.

The translation is by Anne Larsen, "Les Dames des Roches: The French Humanist Scholars," in *Women Writers,* ed. Katharina Wilson, 245.

Patriarchy and the Maternal Text
The Case of Marguerite de Navarre
ॐ

Carla Freccero

Marguerite de Navarre inscribes a mother-daughter relation into the prologue of her novella collection, the *Heptameron,* and stages that relation, narratively as well as dialogically, in several of her stories. In the prologue, Parlamente, a married woman whose husband also figures among the participating storytellers and whose name suggests a privileged narrative role as "porte-parole" and mediator (there are those who assert that she is the Marguerite persona of the *Heptameron*), invokes the mother-daughter relation in her address to Oisille: "Madame, . . . vous [qui] maintenant à nous, femmes, tenez lieu de mere" (Madame, she said, you have had much experience of life, and you now occupy the position of mother in regard to the rest of us women).[1] Oisille serves as spiritual guide to the group of storytellers, reading lessons from Scripture to them each morning when they rise. Parlamente adds storytelling to the day's activities, mediating between her husband's private, carnal desires and the spiritual requirements set forth by Oisille.

P. A. Chilton, in his introduction to the *Heptameron,* has noted that "these three, Oisille, Parlamente, Hircan (Parlamente's husband), are at the apex of a miniature aristocratic society. They represent . . . a three-cornered antagonism that runs throughout the *Heptameron*" (13). This antagonistic triangle challenges both Freud's and Girard's oedipal models for the structuring of desire and the novel and announces the entry of feminine desire and feminine subjectivity as a thematic preoccupation and structuring agent of prose narrative.[2] Indeed, what implications might be drawn for feminists and literary theorists from the possibility that early novels include mothering in their motives (rather than "fathering" alone) and that the mother-daughter relation constitutes one of their founding paradigms?

What I propose to examine then is a literary work that figures the maternal as a social and political function in a particularly marked way. I use the term maternal to characterize a privileged figure and a privileged relation in the text. I say maternal rather than filial because of the authority invested in the mother's voice and her actions, an authority confirmed by both narrative events and the subsequent commentaries of the discussants. Maternal also implies a practice associated with a specific mode of sex/affective production and has "its own distinctive logic of exchange of the human services of sexuality, nurturance, and affection."[3] I would like to suggest that Marguerite's is a maternal text precisely insofar as it also enacts a praxis of mothering that can be ideologically described through textual analysis.

Departing from a previously articulated feminist position concerning the literary interaction of mothers and daughters, Marianne Hirsch, in *The Mother/Daughter Plot: Narrative, Psychoanalysis, Feminism*, argues that feminism—psychoanalytic feminism in particular—has occluded the maternal subject position in its theorizing about and interpretation of women, so that to speak or write as a feminist is to articulate a daughterly (psychoanalytic feminism) or a sisterly subject position that relegates the maternal to the status of a silenced obstacle to be overcome. Thus, for example, in her earlier work, Hirsch suggested that merger with the mother is precisely what threatens the heroine's "progression and development" in Madame de Lafayette's *La Princesse de Clèves*.[4] In *The Mother/Daughter Plot*, however, Hirsch revises the "matrophobia" of her earlier article and analyzes feminism's "avoidance [of] and discomfort with" the maternal (165). She argues that "an alignment of feminist with daughterly . . . only perpetuates mystifications of the maternal" (165) and concludes that

> Unless feminism can begin to demystify and politicize motherhood, and by extension female power more generally, fears and projections will continue. Feminism might begin by listening to the stories that mothers have to tell, and by creating the space in which mothers might articulate those stories. . . . A reconceptualization of power, authority, and anger can emerge only if feminism can both practice and theorize a maternal discourse, based in maternal experience and capable of combining power and powerlessness, authority and invisibility, strength and vulnerability, anger and love. Only thus can the maternal cease to polarize feminists; only thus can it be politicized from within feminist discourse. (167)

In her statement "Only thus," however, the maternal has not yet ceased to polarize feminists, and precisely that "female power more generally" that is being alluded to as an extension of the discussion of motherhood may suggest some of the reasons for that development. A paradigm of power based upon the extension of individualized and hierarchized "authority" seems to leave little room for collective and democratic struggle, while the very "invisibility" and "vulnerability" of that authority within a political context—the mother's own subjection—often exacerbates rather than mitigates its abuse. Hirsch's utopian vision of "a feminist family romance of mothers and daughters, both subjects, speaking to each other and living in familial and communal contexts which enable the subjectivity of each member" (163) thus seems at the same time to convey its dystopian political counterpart of a "family romance" that "subjects" both parties.

I take seriously the injunction to listen to maternal discourse and to politicize the maternal from within feminism. The exercise of feminist recuperation of the maternal is not without its ambiguities, as Hirsch's language suggests, particularly when, as in the case of Marguerite de Navarre, that position is one of both subjection and "public" political authority, if not sovereignty. Indeed, maternal sovereignty may constitute the genealogy of right-wing female authority in some sociopolitical orders of the late twentieth century. Nevertheless, Hirsch's proposal, when practiced skeptically, may generate ideological contradictions that suggest the possibility for (political) solidarity among daughters and mothers even within patriarchal orders that construct their interests as radically opposed.

The feminine subjectivity and desire constructed in Marguerite's text do not function in a utopian realm apart from patriarchal strictures. While Oisille, as reigning spiritual mother and widow, may indeed exist outside an economy of circulation and exchange, this is not the case for the mothers and the daughters who populate Marguerite's novellas. They operate within economic, political, and social spheres where feminine desires constitute the objects of contention between the individual and society.[5] In these spheres, the mother speaks the voice of social authority, often in the service of a father, brother, or king, against the daughter's wishes, while the daughter transgressively speaks in her own.

Marguerite herself was a mother whose mother-function was political, in the narrow sense of the word. Her political position and social station must be invoked as a precondition for any concept of maternal authority that appears in the text. She was a queen, wife, eventually, of the King of Navarre, and she was the sister of Francis I. The correspondence around her daughter's marriage indicates that marital negotiations played an important role in the political situations of both Marguerite and her husband vis-à-vis not only the king Francis I (and later Henry) but also the emperor Charles.[6]

The two stories I focus on, novellas 10 and 21, are narrated by Parlamente. The first involves a mother, her daughter, and a knight; the second a queen, Rolandine (her subject), and Rolandine's bastard lover (in story 21 Rolandine's father also plays a role). In each there is a conflict between a female authority, the mother or queen, and her daughter or subject. The men, with the exception of Rolandine's second husband, are eliminated in the course of the narrative. While in many respects these stories differ considerably, they both stage a conflict between the individual feminine subject and a sociopolitical authority that, while being marked patriarchal, comes to be ambivalently (and not uncritically) upheld by a maternal figure.

Story 10 is about Floride, a girl, her mother, the countess of Aranda, and Amadour, a knight of a lower station who falls in love with Floride. In the course of the narrative the daughter is married against her will. The narrative account suggests that the countess also has little choice in the matter:

> Ilz [the king and queen] prierent la contesse de faire le mariaige.... La contesse, comme celle qui en riens ne leur voulloit desobeyr, l'accorda, estimant que en sa fille, qui estoit si jeune, n'y avoit volunté que la sienne. (69)

> Pressed by the King to agree to the marriage, the Countess, as a loyal subject, could not refuse his request. She was sure that her daughter, still so young in years, could have no other will than that of her mother. (137)

Amadour, the knight, who cannot marry Floride because of their difference in social stations, insinuates himself into the countess's good graces and obtains free access to the house and to Floride. After Floride is married, he tries to rape her whereupon the young woman, although in love with Amadour, resolves never to disclose her feelings or encourage the friendship between them. At this point Amadour appeals to the countess, who approves of his love and encourages him. While Amadour is away, she forces her daughter to write him letters. There is the suggestion in the narrative of an implicit antagonism between the countess and Floride's husband; when Amadour visits the countess he finds her "fort malade d'une tristesse qu'elle avoit de l'absence de sa fille Floride" (76) (ailing, and pining for her daughter) (144). Shortly thereafter the countess summons Floride, "esperant," recounts Parlamente, "qu'elle reviendroit auprès d'elle" (76) (in the hope that she might want to come back and live with her permanently) (145). Floride refuses, and one wonders how much the countess's indulgence toward Amadour is a function of her desire to reclaim her daughter.

Amadour despairs of ever recovering the favor of Floride and devises a scheme to rape her. He enlists the complicity of the countess in arranging a private meeting with Floride. This time Floride screams, and her mother rushes to the rescue. Amadour claims to have been trying to kiss her hand, while the countess, skeptical, asks her daughter for an explanation. Floride does not reply. Her silence provokes a seven-year estrangement between mother and daughter.

> La mere . . . pensa pour certain qu'elle fust si desraisonnable qu'elle haïst toutes les choses qu'elle aymoit. Et, dès ceste heure-là, luy mena la guerre si estrange, qu'elle fut sept ans sans parler à elle, si elle ne s'y courrouçoit, et tout à la requeste d'Amadour. (81)

> She [the countess] was convinced that Florida was just being perverse, and had taken it into her head to dislike anyone that her mother was fond of. From that time on, the Countess became so hostile toward her daughter, that for seven whole years she did not speak to her except in anger—and all this for the sake of Amador. (150)

Floride does not succeed in mitigating her mother's anger until she learns deception; finally, she tricks Amadour into courting another woman so that the countess may see that he is untrue. He goes off to war a final time and dies. Then, "sans en parler à mere ne à belle-mere" (83) (saying not a word either to her own mother or to the mother of her dead husband) (152), Floride retires to a convent.

What Floride seems to "learn" in the course of the narrative is rhetorical dissimulation, to discern the difference between what a man says and what he does: "Floride, qui commançoit à congnoistre la malice des hommes par luy, tout ainsy qu'elle avoyt esté difficille à croire le mal où il estoit, ainsi fut-elle et encores plus, à croyre le bien où il n'estoit pas" (75) (Florida was beginning to understand the evil ways of men. If she had before found it hard to believe that Amador's intentions were bad, she now found it even harder to believe him when he said that in reality they were good) (143–144); she also learns to practice that dissimulation in her own interests. Parlamente, in fact, claims such an exemplary status for the story. In concluding, she comments:

> "Je sçay bien, mes dames, que ceste longue nouvelle pourra estre à aucuns fascheuse; mais, si j'eusse voulu satisfaire à celluy qui la m'a comptée, elle eut esté trop plus que longue, vous suppliant, en prenant exemple de la vertu de Floride, diminuer ung peu de sa cruaulté, et ne croire poinct tant de bien aux hommes, qu'il ne faille, par la congnoissance du contraire, à eulx donner cruelle mort et à vous une triste vie." (83)

> I'm afraid, Ladies, that this story has been rather long, and that some of you might have found it somewhat tedious—but it would have been even longer if I'd done justice to the person who originally told it to me. I hope you will take Florida's example to heart, but at the same time I would beg you to be less harsh, and not to have so much faith in men that you end up being disappointed when you learn the truth, drive them to a horrible death and give yourselves a miserable life. (152)

John Lyons has noted that any attempt within the *Heptameron* to turn "history" into example fails, given the conflict between discourse and history within the stories themselves (in this case, between following Amadour's words and actions) and between the stories and the following frame discussions. The latter have the status of discourse, individual, polemical, inconclusive, and open-ended assertions that serve to generate more stories. Lyons remarks that "the goal of the examples is not to extract truth from them but to use them to establish one's authority within a discursive situation."[7]

The contest to establish authority in the frame is between the men and the women; both Hircan and Geburon justify the actions of Amadour, and the discussion ends with Geburon's extravagant praise of Amadour's knightly virtues. The women criticize or defend Floride, while the countess, whose actions and words motivate the tale, is never mentioned. Within the story itself, however, she is clearly a contestant in the struggle for authority. That struggle, conducted in the service of her interests and those of her daughter, must be negotiated within patriarchal strictures. Constrained by the king to accept the marriage of her daughter to the Duke of Cardonne, she justifies her choice to the daughter through exercising her authority to silence Floride's complaints. Suffering the loss of her daughter and desiring to win her back, the countess subverts the husband-wife bond by encouraging and assisting Amadour in his courtship of Floride. In doing so, she nearly hands her daughter over to be raped. Finally, faced with Floride's resistance to her choice of suitor, she becomes hostile. Floride, in turn, claims authority over her own honor by refusing to speak (the frame discussion returns to this question of public and private honor); she then appeals to public honor to disparage Amadour in her mother's eyes.

The discursive mother-daughter struggle for authority empowers neither. Rather, the narrative delineates a predicament.[8] Sara Ruddick, in an essay entitled "Maternal Thinking," theorizes the patriarchal predicament of mothers, offering a means by which to understand the simultaneous collaboration with and subversion of the social structures produced as givens in this text.[9] Ruddick, a philosopher, identifies three "interests" that govern maternal practice: preservation (ensuring the continued life of the child), growth (fostering the child's development), and acceptability (producing an adult who will be acceptable to her social group) (215). In the mother-daughter relation, the conflict among these interests may be particularly acute because the mothering takes place within the context of a patriarchal society that does not exist to promote the interests (subjective authority, desire) of women. Thus a mother is seen as constrained by the requirements of patriarchy to produce a cooperative and obedient woman, one whose desires will not conflict with the structures that govern her (and her mother's) life (in this case, economic, political, and social allegiances between the king and other men).

Ruddick's theory is helpful in providing a partial analysis of the colonized's collaboration with the colonizer, but, while eliding the specificities of social formation and historical circumstance, it also does not account for the vested interest that is a component of collaboration.[10] In the text, this vested interest is maternal authority, the power of social and political decision making granted to the aristocratic woman in exchange for her collaboration. That authority, and its ambivalent interaction with the rebellious feminine subject, is the theme of story 21.

Rolandine's story is one of the most well-known in the *Heptameron*. Rolandine is an unmarried thirty-year-old woman whose father's economic interests prevail over his daughter's desire to marry, and whose queen—the narrative refers to her as "une Royne" (158) (a Queen of France) (236)— actively dislikes her because of a grudge she holds against the father.[11] Rolandine eventually finds consolation in the company of a "bastard," whose illegitimate birth and physical unattractiveness have kept him unmarried as well. Eventually, the two hold a clandestine wedding ceremony: "se donnerent chascun ung anneau en nom de mariaige, et se baiserent en l'eglise devant Dieu, qu'ilz prindrent en tesmoing de leur promesse" (162) (each gave the other a ring in token of the marriage. Then they kissed, in the church and in the sight of God, taking Him as witness of their vows) (240). They agree not to consummate their union until Rolandine's father dies or lends his approval. When discovered together, the couple separates but continues to exchange letters through the intermediary of servants. The narrative details the queen's obsessive regulation of their speech and the eventual interception of a letter that reveals their marriage. In the lengthy confrontation that ensues between mistress and subject, the narrator is highly critical of the queen's behavior—"La Royne, . . . ne luy peut respondre par raison" (169) (the Queen was quite incapable of making a reasonable reply) (247)—while Rolandine's calm reasonableness is repeatedly contrasted with the queen's rage: "Rolandine . . . luy respondit, d'un visaige aussi joyeulx et asseuré, que la Royne monstroit le sien troublé et courroucé" (167) (when she replied, she was as calm and composed as the Queen was violent and vehement) (246).

Rolandine's transgression of the social order constitutes a threat in that she has not obtained "parental" or monarchic consent: "La Royne . . . l'appella plusieurs foys 'malheureuse,' en lieu de 'cousine,' lui remonstrant la honte qu'elle avoit faicte à la maison de son pere et à tous ses parents de s'estre maryée, et à elle qui estoit sa maistresse, sans son commandement ne congé" (167) ([the queen] . . . far from addressing her as "cousin," told her repeatedly . . . that she was a "miserable wretch," and accused her of bringing dishonor upon her father's house, upon her relatives and upon her mistress, the Queen) (245). In one of the longest speeches in the *Heptameron*, Rolandine accuses the queen of injustice and claims the right to act according to her own desires. She appeals to a higher authority to justify her actions:

"puys que je n'ay advocat qui parle pour moy, sinon la verité, laquelle moy seulle je sçay, je suis tenue de la declarer sans craincte. . . . Je ne cranctz que creature mortelle entende comme je me suis conduicte en l'affaire dont l'on me charge, puisque je sais que Dieu et mon honneur n'y sont en riens offensez." (169–170)

My only advocate is the truth which is known to me alone, and I am bound to declare it to you fearlessly. . . . I am not afraid that any mortal creature should hear how I have conducted myself in the affair with which I am charged, since I know that there has been no offence either to God or to my honor. (248)

Rolandine's claim is indeed outrageous ("audatieuse" is repeated twice in the text). Her aunt (in story 40) is condemned, both within the story and by the discussants, for the far more modest transgression of marrying someone whom she thought would meet with approval. At the end of that story, both Parlamente and Oisille side with the social authorities: "'Je prie à Dieu, mesdames, que cest exemple vous soit si profitable, que nul de vous ayt envye de soy marier, pour son plaisir, sans le consentement de ceulx à qui on doibt porter obeissance'" (277) (Ladies, I pray God that you will take note of this example, and that none of you will wish to marry merely for your own pleasure, without the consent of those to whom you owe obedience) (370–371). Yet in story 21 the narrative works to justify Rolandine's claim. Upon refusing to allow the dissolution of her marriage, Rolandine is returned to her father, who locks her in a castle in the forest. The bastard proves unfaithful and dies, whereupon Rolandine's father seeks to make amends. Rolandine marries a gentleman who is "du nom et armes de leur maison" (173) ([of] the same name and arms as her father) (252). When her brother tries to disinherit her "lui mectant au devant qu'elle avoit desobey à son pere" (174) (on the grounds that she had been disobedient to her father) (252), God intervenes, and the brother dies, leaving all the inheritance to her. God is indeed, as Rolandine asserts, on her side.

The queen disappears when Rolandine returns to her father, and the storytellers never mention her. Although the discursive confrontation with Rolandine discredits the queen, other events in the narrative, on the contrary, seem to justify her opposition to the union. The bastard proves an unworthy mate for Rolandine: "monstra bien, par sa legiereté, que vraye et parfaicte amour ne luy avoit pas tant faict pourchasser Rolandine que l'avarice et l'ambition" (172) (It was quite plain from his lack of constancy that it was not true and perfect love that had led him to attach himself to Rolandine but rather greed and ambition) (251). In retrospect, therefore, the queen's judgment is justified on moral grounds. Rolandine's honor is preserved, but more because of her constancy relative to the bastard than because of her claims. The narrator comments, "Et combien qu'elle n'eut failly, la pugnition fut si grande et sa constance telle, qu'elle feit estimer sa faulte estre vertu" (172) (Although she [had done] wrong, the punishment was so harsh and her constancy so great, that it made her offence seem a virtue) (250). At the end of the tale, Oisille remarks: "'mais ce qui donne autant de lustre à sa fermeté, c'est la desloyaulté de son mary'" (174) (what enhances her constancy is her husband's disloyalty) (253).

In story 21 the moral justifications for opposition to Rolandine's choice (presented, initially, by her governess or "mother") ideologically mask the threat to the established order represented by her claims, a threat figured in the rage of the queen. At the end of story 40, Dagoucin alludes to this threat in matters of marriage:

> "pour entretenir la chose publicque en paix, l'on ne regarde que les degrez des maisons, les aages des personnes et les ordonnances des loix, sans peser l'amour et les vertuz des hommes, afin de ne confondre poinct la monarchye." (280)

> in order to maintain peace in the state, consideration is given only to the rank of families, the seniority of individuals and the provisions of the law, and not to men's love and virtue, in order that the monarchy should not be undermined. (374)

The exigencies of the "state" apply as much to the countess (story 10) and the queen (story 21) as they do to their daughters and subjects. Thus the countess in story 10 must marry off her daughter at the behest of the king, while the queen in story 21 serves the king and Rolandine's father in separating Rolandine and the bastard. To the extent that they collaborate with or uphold the monarchy, they are invested with an authority of their own, the power to regulate the actions of less empowered feminine subjects.

Simultaneously in these stories a subversion of the state undoes both the mother/queen's authority and that of its patriarchal context. In story 10, the countess enacts the subversion, appropriating for herself the daughter's desire in the service of her own. The daughter's resistance undermines the countess's authority. The result is a double disempowerment, a double failure. Floride's refusal to negotiate the terms of her desire within patriarchy (either to collaborate with her lover and thus maintain a split between public and private honor, or to indict him and thus appease her mother) preserves her honor, but at the cost of definitive separation from both her mother and the social economy as a whole.

In story 21, there is a more radical split between authority and its subversion, perhaps because the mother-figure is a queen, ersatz embodiment of monarchic authority. The daughterly resistance, in the subjective assertion of the right to desire autonomously, undermines the queen's power to control. In this story, the conflict is "resolved" by scapegoating the bastard.

Both desires triumph: the social order is upheld (the bastard proves unfaithful), and Rolandine gets what she wants.

As I hope to have shown, the mother-daughter conflict in this text paradigmatically figures sociopolitical struggles between the individual and the social order. Marriage is the appropriate focus for these struggles, as it constitutes the political and social cement that binds the aristocracy together as a distinct class. Under patriarchy, the position of the aristocratic maternal authority-figure is contradictory indeed. From this position a woman may exercise authority over other women in the negotiation of marriage contracts. Yet for such controlling power to be successful, it must appear to serve the interests of those daughterly subjects, for their resistance or rebellion threatens to undermine the hierarchy that constitutes the very basis of maternal authority.

Mothering is a praxis that, in the case of Marguerite and her text, is not solely based on political domination. It is a praxis engaged, in part, in mediation. In the uneasy open-endedness of its dialogic structure and the inconclusiveness of its discursive confrontations between collaborator and rebel, Marguerite's text mediates between feminine desires, negotiating those desires through patriarchal territory. Marguerite suggests this difference between her work and its male-authored counterparts, in both her condemnation of courtly romance (story 21) and the anti-Boccaccian polemics of the prologue to the *Heptameron*. The Galeotto (Boccaccio's *Decameron*) mediates desire, but it does so in the service of the patriarchy, that is, to the detriment of feminine subjectivity and maternal authority. The *Heptameron* mediates in the interests of preserving a precarious, feminine, place of authority, even if that place is only the space in literary history where some women's voices, speaking their desire, are occasionally heard.

NOTES

1. Marguerite de Navarre, *L'Heptaméron,* ed. Michel François (Paris: Garnier Frères, 1967), 6. All subsequent citations are from this edition. For the English translation, see *The Heptameron,* trans. P. A. Chilton (Harmondsworth: Penguin, 1984), 65–66.

2. For critiques of Freud and Girard in relation to "woman," see Sarah Kofman, "The Narcissistic Woman: Freud and Girard," *Diacritics* 9 (September 1980): 36–45; and Toril Moi, "The Missing Mother: The Oedipal Rivalries of René Girard," *Diacritics* 12 (Summer 1982): 21–31.

3. See Ann Ferguson, "On Conceiving Motherhood and Sexuality: A Feminist Materialist Approach," in *Mothering: Essays in Feminist Theory,* ed. Joyce Trebilcot (Totowa, N.J.: Rowman and Allanheld, 1984), 155. For the term "maternal text," a text that privileges the subjectivity or "voice" of the maternal subject position, see Marianne Hirsch, *The Mother/ Daughter Plot: Narrative, Psychoanalysis, Feminism* (Bloomington: Indiana University Press, 1989).

4. Marianne Hirsch, "A Mother's Discourse: Incorporation and Repetition in *La Princesse de Clèves,*" *Yale French Studies* 62 (1981): 73.

5. See John Lyons, "The *Heptameron* and the Foundation of Critical Narrative," *Yale French Studies* 70 (1986): 150–163.

6. For a more detailed account of the events in question, see my entry on Marguerite de Navarre in *A New History of French Literature,* ed. Denis Hollier (Cambridge: Harvard University Press, 1989), 145–148; see also my "Marguerite de Navarre and the Politics of Maternal Sovereignty," *Cosmos 7,* Special Issue on *Rethinking Queenship,* ed. Louise Fradenburg (forthcoming).

7. Lyons, "The *Heptameron,*" 159.

8. For a very different, and persuasive, reading of the narrative impasses of story 10, see Patricia Cholakian, *Rape and Writing in the Heptameron* (Carbondale: Southern Illinois University Press, 1991).

9. Sara Ruddick, "Maternal Thinking," in *Mothering: Essays in Feminist Theory,* ed. J. Trebilcot (Totowa, N.J.: Rowman and Allanheld, 1984); see also her book, *Maternal Thinking: Toward a Politics of Peace* (Boston: Beacon Press, 1989).

10. For theories of colonized subjectivity, see Frantz Fanon, *Peau noire, masques blancs* (Paris: Seuil, 1952); and *Les Damnés de la terre* (Paris: Maspero, 1961; reprint 1987). See also Albert Memmi, *Portrait du colonisé* (Paris: Gallimard, 1957; reprint 1985). Their focus is primarily on the violence of others effected by the colonial relation in a situation of territorial occupation, whereas in my use of the colonial relation to describe "internal" colonization I focus on the particular subjectivity of the colonized who identifies with the interests of the colonizer, who is, in Althusser's sense, "interpellated" by colonialism.

11. Here the mother-figure splits: there is Rolandine's governess (whom she calls "ma mere" [159]) who warns her to protect her honor from scandal, and there is the queen, who forbids Rolandine to speak with the bastard. Natalie Zemon Davis notes in *Fiction in the Archives: Pardon Tales and Their Tellers in Sixteenth-Century France* (Stanford, Calif.: Stanford University Press, 1987) that narratives of female conflict typically "pitted a young woman against a stepmother or surrogate mother" (102). Her work, as well as the splitting that occurs in novella 21, suggest that for the daughterly voice to be privileged and thus brought before the law and recorded in sixteenth-century France the familial authority denounced must be perceived as in some sense "illegitimate."

PART
THREE
❧

LITERARY
CAMOUFLAGES
AND
THE POLITICS
OF
RECEPTION

GENDERED OPPOSITIONS IN
MARGUERITE DE NAVARRE'S *HEPTAMERON*
The Rhetoric of Seduction and
Resistance in Narrative and Society

ℰᴂ

Gary Ferguson

Marguerite de Navarre's *Heptaméron* opposes a male to a female code of behavior in matters concerning the relationship of the sexes.[1] Intimately related to this problem is a theme so recurrent that it must be considered a leitmotif of the work as a whole: the admonition of women to beware of the noble sounding but thoroughly deceitful rhetoric of men. Again and again, male characters in the stories and male *devisants* in the frame manipulate the rhetoric of a particular ideology (Neoplatonism, courtly love, Christian charity, etc.) with the sole intent of beguiling and seducing women. Saffredent, one of the most cynical of the male *devisants,* even offers a frank admission of how members of his sex abuse language in order to deceive women and obtain their sexual favors.[2] The problem of how to respond to male rhetoric, a primary concern of the women *devisants,* often forms the subject of their discussions.[3]

The male *devisants,* however, often accuse the women of cloaking their own sexual needs and desires with a rhetorical mantle of female honor, based on a morality of chastity or fidelity to their husband. Saffredent, in particular, constantly reiterates his doctrine of "amour naïve": "Nous sommes faictz . . . Toutes pour tous, et tous pour toutes" (54) (It's every man for every maid, and every maid for every man) (120); he criticizes the hypocrisy of the women who go against nature and repress their sexuality. Yet even in their accusation of the women, the men's discourse rests on a confusionist rhetoric of seduction that undermines conventional semantic values. To argue, for example, that the women's concept of honor is based upon hypocrisy, Saffredent elaborates a myth of primal fall, which draws

143

obviously on biblical images of Eden and Neoplatonic images of the androgyne. A Johannine vocabulary of light and darkness, of truth and error
is also exploited to describe women who hold to the prelapsarian virtue
of *amour naïve*. Saffredent's discourse overtly disjoins rhetorical modes of
expression from their usual ideological contexts and alters their conventional meanings. To expound a doctrine, which in Christian terms is
frankly immoral, he does not hesitate to use vocabulary and images drawn
from the Book of Genesis, St. John, and Plato (292–294).

In the debate following story 26, to illustrate an idea very similar to
Saffredent's *amour naïve*, Hircan draws a parallel contrast between vice and
virtue, nature and constraint. Initially adopting conventional moral categories, Hircan limits himself to the suggestion that these might be false.
Women, he says, have exchanged the vice of acceding to male desire for
the greater vices of pride and cruelty, which they deem honest.

> "C'est une gloire et cruaulté, par qui elles esperent acquerir nom d'immorta-
> lité, et ainsy se glorifians de resister au vice de la loy de Nature (si Nature est
> vicieuse), se font non seullement semblables aux bestes inhumaines et cruelles,
> mais aux diables, desquelz elles prenent l'orgueil et la malice." (220)

> Thus, glorying in their resistance to the (sinful) law of Nature, (if Nature is
> sinful,) not only do they make themselves no better than cruel and inhuman
> beasts, but they turn into veritable demons, and take on the arrogance and
> malice of demons. (305)

Philippe de Lajarte has noted in Bakhtinian terms that Hircan is using the
"mot de l'autre," while at the same time seeking to undermine the ideology of that other.[4] This strategy is typical of the rhetoric of the *Heptaméron*'s male *devisants*. Hircan's tactics are recognized by the women for what
they are, however, and it is Nomerfide who asserts: "C'est dommaige . . .
dont vous avez une femme de bien, veu que non seullement vous deses-
timez la vertu des choses, mais la voulez monstrer estre vice" (220) (It's a
great pity that your wife is such a good woman . . . seeing that you not
only want to discredit virtue but also want to prove it to be a vice) (305).
Not only does Nomerfide reaffirm the conventional meanings of "virtue"
and "vice," but she also does so in specifically feminine terms with reference to Hircan's wife, Parlamente. The strategy of seduction practiced by
the men consists in severing the rhetorical figures of a particular ideological
language from their usual context. Thus isolated, words, images, and other
figures of speech can be voided of their conventional meanings and used
to signify concepts whose ideological import is quite different. The female
strategy of resistance, however, is based on a concept of womanly honor,
defined in terms of chastity or fidelity, and a reaffirmation of conventional
semantic values.[5]

In a recent article, Yves Delègue judged the attitudes of the men of
the *Heptaméron* to be superior to those of the women because they are

more honest.[6] Such a judgment seems difficult to sustain, however, because it connives at the fundamentally hypocritical and confusionist nature of the men's discourse. It should not be forgotten that when the men of the *Heptaméron* appeal to the women to be true to their sexuality, they are speaking as would-be seducers, rather than as husbands. They address the women as potential mistresses, rather than wives. The women are aware of this, and of the fact that they do not share the same sexual freedoms as the men. Any woman caught committing adultery can expect the most shameful moral and physical punishments to be inflicted on her. This is the subject, for example, of novella 32. If the men were offering the women the possibility of expressing their sexuality freely, then their discourse might be deemed honest. Because they are merely seeking their own sexual gratification in total disregard for the dangers to which their partners would be exposed, it is difficult to see how their behavior can be regarded as anything other than exploitative. The fact that the men admit their dishonesty does not make their actions honest. Rather, Saffredent and the other male *devisants* revel lucidly in the role of the seducer. Simontault affirms that "il avoit souvent souhaicté toutes les femmes meschantes, hormis la sienne" (96) (he had often wished that all women, save his own wife, were wicked) (164). He desires the liberty to be unfaithful to his wife with the unfaithful wives and daughters of other men; his own spouse, however, must keep herself chaste for him. The women are aware that the rules of the game are not the same for both sexes; the men, when it suits them, are the first to admit that this is so.[7] The first part of this essay examines how male rhetorical strategies of seduction and female rhetorical strategies of resistance frequently inform not only the discussions of the *devisants* but also the narrative techniques they use in the telling of the tales and the structural articulations between stories and debates. The second part considers the sociological significance of the *Heptaméron*'s male/female opposition and the moral code of chastity/fidelity that underlies the rhetoric of the women *devisants*, while paying attention in particular to the relationship of these issues to social class.

Novella 26, narrated by Saffredent, has drawn the attention of critics because of the remarkable turn-around executed by the narrator in the discussion following the tale.[8] Ostensibly the story praises the chastity of a "saige dame," who resists the physical advances of a *serviteur*, and criticizes the lack of honor of a "folle dame" who does not. But no sooner has Oisille, the matriarch of the group, praised the actions of the wise woman of the story, than Saffredent exclaims:

> "Pensez . . . voylà une saige femme, qui, pour se monstrer plus vertueuse par dehors qu'elle n'estoit au cueur, et pour dissimuler ung amour que la raison

de nature voulloit qu'elle portast à ung si honneste seigneur, s'alla laisser morir, par faulte de se donner le plaisir qu'elle desiroit couvertement!" (220)

> But just consider . . . here we have a wise woman, who, for the sake of showing herself outwardly more virtuous than she was in her heart and for the sake of covering up a passion which the logic of Nature demanded she should conceive for this most noble lord, goes and allows herself to die just because she denies herself the pleasures that she covertly desires. (304)

The *volte-face* operated by the narrator ought not to take us completely by surprise, however, because the novella's discourse itself is shifting and ambiguous. The narrative voice presents two distinct ideologies, which imply radically different interpretations of the story's diegesis. By the end of the tale, however, there can be little doubt in the listener's/reader's mind that the narrator's strategy has been to undermine his own initial discourse.

From the outset, Saffredent signals explicitly the potentially ironic nature of his story concerning "une folle et une saige" (207) (a woman who was wanton and a woman who was wise), when he adds, "vous prendrez l'exemple qu'il vous plaira le mieulx" (207) (you may please yourselves which example you follow) (291).

The novella begins by establishing in conventional moral terms the different character of its two female protagonists. The wise woman is introduced to the young and handsome seigneur d'Avannes at a ball. The narrator tells us that, although she was attracted to him, "Elle, qui avoit Dieu et honneur devant les oeilz, se contentoit de sa veue et parolle où gist la satisfaction d'honnesteté et bon amour" (209–210) (she . . . kept God and honor firmly in mind and satisfied herself with seeing him and hearing him speak, for in the faculties of sight and hearing lies the whole satisfaction of love that is noble and good) (293). The second woman is characterized by the narrator as not only "beautiful" but also "foolish" and "flighty."

Only a little later in the tale, however, the first encounter between the seigneur d'Avannes (who has disguised himself as a stable-hand) and the *folle dame* is narrated: "[se coucha auprès d'elle] non comme crainctif pallefrenier, mais comme bel seigneur qu'il estoit . . . [et] fut receu, ainsy que le plus beau filz qui fust de son temps debvoit estre de la plus belle et folle dame du pays" (212) (Gone was the cringing stable-lad. In his place was a bold young lord, the finest youth of his age, and as such he was received by the loveliest and most lascivious [folle] lady in the land) (296). The exploits of the lovers are now recounted with such complicity and verve that the quality of folly seems both life-giving and desirable. Here, for the first time, is suggested briefly the possibility of a dissenting ideology, which would serve as the basis for an alternative interpretation of the story. The narrator himself insinuates the existence of a second hermeneutic standard and begins to question the moral categories of "sagesse" and "folie."

The tension in the narrative voice of the novella carries over into the direct discourse of its protagonists. Having become ill as a result of the life he is leading, D'Avannes leaves the *folle dame* and returns to the house of the *saige* and her husband where he recuperates. Suspecting the cause of his sickness, the wise woman exhorts the young lord to love honestly in the future—that is according to the dictates of *sagesse*, not *folie*. D'Avannes agrees to do so and professes his love for the wise woman in terms imbued with the vocabulary of Neoplatonism:

> Aussy, ceste vertu que je desire aymer toute ma vie, est chose invisible, sinon par les effectz du dehors; parquoy, est besoing qu'elle prenne quelque corps pour se faire congnoistre entre les hommes, ce qu'elle a faict, se revestant du vostre pour le plus parfaict qu'elle a pu trouver; parquoy, je vous recongnois et confesse non seullement vertueuse, mais la seulle vertu; et, moy, qui la voys reluire soubz le vele du plus parfaict corps qui oncques fut, la veulx servir et honnorer toute ma vie. (214)

> Thus is that virtue, which my whole life through I desire to love, a thing that is invisible unless it show external effects. It must therefore take on a bodily form, so that it may make itself known unto men. Indeed, it has done so, for it has clothed itself in your body, Madame, the most perfect it could find. Therefore, I acknowledge and confess that you are not merely virtuous, but Virtue itself. And I, who see that Virtue shining through the veil of the most perfect body that ever existed do desire to serve and honor it for the rest of my days. (299)

This declaration, however, is problematical. Rather than revealing the upward movement of abstraction that characterizes a true Neoplatonic rhetoric, as the subject passes from the contemplation of human beauty to the contemplation of divine beauty, D'Avannes's discourse comes spiralling down from an alleged love of perfect virtue to its all too physical incarnation in his beloved's body.[9] The alluring and enticing character of D'Avannes's words is clear from the context of his conversation with the wise woman. Having got her to agree to help him in his professed desire to follow virtue, he introduces his declaration of love in the following way: "'Or, Madame, . . . souvienne-vous de vostre promesse, et entendez que . . . '" (214) (Then may you heed your promise, Madame, and know that . . .) (298). D'Avannes is consciously seducing the wise woman, leading her step by step into a rhetorical trap and seeking her logical assent along the way. The young lord's actions immediately belie his words moreover; when a kiss he seeks as a gauge of their virtuous love is refused, he resorts to trickery to obtain what he desires through the intervention of the woman's unsuspecting husband. D'Avannes's moral conversion does not seem to go very deep. His discourse is in many respects anti-Neoplatonic, and we are forced to conclude that his noble-sounding words are no more than a simple attempt at seduction. In her reply to the lord, moreover, the wise woman expresses satisfaction mixed with a certain cautious reserve. She will not judge his theology, she affirms, but she is a far from perfect creature and "la vertu feroit plus grand acte de me transformer en elle, que de prandre ma forme, sinon quant elle vouldroit estre incongneue en ce monde, car, soubz tel habit que le myen, ne pourroit la vertu estre conngneue telle qu'elle est" (215) (Virtue would be performing a greater act in transforming me into herself than in taking on my form, unless she wished perchance to remain unknown to the world. For, hidden beneath such a garb as mine, Virtue could never be known as she truly is) (299). More than simple modesty is being expressed here, and the woman's words question what D'Avannes has just affirmed.

Far from expressing a morality of chaste love, D'Avannes cloaks his *folie* in a rhetorical mantle of *sagesse*. The listener/reader recognizes in the actions of D'Avannes a representation within the novella of the rhetorical strategy of seduction described by Saffredent himself in the frame. D'Avannes's discourse also seeks to subvert the moral categories established at the beginning of the tale.

Toward the end of the story the narrator operates a remarkable coup de force, signaled in the text by the word "however" (mais), which prefigures yet more clearly his subsequent turn-around in the ensuing discussion. His attempts to woo his mistress having failed, D'Avannes takes leave of her and her husband. All should then be well for the virtuous wife:

> "Mais soyez seur que plus la vertu empeschoit son oeil et contenance de monstrer la flamme cachée, plus elle se augmentoit et devenoit importable, en sorte que, ne povant porter la guerre que l'amour et l'honneur faisoient en son cueur, laquelle toutesfois avoit deliberé de jamays ne monstrer, ayant perdu la consolation de la veue et parolle de celluy pour qui elle vivoit, tumba en une fievre continue, causée d'un humeur melencolicque" (217)

> However, you may take my word for it, the more virtue prevented the hidden flame from showing itself in her eyes and in the expression on her face, the hotter it grew and the more unbearable it became. In the end she was unable to endure the war in her heart between love and honor. It was a war that she had, however, resolved never to reveal, and, deprived of the consolation of being able to see and speak to the man who was life itself to her, she fell into a continuous fever due to a melancholic humor. (301–302)

The tone of the opening of this sentence is unmistakably Saffredentian. "'You may take my word for it'" constitutes a direct appeal out of the narrative to textual and extratextual narratees. It admonishes of the danger of battling against one's natural disposition and of imposing impossible constraints on one's humanity. Thus, we hear a clear expression of the narrator's own personal ideology of *amour naïve*.

The narratorial ideology of Saffredent dominates the tale at this point even with regard to the direct discourse of the wise wife: "O Monseigneur, l'heure est venue qu'il fault que toute dissimulation cesse, et que je confesse la verité" (218) (Oh Monseigneur, the hour has come when all dis-simulation must cease, and I must confess the truth) (302). The diegetic movement of the story now tries to reverse the judgment the listener/ reader has made of the male and female discourses in the narrative so far. Not D'Avannes but the wise woman is shown to have dissimulated; she has used a rhetoric that has conveyed untruth rather than truth, because it has hidden her real feelings. The wise woman even encourages D'Avannes to pursue other women; she assures him that "la grace, beaulté et honnes-teté qui sont en vous ne permectent que vostre amour sans fruict travaille" (218) (your grace, your beauty and your nobility are such that they will never let the toils of love go fruitless) (303). With great skill the narrator has brought his audience to the point in the novella where sagesse and folie have become indistinguishable and each has taken on the characteristics of the other.[10]

The ideology that at the beginning of the novella led to the establish-ment of the categories of *sagesse* and *folie* reappears only at the very end of the tale, in the description of the wise wife's pious death. After seeing the seigneur d'Avannes, the woman speaks to her husband for the last time. She reaffirms in her direct discourse her conception of love as fidelity to her husband in the face of her desire for another man. The narrative voice itself falls back into line and readopts a traditional moral stance in its de-scription of the woman's holy death. After receiving the Blessed Sacrament and Extreme Unction "avecq telle joye comme celle qui est seure de son salut . . . [rendit] avecq ung doulx soupir sa glorieuse ame à Celluy dont elle estoyt venue" (219) (joyously, as one who is sure of her salvation . . . with a gentle sigh she rendered her glorious soul unto Him from whom she had come) (303).

It is impossible to ignore the irony of the conclusion of story 26. All that proceeds in the novella is designed to empty the words *sagesse* and *folie* of meaning and to undermine the traditional morality to which they point at the beginning of the tale. The male/female opposition, so exten-sively discussed by the *devisants*, has become the subject of Saffredent's story. We witness D'Avannes's strategy of rhetorical confusion as he manip-ulates a Neoplatonic rhetoric in order to seduce the woman he loves. Within the context of a narrative discourse, which is itself fundamentally ironic, however, D'Avannes is vindicated through a collusion of narrator and protagonist. The would-be protagonist-seducer within the novella is seconded by the would-be narrator-seducer outside it, just as two centuries later, in another masculine narrative, the account of the chevalier Des Grieux is guaranteed by the "homme de qualité."[11] In conformity with the strategy described in the debates of the *devisants*, Saffredent, as narrator, disjoins the rhetorical forms of expression of a traditional morality from their usual ideological context. His interested motivation in telling the tale is thus revealed. Saffredent does not say what he means; rather, he exploits the rhetoric of a traditional morality—the holy death of the wise and virtuous woman and the ill repute of the unchaste woman—in order to suggest its opposite—the folly of the *saige dame*, who represses her sexual desires to the point of being unable to sustain her own life, and the wisdom of the *folle dame*, who acts according to nature.

In story 26, Saffredent creates a narrative justification of not only male rhetorical strategies of seduction but also his personal ideology of amour *naïve*. His story constitutes a vindication of himself and those like him, that rests in particular on the punishment of the woman who resists the rhetoric of the seducer and whose death is intended to serve as an example to women who might be tempted to follow her.

Saffredent concludes his story and thus introduces the discussion:

> "Voylà, mes dames, la difference d'une folle et saige dame, auxquelles se monstrent les differentz effectz d'amour, dont l'une en receut mort glorieuse et louable, et l'autre, renommée honteuse et infame, qui feit sa vie trop longue, car autant que la mort du sainct est precieuse devant Dieu, la mort du pecheur est très mauvaise." (219–220)

> Well, Ladies, that shows you the difference between a wanton woman and a wise one, two women who demonstrate the different effects of love. In the one it led to a glorious death that we should all admire; in the other it led to disgrace, shame and a life that was all too long. For as much as the death of a saint is precious before God, the death of a sinner is nothing worth. (304)

Even without the complete reversal of sentiment that follows, these words are enough to surprise us in the mouth of Saffredent because they run contrary to the narrative strategy he has implemented and to so much of his discourse in the *Heptaméron* in general. Again, Saffredent's words can only be considered ironic. Following the description of the wise woman's pious death, they form a trite and purely formal conclusion to the story: it is a challenge to the *devisants* to discuss the ambiguities he has been at pains to reveal in the narrative. His companions' failure to do this and Saffredent's consequent frustration lead to the outburst that we quoted above. It is a woman, Parlamente, who challenges Saffredent's interpretation, again by reaffirming traditional moral categories: "Si elle eust eu ce desir . . . elle avoit assez de lieu et occasion pour luy monstrer; mais sa vertu fut si grande, que jamais son desir ne passa sa raison" (220) (if she really had felt such desires . . . she had plenty of opportunities to show it. But so great was her virtue, that her desire never went beyond her reason) (304).

On the fifth day of the *Heptaméron*, Parlamente in fact narrates a tale that provides an interesting contrast to story 26 (I analyze novella 42 in detail in the second part of this essay.) It is enough to note here that the women's concept of female honor based on chastity is strongly upheld by the story and the heroine is praised for resisting the advances of her admirer because she sees they could never lead to marriage. This course of action is not presented as an impossible and unnatural feat that leads to death, but rather as the demonstration of a perfect mastery over self that is a source of happiness. The moral categories of *sagesse* and *folie* return to describe the alternative courses of conduct open to the heroine; but now the traditional meanings of these words are clearly upheld, and no confusion of semantic values occurs. As the narrative strategy of Saffredent reproduced the rhetorical strategy the male *devisants* describe and practice in the discussions, so that employed by Parlamente in novella 42 reproduces the strategy used by the women *devisants* to oppose the men's rhetoric of seduction. This strategy, as we have seen, consists in a reaffirmation of traditional moral categories and traditional semantic values. The significance of Parlamente's story does not escape Saffredent, and it is precisely this tale that provokes his famous remarks concerning the prelapsarian age of *amour naïve* and his criticism of the hypocritical rhetoric of women, who seek to dissimulate their sexual desires.

The clash between male and female rhetorical strategies, which frequently provides the *devisants* with the material for their discussions and stories, may also explain the narrative techniques the narrators employ and the articulation in the work between stories and debates.[12]

The woman who defines her honor in terms of chastity or fidelity to her husband often does so in the context of the refusal of a male who poses as *serviteur* and, operating broadly in accordance with medieval codes of courtly love, seeks physical gratification for his service. The well-known fourth novella is just one of many examples here. This story tells of a highborn widow who refuses the service of a gentleman acquaintance. When the court comes to stay at his house, however, the nobleman introduces himself into the lady's chamber at night by means of a trap door and proceeds to climb into bed with her. The woman calls her maidservant and resists her assailant physically, scratching his face so badly that he is forced to retreat and to keep to his room until his disfigurement has healed. The court continues on its royal progress, and gradually the woman is able to exclude the *serviteur* from her presence.

What is interesting is that this direct challenge to the aristocratic and medieval codes of courtly love comes from not only noblewomen but also their bourgeois counterparts. Story 42, told by Parlamente, is of particular interest here.

Novella 42 describes a young prince's pursuit of a bourgeois girl, Françoise. The young man is introduced initially as being "de grande et bonne maison" (286) (of high and noble birth), and moreover full of "perfections, grace, beaulté et grandes vertuz" (286) (perfections . . . grace and beauty and great virtues) (381). The prince expresses in his person the equation of aristocratic birth and beauty and virtue. The young girl, we are told, had been brought up in the castle of the prince's own family. Later she inherits a house nearby from her father, but because of her young age she lives with her sister in the town. The prince's attention is drawn by Françoise's beauty and her grace, which "passoit celle de son estat, car elle sembloit mieulx gentil femme ou princesse, que bourgeoise" (287) (was unusual for one of her station, to the point that she looked more like [sembloit] a noblewoman or a princess than a [bourgeoise]) (381). Initially, then, Françoise seems to contradict the equation of aristocratic birth and beauty and virtue—at least in the eyes of the prince, on which this description depends. The sentence is initiated by the phrase "Le jeune prince, voiant . . . que" (Now the young prince saw that . . .). The prince still assumes that he will easily have his way with the girl, however, "pour ce qu'il la congnoissoit de bas et pauvre lieu" (287) (as he knew she was of poor family and of low birth) (381–382). In other words, he assumes that her resemblance to a noblewoman is superficial and that her conduct will necessarily be determined by her social class. The key word in the prince's estimation of Françoise is "sembloit" (looked like). The prince then supposes that honor is mediated through class, but that beauty is not.[13]

When the prince sends a messenger to Françoise to declare his passion, the narrator tells us that she refuses to believe him because she is *saige*. Françoise recognizes that the prince is handsome and noble and that at the castle there are many women who are beautiful. She cannot believe therefore that he would waste his time with "une chose si layde qu'elle" (287) (an ugly creature like herself) (382). Françoise's estimation of the prince confirms the equation of high birth and beauty and honor. As a logical conclusion, she must then believe that she is ugly. But if she is *layde*, she is also *saige*, and in relation to herself, Françoise affirms that beauty is mediated through class, but that honor is not—at least in the specific sense of womanly virtue, sagesse, or to spell it out, chastity. Thus her belief regarding the relationship between class, beauty, and honor is diametrically opposed to that of the prince.

Not easily discouraged, the prince decides to write directly to Françoise himself. We are told that the latter can both read and write but that she declines to reply to her suitor because she considers herself too lowly. Françoise sees clearly that the prince could never love her "par honneur ou par mariage" (288) (honorably or with the intention of marrying her) and she refuses all forms of love based on "folie et plaisir" (wanton pleasure). Again she affirms that the prince is wrong if he thinks he will enjoy her physical favors easily because of her low social status.

> "Car elle n'avoit le cueur moins honneste que la plus grande princesse de la chrestienté, et n'estimoit tresor au monde au pris de l'honnesteté et de la con-

science, le supliant ne la vouloir empescher de toute sa vie garder ce tresor, car, pour mourir, elle ne changeroit d'oppinion." (288)

No princess in the whole of Christendom, she declared, had a heart more noble than hers, and there was nothing in the world more precious to her than honor and a clear conscience. She begged him, therefore, not to try to prevent her preserving this treasure for the rest of her life. Nothing would make her change her mind, not even death). (382)

Françoise does not hesitate to equate herself on the moral plane with a woman of a higher social rank. She also expresses a clear dichotomy between "pleasure" on the one hand and "this treasure" ("honor" and "a clear conscience") on the other.

When, through the prince's wiles, he and Françoise are finally brought together in a direct encounter, the latter restates her position, employing now a vocabulary of exchange, whose mercantile character is unmistakable: "Non, Monseigneur, non; ce que vous serchez ne se peult faire, car, combien que je soye ung vert de terre au pris de vous, j'ay mon honneur si cher, que j'aymerois mieulx mourir, que de l'avoir diminué, pour quelque plaisir que ce soit en ce monde" (290) (No, Monseigneur, no! What you seek cannot be. Even though I am no more than a worm in comparison with you, my honor is precious to me, and there is no pleasure in this world for which I would damage it. I would rather die) (384). Her honor (chastity) is an investment that must not be allowed to depreciate because on it depends the possibility of an honest marriage, the final commodity she seeks. Though pleasure might be desirable, it is not the ultimate goal and to squander her resources to this end would in every sense signal dissipation (*folie*).

Françoise exemplifies a bourgeois morality of thrift, economy, and investment and of the deferral of pleasure. In Jean-Joseph Goux's words, she is an example of the principle of "patient retention with a view to the supplementary *jouissance* that is calculated."[14]

Ironically Françoise reestablishes the equation of aristocracy and honor when she reminds the prince that she was brought up in his own household and that it was there that she learned the nature of love. As she cannot hope to be his wife, nor even his mistress, she begs not to be reduced to the "ranc des pauvres malheureuses" (290) (rank of those poor and wretched women who have succumbed)—those who have their chastity investment reduced to nothing. Françoise affirms, however, there are other bourgeois women in the town who are less scrupulous than she: "Arrestez-vous doncques à celles à qui vous ferez plaisir en acheptant leur honneur" (291) (Be satisfied with those women who will be only too glad to have you buy their honor) (385).

When the young prince sees he is making no progress whatsoever, he promises Françoise his complete fidelity and assures her of the uniqueness of his love. In a last ditch attempt to implement his seigneurial morality of *jouissance* now, of impetuous and unproductive *consommation*—that is of consumption and consummation, he offers the promise of an economy of thrift in the future. ("Sleep with me now and I will love you for ever.") Again, however, Françoise is too *saige* to believe such an unreasonable proposition. When the prince finally offers Françoise money in exchange for her favors, she rejects his bid with scorn. Although she says she prefers to remain in a state of "poverty with [her] honor intact" (in contrast to a state of financial dependence on the prince, which would make her one of "those poor and wretched women who have succumbed"), this impecuniosity is relative because Françoise is not without her own independent means.

Eventually, seeing that nothing is to be gained, the prince gives up his pursuit of the honest bourgeois girl and gives her in marriage to one of his servants. Thus Françoise obtains the return on her investment for which she had hoped, and in social terms the rate of exchange is respected.

Françoise acts according to bourgeois economic principles, while claiming an aristocratic morality as the source of her conduct. Parlamente, narrating the tale, proposes it as an example to aristocratic women of her own class:

> "Que dirons-nous icy, mes dames? Avons-nous le cueur si bas, que nous facions noz serviteurs noz maistres, veu que ceste-cy n'a sceu estre vaincue ne d'amour ne de torment? Je vous prie que, à son exemple, nous demorions victorieuses de nous-mesmes." (294)

> Well, Ladies, what are we to make of that? Are our hearts so base that we allow our servants to become our masters? The girl in the story could not be overcome either by the force of love or by the torment of importunity. My appeal to you is that we should all follow her example, that we should be victorious over ourselves, for that is the most worthy conquest that we could hope to make. (389)

It is noticeable that the female *devisants* of the *Heptaméron* affirm the principles of chastity and fidelity as an example and ideal for women of all social classes. In this the women's morality differs from that of the men, for whom class distinctions are more important.

In the discussion following story 4, for example, to which we referred above, Hircan criticizes the nobleman who failed to obtain from his lady the sexual favor he had set out to gain. He should have killed the woman's chamber-maid and then taken her by force. Story 2 tells of the chaste wife of a muleteer who, when she resists the advances of a servant, is raped and killed. The attacker is harshly condemned by the women, and neither Hircan nor any other men speak out in his defense. Hircan's silence may in part be due to the fact that the tale exposes the horrific consequences of the implementation of his morality of male sexual dominance through violence. It is more likely to result, however, from the fact that the honor of his own social class is not involved. The right of a *serviteur* to sleep with the woman he chooses is not at issue here because the servant is excluded from the elite to whom the courtly love tradition belongs. In other words, whereas the woman's rejection of her servant does not threaten the social order, the heroine's refusal of her aristocratic *serviteur* in story 4 is clearly more disturbing to the men because it undermines aristocratic and male prerogatives.

It is hardly surprising that the division of the social classes should be more important for the men of the *Heptaméron* than it is for the women. Contemporary society was dominated by the aristocratic male. All women of whatever class necessarily found themselves subordinate. The class division that is important for aristocratic men is less so for the noblewoman. Indeed for the women, the male/female division is primary, and women of all classes can feel solidarity in a shared moral code of chastity and a shared resistance to male whim and abuse.

In short, the morality of the women *devisants* undermines male aristocratic codes of *amour courtois* in two ways. First, through the impulse to chastity and fidelity and the deferral of *jouissance;* second, in the impulse to transcend important male class divisions that distinguish noble from bourgeois, ruler from ruled. These two tendencies are in fact typical of aristocratic women's writing in France in the late medieval and early modern periods. For Christine de Pisan, Marguerite's fifteenth-century predecessor in women's letters, chastity is also important because if women are to be able to resist male calumny they must be morally and socially independent—free from reproach and free to reply. At the same time, the City of Ladies is to be built with the blocks of virtuous examples, and into its precincts are to be admitted women of all social classes. Women, irrespective of their birth, may become ladies through the practice of virtue.[15]

In the sixteenth century, this female morality of chastity/fidelity is also in line with new ideals of courtliness coming from Italy, exemplified by writings such as Castiglione's *Book of the Courtier,* which was translated into French and published in 1537. Book Three of the *Courtier* contains a long defense of women and at the same time proposes a courtly model of conduct. Women of the court ought to remain chaste. Extramarital affairs are to be avoided; love between the unmarried is licit only if it might lead to matrimony. These ideals, at once Christian and courtly, were designed to appeal to Marguerite de Navarre.

Much of the violence depicted in the *Heptaméron* is in fact occasioned when women claim the right to define their honor in terms of this alternative code of *courtoisie*. At one point in the discussion of the *devisants,* Hircan and Simontault suggest that the women who imposed long trials on their *serviteurs* are of a bygone age (200–202). They are wrong. Rather, this distinctly female morality will go from strength to strength and the chaste heroines of the *Heptaméron* will be followed in the seventeenth century by that well-known heroine of another aristocratic text, the Princesse de Clèves. Floride, the heroine of the long and famous tenth novella, refuses her *serviteur,* Amadour, despite the fact that she is married to a man she does not love. It is impossible to read her story without being reminded of that of Mme de Clèves. Like the protagonist of Mme de Lafayette's novel, Floride retires to a convent at the end of the tale. "[Elle print] pour mary Celuy qui l'avoit delivrée d'une amour si vehemente que celle d'Amadour, et d'un ennuy si grand que de la compagny d'un tel mary" (83) (Thus she took Him as lover and as spouse who had delivered her from the violent love of Amadour and from the misery of her life with [such a] husband) (152).

Men's attitudes toward women in the Middle Ages were profoundly paradoxical. Medieval society demanded of women faithful wives and unfaithful mistresses. This paradox may also be expressed in terms of a tension between economy and *jouissance.* On the one hand, the system of primogenital inheritance requires a deferral of pleasure on the part of women because this alone can guarantee the legitimacy of offspring. On the other hand, the *serviteur* requires that a woman fulfill his desire now, irrespective of whether she is married already or a virgin to be married in the future. Women were irrevocably torn between two conflicting societal demands. In the face of this dilemma, the women *devisants* of the *Heptaméron* and women aristocratic writers in early modern France choose chastity and the bourgeois mode of deferral.

Of course a morality of chastity and fidelity may offer a woman the possibility of refusing the unwanted advances of a *serviteur,* but it does not lead to emancipation for women. In many ways it makes them even more subject to their husbands for the time they are married. For this reason, some feminist critics, taking sexuality as a standard to judge women's social freedoms, have offered extremely negative interpretations of Renaissance codes of *courtoisie* compared to medieval codes of *amour courtois.*[16]

Several observations must be made, however. First, it is not clear that courtly love codes brought women any real social freedoms; indeed, the opposite seems to be the case. Many critics argue that such codes were elaborated in the face of an increasingly repressive social practice and that they provided a vehicle for the release of the frustrated emotions of women and young men, who were falling into ever increasing dependence on the feudal lords.[17] Also we must not forget the markedly misogynist side of the courtly love tradition that makes women the objects of possession and the prize—willing or otherwise—of male prowess.

Ironically, in the sixteenth century, while aristocratic writers are affirming the right to refuse male sexual advances, a woman writer of the bourgeoisie, Louise Labé, claims the right to sexual expression and aristocratic *jouissance.*[18] Ultimately, it is clear that Labé's position is the more socially subversive, and this no doubt accounts for the intensity of the controversy that has surrounded her from the sixteenth century onward. The *Epître dédicatoire,* which opens her work, establishes a clear link between the poems that follow and women's right of access to culture and public life. The *Epître* urges women to reject the accoutrements of woman as desired object—chains, rings, and sumptuous garments[19]—and the poems that follow firmly constitute woman as desiring subject. It is worthy of note that the *Epître* is addressed to Clémence de Bourges, the daughter of one of the most prestigious landowners of the region. It has been argued in this connection that the disapproval of the bourgeois women of Lyons, whom Labé at several points in her work seeks to mollify, may well translate a sentiment of resentment, provoked as much by Labé's social climbing as by her eroticism.[20] Critics have pointed out that Labé's erudition is remarkable for a woman of her low social status.[21] It seems plausible that her own experience of bourgeois society, in which the sphere of most women's activity was strictly limited to the domestic, would prevent Labé from seeing any advantages in a morality of female chastity and fidelity. But aristocratic women writers in early modern France already enjoyed, to a certain extent, both access to culture and a role as public figures. Their opposition to the aristocratic principle of *jouissance* must be understood as both the rejection of a courtly tradition that was often demeaning to women and a desire to affirm their independence and subjectivity in the context of a society, in which the pursuit of women was one of the nobleman's chief distractions. But whether they claim the right to say "yes" or the right to say "no," women writers of both aristocracy and bourgeoisie are ultimately working toward the same ends—they seek some degree of sexual emancipation and freedom from an unjust male domination.

Only one tale in the *Heptaméron* is set in the medieval past of chivalry and courtly love; the châtelaine de Vergi is recounted by Oisille with the special permission of the *devisants*.[22] Oisille significantly places the story in a modern, Christian and Evangelical context, and concludes that it shows women should never place their trust in any man or indeed in anything earthly. Parlamente remarks that even virtuous love needs to be kept secret because a woman is judged only by appearances. Longarine concludes that under such circumstances it is better not to love at all. Dagoucin, the *Heptaméron*'s only male idealist of love, understands very well the link between contemporary social and economic forces, the women's refusal to play the roles demanded of them by the courtly love tradition, and their choice to follow instead a code of *courtoisie* based on bourgeois principles. With foresight, he objects: "Mais qui penseroit que les dames n'aymassent poinct, il fauldroit en lieu d'hommes d'armes, faire des marchans; et, en lieu d'acquérir honneur, ne penser que à amasser du bien" (419) (but if we thought that women did not love, then, instead of following the profession of arms, we should all turn into mere merchants, and instead of winning our honor, seek only to pile up wealth) (533). Those words of aristocratic and male anxiety foretell the end of an era.

NOTES

1. See among others Marcel Tetel, "The *Heptameron,* a Simulacrum of Love," in *Women Writers of the Renaissance and Reformation,* ed. Katharina M. Wilson (Athens: University of Georgia Press, 1987), 105. An earlier version of part of this essay was presented as a paper at the April 1992 Agnes Scott College Colloquium celebrating the 500th Anniversary of the Birth of Marguerite de Navarre. I wish to thank Frank Bowman, Lance Donaldson-Evans and Mary Donaldson-Evans for their helpful comments.

2. See Marguerite de Navarre, *L'Heptaméron,* ed. Michel François (Paris: Garnier Frères, 1967), 95–96. The English text is taken from *The Heptameron,* trans. P. A. Chilton (Harmondsworth: Penguin, 1984).

3. These issues are discussed, for example, after stories 12 and 14. Only Dagoucin among the male *devisants* expresses an idealistic concept of love and must be excepted from what we say regarding male rhetorical strategies.

4. "Christianisme et liberté de pensée dans les 'Nouvelles' de Marguerite de Navarre," in *La Liberté de conscience (XVIe–XVIIe siècles),* ed. Hans R. Guggisberg, Frank Lestringant, and Jean-Claude Margolin (Geneva: Droz, 1991), 59–60.

5. Of course the stories of the *Heptaméron* display a wide variety of modes of female conduct, and there are women also who manipulate language in order to deceive. One example is Jambicque, the heroine of story 43, who cloaks her sexual license with a rhetoric of *gloire.* These women almost inevitably incur the express disapproval of the women *devisants,* however. See Raymond Lebègue, "La Fidélité conjugale dans l'*Heptaméron,*" in *La Nouvelle française à la Renaissance,* ed. L. Sozzi and V.-L. Saulnier (Geneva: Slatkine, 1981), 425–433. Although there is some indirect evidence that the moral codes of Ennasuite and Nomerfide might be a little less rigorous than those of the other women as Betty J. Davis notes in *The Storytellers in Marguerite de Navarre's Heptameron* (Lexington: French Forum Publishers, 1978), it would be wrong to read too much into the text by concluding that these women generally practice or advocate unchastity. The male/female opposition is particularly strong, however, between Saffredent, Hircan, Simontault, and Geburon on the one hand, and Parlamente, Oisille, and Longarine on the other.

6. Yves Delègue, "La Présence et ses doubles dans l'*Heptaméron,*" *Bibliothèque d'Humanisme et Renaissance* 52 (1990): 280 and ff.

7. This situation is the subject of story 15, which constitutes a forceful defence of the position of married women. Katharine Rogers examines the mistress-wife dichotomy and concludes that Renaissance writers rarely attempted to reconcile the two conflicting ideals of woman as wife and mistress because women were considered less as independent human beings than as fillers of various functions in relation to men. See Ruth Kelso, *Doctrine for the Lady of the Renaissance,* preface by Katharine M. Rogers (Urbana: University of Illinois Press, 1978), viii–ix. I return to this question in the final part of this essay.

8. See, for example, Lajarte, "Modes du discours et formes d'altérité dans les 'Nouvelles' de Marguerite de Navarre," *Littérature* 55 (1984): 68–69. Patricia Francis Cholakian in *Rape and Writing in the Heptaméron of Marguerite de Navarre* (Carbondale: Southern Illinois University Press, 1991) also analyzes story 26, and my own reading converges at certain points with hers. She, however, attributes the duality of the story's narrative perspective to Longarine's injunction that Saffredent should speak no ill of women (131–132, 135).

9. It is enough to compare D'Avannes's speech with the discourse of Bembo at the end of Book Four of Castiglione's *Book of the Courtier,* trans. G. Bull (Harmondsworth: Penguin, 1976). Bembo emphasizes the danger of allowing the senses too much influence in the appreciation of beauty. He urges a progression from the contemplation of particular human

beauty to that of general and universal human beauty, and thence to the contemplation of the spiritual beauty of the soul.

10. Tetel, *Marguerite de Navarre's Heptameron: Themes, Language, and Structure* (Durham, N.C.: Duke University Press, 1973), 125–126.

11. See Naomi Segal's brilliant and provocative reading of Prévost's *Manon Lescaut* in *The Unintended Reader: Feminism and Manon Lescaut* (Cambridge: Cambridge University Press, 1986).

12. See John D. Lyons, *Exemplum: The Rhetoric of Example in Early Modern France and Italy* (Princeton: Princeton University Press, 1989), 92.

13. On the question of the representation of social class in novella 42, see also Cholakian, *Rape,* especially 167–170, 178–179.

14. See Jean-Joseph Goux, *Symbolic Economies: After Marx and Freud,* trans. Jennifer Curtis Gage (Ithaca: Cornell University Press, 1990), 203.

15. See Diane Bornstein, *The Lady in the Tower: Medieval Courtesy Literature for Women* (Hamden: Archon Books, 1983), 26–30; and Christine Reno, "Virginity as an Ideal in Christine de Pizan's *Cité des Dames,*" in *Ideals for Women in the Works of Christine de Pizan,* ed. Diane Bornstein (Detroit: Michigan Consortium for Medieval and Early Modern Studies, 1981), 69–91.

16. See Joan Kelly-Gadol, "Did Women Have a Renaissance?," in *Becoming Visible: Women in European History,* ed. Renate Bridenthal and Claudia Koonz (Boston: Houghton Mifflin, 1977), 137–164.

17. See Bornstein, *The Lady in the Tower,* 31–33, and William E. Monter, "The Pedestal and the Stake: Courtly Love and Witchcraft," in *Becoming Visible,* 119–136.

18. On the question of sexuality and social class, see Margaret W. Ferguson, "A Room Not Their Own: Renaissance Women as Readers and Writers," in *The Comparative Perspective on Literature. Approaches to Theory and Practice,* ed. Clayton Koelb and Susan Noakes (Ithaca: Cornell University Press, 1988), 93–116.

19. Louise Labé, *Oeuvres,* ed. François Rigolot (Garnier Flammarion, 1986), 41; see also 8.

20. Fernand Zamaron, *Louise Labé: dame de franchise* (Paris: Nizet, 1968), 66.

21. Labé, *Oeuvres,* 7–8. See also Natalie Z. Davis, "City Women and Religious Change," in *Society and Culture in Early Modern France* (Stanford: Stanford University Press, 1975), 65–95.

22. Because it is set in the past, story 70 is not strictly speaking a *nouvelle*. It has, moreover, been recorded in writing and "men of letters" were to be excluded from the narrative enterprise.

ENGENDERING LETTERS
Louise Labé Polygraph
ℐℬ

Tom Conley

Texts that come to us from the Renaissance are bathed in silence. Silence, first, of print that refuses to give way to speech that characters are said to relay from orators or writers to readers. And a silence, too, of a world whose ways we cannot fathom. When we open the velum covers of the early modern editions we read in special collections or *salles de livres rares et précieux,* we are told not to touch the paper, respect codes of silence, and take notes in silence. Gender does not easily cross the exalted decor of the library. What gender seems to mean in the typography of books printed then is not what we think we know it may be now. By contrast, in the modern canon, we are assured that gender is produced extensively in fiction. Because it treats of language and is less concerned with representation than establishing networks of symbolic correspondences in the realm of language, poetry rarely engraves true images of sexed forms. The novel or short story, however, tends to construct mimetic fields in which gender produces a field of illusion that "reflects," like a mirror, what we observe, through the window of the reading room, in the streets below.

Virginia Woolf has shown us that in the novel relations of male and female code most literary representations. These become the laws of "life" that affect the ways people live (e.g., Emma Bovary having fallen in love because she read Sir Walter Scott, where there reigned men, women, in love, with copious tears and kisses). From a sociological perspective, the novel furnishes valuable information about the history and dynamics of sexual difference. Point of view, expression, psychological experiment, or representation of desire and conflict—the raw material of narrative—

depend on the display of pertinent signs of difference and identity. The writer of fiction tends to assume these signs in a language whose codes furnish all the necessary indications that will flag the signs of sexual difference. In turn, readers assume a task of finding the origins and ideology of sexual difference through study of literary forms that language has already, to an extent, predetermined.

Writers, we believe, gain the privilege of a creative space where they can experiment with alterity by folding themselves into sensibilities other than their own; or, in the act and art of writing, they tease out of us *our* yearnings to confuse roles and attitudes generally refused by the laws of gender. A writer or a critic can make us dare either to cross social boundaries through polymorphous adventures of language or to do with vocables and letters what we cannot perform so easily in our lives. And strong readers detect in fact the limits of writing when they determine if a discourse succeeds in transgressing or—failing that—impugning coded sexual and social boundaries. He or she can use received "signifiers of demarcation"[1] to construct social space of past time in order to test those of our own.

In the Renaissance, these can include, first, a mystical relation with language, by which both reader and writer seek to collapse sexual difference for the purpose of constructing an imaginary universality. The mystic recalls how his or her body was enveloped by a world that knows no time. Through the mystic's tale of venture, proven by the writing of the experience left on the body, we listen and strive to imagine ourselves in that world. If the mystical experience is gained through writing, we allow the very characters of the account to move through us; we become one with the mystic, when we invest ourselves in the shape of its printed words that trace the tale of a crossing. The sixteenth century speaks to us and, at times, even ravishes us in the spell of its signs. It becomes our actual, lived present in the ways we displace our imagination into the silence of its printed speech. We seek to change sexual difference of our time by means of an art, like that of self-analysis or anamorphosis, of being obliquely projected through or across the canon of the Renaissance. Or, second, there is travesty. French literature of the sixteenth century offers the viewpoint of the other's body that may be desired, feared, and, at the same time, even loathed when it dissimulates its truthful being. Male and female live in drag, or, if not, they exchange their identities through the characters they play on the fictive stage of writing. Yet, third, the uneasy relation of mimesis and writing—because the one is never the other—can lead to an unveiling of dissimulation, in scenes where sexual difference becomes nothing other than a detection of lies—a sort of polygraph test—in which meaning and form, truth and dissimulation are together extinguished. In these scenes, we discover how the illusion of difference becomes the very allure of the text, and the textual truth, in turn, becomes what questions our assumptions—brought to the text—about sexual difference. In these moments, letters and bodies appear to live in total and unending congress and disaggregation.

Our relation with these forms is, for the French Renaissance, complicated doubly by the filters of gender through which we apprehend the period. A reader of Marguerite de Navarre cannot fail to approach the *Heptameron* through stagings of oedipal scenarios that merely illuminate *our* cultural experience, such as what has concretized perhaps our identification of the tale of Amadour and Floride as the double of Marguerite Duras's *Ravissement de Lol V. Stein.* Or a narratologist disengaging the variety of points of view in the same work—those of belief, of erotic charge, of historical verisimilitude in respect to the ties of the names of the tellers and real-life personages—does so through experience of literary camouflage almost invariably learned by way of Melville or Henry James. For a *seiziémiste,* psychoanalysis provides convenient models that can study refractions of drive and desire to map out a history of the birth of subjectivity, that is, to show how one comes into language and is determined by social practices. These, the science would lead us to believe (and hope), can apply to individuals of any historical time. By way of the authority of psychoanalysis, the birth of the "modern subject" is assured through the interpretation of *any* text of the past: the psychoanalytical gloss assures us that a common idiom links the past and the present; a dynamics is established in the relation of reader and writer, like that of analyst and patient, that identifies the experience of the subject "then" to be quite like what we negotiate "now," with the result that literature of the past enhances the "modernity" of our age.[2]

In this respect, as historians and feminists alike, we have to work against ourselves. We must, it appears, study sexual difference with the assumption that it can deny what we take or know to be essentially our own. Helpful, then, are the resistances that the early modern period offers us: its polyglot nature; its dazzlingly complex matters of belief and social practice; its allure, as Lucien Febvre imagined, of heightened sensibility and violence in the same blow; its brutal frankness about bodily matters; its erasure of lines demarcating life and death. Our frustration becomes a vital element in what we call the truth of the period.

One area of resistance may include that of the female signature. In this essay I ask what indeed constitutes that signature and how that signature confers a specific validity upon the works it appends. Does the distinguishing mark give the text a different aura? Does it cast light on practices and positions where, in a world of lettered males, the female name goes *otherwise?* Whereas the male signature can be said to go—or be signed—"without saying," does the feminine paraph color its discourses in other and different ways? We can approach these questions by noting that the feminine signature, first, questions the social space that a masculine gender uses to arrogate a refined cultural form or a mode of ascendancy—literature—for itself. And, more urgent, second, that, occupying, as it does, the place of a male position, the feminine mark turns relations of gender toward a divided but autonomous writing of *generation*. In the years before 1550 writings that fall under the feminine signature bring forth a style that propagates forms from within themselves, one that questions modes of power and control that generally appear aligned with the masculine paraph. The woman's signature works in conjunction with a process in which early modern print culture establishes complex grids of correspondences among letters, numbers, ciphers, and typographical marks. The same process establishes fields of exclusions and inclusion. Now when writing is eroticized under a female sign, a polymorphous character and a new autonomy of generation come into view.

Such is the effect of Louise Labé's brief collection of twenty-three sonnets. Near the axis of the collection, the twelfth marks a center of tensions that radiate, like rays of light and of desire, through the surrounding sonnets.

XII

Oh, si j'estois en ce beau sein ravie
De celui là pour lequel vois mourant:
Si avec luy vivre le demeurant
De mes cours jours ne m'empeschoit envie:
Si m'acollant me disoit: chere Amie,
Contentons nous l'un l'autre! s'asseurant
Que ja tempeste, Euripe, ne Courant
Ne nous pourra desjoindre en notre vie:
Si, de mes bras le tenant acollé,
Comme du Lierre est l'arbre encercelé,
La mort venoit, de mon aise envieuse,
Lors que, souef, plus il me baiseroit,
Et mon esprit sur ses levres fuiroit,
Bien je mourrois, plus que vivante, heureuse.

Oh, were I only in this body ravished
By him for whom I am dying:
If, with him, living in days remaining,
My life's longings wouldn't be famished:
If, holding me, he were to say: Dear Friend
Let's be happy, stick to ourselves, assuring
Me that with the tides of Euripes flowing,
They never untie us from our desires' end:
If, with my arms, embraces I lavished
About his body, as ivy grips and laces a tree,
Death squeezed me, I feel it would be wished.
When with joy, the more he were loving me,
My spirit, curling over his lips, would flee,
I would die in bliss, beyond life, cherished.

Study of the extraordinary rhythms of the text, its literal inspiration, have underscored how the measure duplicates the breath of desire. The initial apostrophe begins as a pause, a suspension, that inclines to ravishment, that comes over and again, three times, in the volley of the first tercets. The expiring breath that utters *Oh* is stopped—almost repressed—by the strident *si* that marks the verbal flow like the crests of waves. A fantasy reading would have the *O* stand as a bull's eye, a target, that the arched trait of the sibilant *si*, as a volley of arrows—or eros—strikes at its center.[3] As a graphic mark that cannot yet be iconized as an archer's target, *Oh* leans toward symbolic form when *si*, a pure expression that has not yet been assigned meaning, turns into the conjunction of a dilemma: would I were ravished. . . . But no sooner than *si* becomes a linguistic sign, or no sooner than it moves from a graphic mark or literally zero- degree icon, to a figure of a subordinate construction, then it shifts into language and follows, *de but en blanc*, the straight and true trajectory of grammar: "if only, if only, if only. . . . " So wonders the voice in the toss and heave of the decasyllable. A ballistics of love emerges. The pathos of desire unfulfilled, of the ravishment of nonravishment, of bliss deferred, comes with the final adjective that sets in place the ambivalence of the writer's pathos: in unabated anxiety she will die "heureuse," when her illusion hits the final mark, period.

The capping irony of the sonnet forces the reader to work back through the entire text—to turn about it, just as it makes the other twenty-odd poems turn about its axis—in order to follow the ways that the meanings of the words either "stick" or detach from their verbal surface. The pathos adheres to the irony that in turn is carried by the emblem of ivy (*Comme du Lierre est l'arbre encercelé*) that embraces—encircles and almost "ensorcelle"—the tree. As soon as the figure begins to disengage the pattern of a flow of motivation, the poem begins to divide and to engender itself. In fact, the literal center or vanishing point of the text is a word that probably appears no less enigmatic for us than for the reader or listener of the 1550s. "Euripe" is the only proper name uttered in the text; it is lodged at the sonnet's bull's eye or point of generation and seems, because of its placement in the frame, to concretize its reference. A narrow, or an antique "Detroit" between the island of Euboea and the coast, Northeast, of Attica and Boetia, the opening in the center literally "squeezes" the textual body, as if the word itself, a sign of flowing waters, were immobilized amidst the movement of tempest (*tempeste*) and current (*Courant*) to the left and right in the same line. The geographical referent, as it might be found in any contemporary edition of Ptolemy's *Geographia* (from the North, in Münster's edition of Basle, 1540, or the South, from a Bologna edition of the 1480s) motivates the very geography of the letters and vocables in the text: the reality of the poet's pathos is not here and now, in the reality of *Europe*, but rather resides far away, in a familiar dream, of a nonplace named *Euripe*.

The center of the sonnet thus displaces two letters, an *I* and an *O,* so as to thrust us away, into a dream of bliss, on the shores of a classical space and time avowedly irretrievable, absent, and bathed in loss.[4] The shift of the letter carries us away. The displacement visually charms or enchants us in the perplexity of space moving in silence. The play of the *i* and *o* in Euripe is literally underscored by the predication of disjunction immediately beneath the proper name. If a mathematical term can be assigned to the style of the poem, Euripe stands above the predication of disruption below, over an invisible "vinculum" linear bar that keeps the verb below it, *desjoindre,* from disintegrating under the effect of its own meaning:

Euripe

———

desjoindre

The tensions held between Euripe and Europe are ostensibly marked beneath an implicit "vinculum," where the two vowels, *o* and *i,* find themselves framed—joined but detached from one another—at the axis of *desj-oi-ndre.*[5] The central area of the sonnet begins to flicker and twist. The text develops extensively, in horizontal scansion from West to East across Eur-*i*/*o*-pe, but also in vertical movement, through the invisible line of white space between lines seven and eight. There we find a play of substitution that the letters below tender to Euripe above:

Euripe

desjoindre

The two characters effectively spot two axes in *Euripe* and *desjoindre,* with torsion on either side in "tempeste" and "Courant," the sum of which suggests that an elliptical configuration flips and folds the sonnet in and about space:

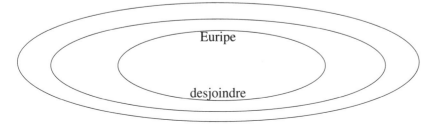

The figure avers to be, once again, an anamorphosis of the archer's target. It is seen from a "Parthian" or "departing" point of view, whose movement away from the desired object constitutes an ambivalent desire to approach and be detached from it.[6] At the same time, an obviously saturnal undercurrent of creation and melancholy is folded into the astral dimensions of the configuration. The fractional character of the printed letter hints at its almost infinite possibility of recombination in the representation of desire. As noted, it can be algebraic and geometrical, at once iconic, ciphered, and symbolic. The text is staging a sexual and social difference, it appears, in the gap between the *I* and the *O* that the space of the sonnet doubles in order to produce an illusion of space, volume, and unending movement.

In this sense it shares much with contemporary work on the letter as a perspectival object. According to poets, typographers, and cartographers of the immediately preceding years (1520–1540), the letter could be viewed as a frame for a picture or an element of a rebus that would carry in its form a "signature" in the shape of a subjacent mental "picture," somewhat like the implicit orbits of ellipses that are described from the view of the double axis of Louise's sonnet. In a similar vein, for his *Protomathesis* (1532), Oronce Finé drew an alphabet of historiated initials, of which the *C* and *H* allowed for the decoration of a dolphin within their frame. Thus Oronce could mark his geographical umbilicus or place of birth, the *Daulphiné*, in the picture of the dolphin, and concretize the genetive form of his signature to be read as "D'O. Finé," a motto combining letter and picture and putting Finé in rivalry with his origin. In his majuscule *O*, he places a self-portrait in a circle within the surround of the initial. The circle, held up by two links of a chain on either side, offers a space in which the letters of the signature, *O* and *F*, are inscribed, one in light and the other in shadow, to follow the rhythms of the days, the seasons, and the years. And the great allegorist of the printed letter, Geofroy Tory, argued in the *Champ fleury* (1529) that every letter is set in a gridded frame subject to the laws of perspective. In this way the printed character carries in its form an illusion of depth that moves both into space and through time (insofar as the Roman letter "displaces" its counterpart, the "lettre de forme," that resides in many readers' memory).

These instances would seem far from the pathos of Louise Labé who seeks ravishment in the great fold ("sein" l. 1) of the world. But perhaps not: Tory builds his alphabet from the *differential* relation of the curve and the straight line. The two forms that generate all knowledge, all writing, or all printed expression, he reminds his readers over and again, include the difference of the *I* and the *O*. The *I* is the mark of the stylus, the inscriptive gesture par excellence, while the *O* is the curve of the universe, the shape that "marries" the unyielding but triumphal *I*. His apology for printed writing goes back to the myth of *IO*, the goddess whose very name conveys the origin of difference, whence every letter of the alphabet is generated. When placed on its side, the *I* reveals the *O* of its base and is configured as Virgil's flute. One letter is and is not of the other. They are at once masculine and feminine despite our recidivous desire to mark the *I* as "male" and the *O* as "female."

Now Louise's figure of love, "Comme du Lierre est l'arbre encercelé," emblematizes the copulation of linear and curved traits. And her recurring apostrophes that know passion (but not grammar), her volleys of "Oh, si" generate in their ciphered form a congress and separation of bodies. "Oh, si" of the first line projects the text into a dream of longing especially onto the character of its own materiality. The concrete, printed shape of the text performs everything for which the meaning is longing. The initial sigh encodes itself as a mark of death that anticipates its recurrence throughout the text and its final inscription in the last verb, "mourrois." "Mourrois" functions with the initial "Oh, si" in the same way that a *sonnet rapporté* gathers together in its last lines the themes articulated in the preceding material. Here the *sonnet rapporté* works at the level of the printed letter, "mourrois" objectifying the three "breaths" of the first three tercets (Oh, *si* . . . *Si* m'acollant . . . *Si,* de mes bras . . .) by mirroring the prevailing configuration of the poem. It contrasts the ironic placement of "heureuse" (a vocable not "configured" with the graphemes *i, o,* or *s,* and therefore out of the mental and physical picture of the sonnet) as the word that not only sums up the prevailing signs of the text but also serves as a focal point from which they are in tension with the initial, historiated *O* of the incipit.[7] The death that ends the life of the voice in the poem also engenders a play of combination that displays the poem's capacity to give renewed birth to itself everywhere on the page. The poem's graphic iteration of engenderment overtakes its deadly scenario of sexual difference.

All of a sudden what appears to be a facile formulation acquires traits of movement and scintillation. Alliteration of "mes cours jours" (l. 4) recalls the initial play of straight and curved shapes (*cours jours*), but also draws attention to a virtual network of signs that come together under the heading of the "où" or the "where?" that asks us repeatedly to find the poem's *vrai lieu* or true site of congress. Where is it? In the middle? At the end? Beyond "heureuse," in Platonic deferment? The graphics anticipate the *Cours* in which the *nous* will be tied and then disjoined in death, where the self will probably die ("mourrois").[8] The poem scans itself hurriedly in the ostensively artificial order that makes the initial apostrophe an instance of anaphora (more deferment) that endows the stanzas with a visual rhythm. Yet it decelerates, first, when we discern the serial disposition of letters and, then, when a dilation of opening and closure emerges from the relation of the sonnet's elliptical center and circumference.

Louise Labé, like other woman writers of her period, has often been treated as a poet of sincerity. Albert-Marie Schmidt has written to the effect that the strength of her poetry consists in a will to avow its confusions and ambivalence. "In her case, Petrarchism, instead of providing her with a sort of sophistry, guarantees the avowal of a meticulous feminine, but not effeminate, sincerity."[9] Because no male can *ever* pretend to argue for or represent the point of view of a female, Schmidt's remark appears to veer toward condescension. Is he beguiled by the very art of Louise's poetry? If we recall that, in respect to Anna de Noailles, André Gide rebuked the countess's verse on the grounds that "c'est avec de bons sentiments qu'on fait de la mauvaise littérature" (with good feelings is written bad literature), sincerity would be a mere stratagem foregrounding more important and more delicate issues of creation. If so, Louise deploys mendacity to write good literature. Once the sincerity is written as a lie, the poem begins to write of itself. On cursory view Louise appears to use the first-person shifter in the feminine in order to change the habitual perspective with which we view Petrarchan sonnets. Her *je* is crafted to become an autonomous, self-replicating object within its own confines.

To call the work autonomous or self-isolating would lead us to a facile conclusion. Louise takes much greater symbolic risks. She forges a writing that casts in doubt all thematic treatment of either "man" and "woman" or "sincerity" and "mendacity." The text uses optical means—what theorists as diverse as Martin Jay and Laura Mulvey call the force of the male gaze—to produce a text that continually engenders itself all over its surface by means of serial and pictographic differences. The printed register does not betray the sincerity of the grief but marks the problem of sexual difference in the *indifference* of markers of gender. "He" and "she" or "le" and "la," the subject and the object, the nominative or accusative cases that constitute the lament, are upstaged by a myriad congress and separation of forms that have no gender. Their visual differences prompt us to see how we produce a difference of gender when we are beguiled in believing that writing functions as a reliable substitute for the real codes of social life.[10]

At least two conclusions can be tendered. First, for all the Petrarchan commonplaces in this and other sonnets, the printed writing continually questions our desire to motivate the figures of speech. We can no longer follow hackneyed approaches to literature that seek "originality" in certain figures and "banality" in others. A stylistics of this kind, that compares sources to their deviation, cannot discern the more problematic area of an original sameness-in-difference that calls attention to the neutral area where literary effects are seen as elements of serial production. In Louise's sonnets, the figures of speech turn about a materiality that seems motivated through its own form. The common emblem of ivy gripping the tree, "encercelé" (l. 10), often seen in woodcuts adorning editions of Alciati and Corrozet, gains force, paradoxically, when it tends to be *least* convincing: *l'arbre* appears in the text like a Saussurean *arbor,* a tree that is used to exemplify the *arbitrary* qualities of the printed or graphic sign. The tree is alternately iconic (emblematic), symbolic (metaphorical), and graphic (made up of characters that neither substitute printed script for voice nor "translate" speech into writing). The sum produces different and unforeseen connections in the text's paragrammar. In this way it becomes a set of seven digits that may or may not spell out, at distinct intervals, the poet's signature (*l'arbre*). Louise is in and of the tree just as much as she is not. Likewise, the scatter of "Oh, si . . ." tells us that the final figure of the male lover's lips, "Et mon esprit sur ses levres fuiroit," despite its topical condition in contemporary ideolect, would turn the most "feminine" part of the male body into a labial fold, something more immediate, arresting, more erotic and alluring than the abstraction of the "beau sein," the Platonic fold, announced in the first line. The lips become a fragment of the poet's name, a labial, sensuous curve that supersedes the male figure sought at the vanishing point of the narrative.

Second, the relation of the poet's name to its inscription and dispersion in and about the congress of letters aligns the feminism of the text with its force of movement. Once the reader detaches signs of gender from the printed words—that invite us to find sexual difference in the mimetic domain of the text, which is surely not one of its most productive areas— the poem begins to design the terms of its own engenderment. It is accomplished by the art that combines figural and visual, iconic and symbolic registers with the discursive dimension of the poet's lament. Each tends to put the others in question. In this way the poem does not lead its writing toward a specific or privileged end. Rather, it duplicates its tensions all over itself. Seen from a different perspective, the poem might also confirm what Pierre Francastel noted in an extensive comparison of painting of the *quattrocento* to cinema:

> Le souci du continu oblige le peintre comme le cinéaste à couvrir de signes la totalité de la surface portante. Mais il utilise, lui aussi, des moyens pour que notre attention se fixe de préférence sur certains détails plutôt que sur d'autres. En bref, il y a création, d'une part, de *signes perdus,* et il n'est pas nécessaire, d'autre part, que l'on présente la totalité d'une figure ou d'une action pour qu'elle devienne repérable. . . . On revient, ainsi, à la notion du parcours, par laquelle on a fait saisir comment une composition inerte vit dans notre esprit et possède un degré de réalité dépassant infiniment le petit illusionisme du détail arbitrairement reproduit.[11]

> The desire for continuity obliges both the cineast and the painter to cover the totality of the bearing surface with signs. Yet the painter also uses means that draw our attention to certain details rather than others. In a word, there is on the one hand a creation of *lost signs,* and it is not necessary, on the other hand, to present the totality of a form, a figure, or of an action to make it perceptible. . . . We thus return to the notion of movement over a surface, by which emphasis is placed on the ways an inert composition can live in our mind and possess a degree of reality that infinitely surpasses the tiny illusionism of arbitrarily reproduced details.

Louise the writer shares much with Francastel's painter and filmmaker. She produces a composition that moves along a *parcours,* in the direction of an ambivalent center, but only in order to make it turn and then disperse everywhere else about itself. It unfolds itself and, in doing so, unfixes the codes of gender that are used to lead us toward that center or, in Francastel's words, toward an illusion of totality. Such would also be the illusion of a fixed gender that is contained in the autonomy of the personal pronoun, the "he" or "she" of the "I." The graphic medium breaks the illusion of gender and draws attention to an art of printed writing. A network of "lost signs" is fashioned, but so too is a liberation. It may be that Louise Labé, as a polymorphous voice in the microcosm of her twenty-three sonnets, owes much to the condition of print-culture of the 1540s. The fact remains that she does exploit it and that no French poetry, of either male or female signature, has since so directly questioned our dilemmas about writing and gender.

NOTES

1. Both the *signifier of demarcation* and the *perspectival object* are terms developed in Guy Rosolato, *Eléments de l'interprétation* (Paris: Gallimard, Coll. "Connaissance de l'inconscient," 1985).

2. See, for example, Lawrence Kritzman, *The Rhetoric of Sexuality and the Literature of the French Renaissance* (Cambridge: Cambridge University Press, 1991), 383; he reads the literary canon through a psychoanalytical filter and sets forth as its most compelling issue the very possibility of engaging such a reading. For that reason, perhaps, the author refrains from arguing that the sexual difference in the Renaissance is an "origin" or "source" of what we assume we know in the name of Freud.

3. In the context of the other sonnets the reading may not be illicit. In Sonnet XV the figure of the "parting shot" or *Parthian* strategy of warfare (arrows fired in retreat) compares love to war and to the movements of the gods in the heavens: "Quand quelque tems le Parthe ha combatu, / Il prent la fuite et son arc il desserre" (When, after battling a while, the Parthian / Retreats and with his bow unleashes his arrow). In Sonnet XXII the masked name of Louise ("*Lou*as jad*is* *e*t ma tresse dorée, / Et de mes yeux la beauté. . ." [You formerly praised both my golden braids / And the beauty of my eyes . . .]) becomes the target of arrows (*trets*) that seem identical to the amber shine of her hair (*tresse*), the two born of an inert, historical object (*res*). The poems compose an extensive archery lesson in which archer and target are willfully confused.

4. See Erwin Panofsky's extraordinarily perceptive history of the structure of the relation that Europe holds with the classical past in *Renaissance and Renascences in Western Art* (Stockholm: Almquist, 1960).

5. The concept of the "vinculum" is borrowed from Gilles Deleuze, *Le Pli* (Paris: Minuit, 1988), a study of mannerist and Baroque esthetics that runs through Leibniz. Deleuze shows that any text engendering or atomizing itself does so by way of a movement between seeing and reading. This is especially pertinent for "ciphered" texts, in other words, all poetry because poetry uses meter and spacing to produce manifold and conflictual levels of meaning. With Louise Labé, a "divided" or "fragmented self," a component of the theme of the lament, is produced in the literally fractional character of the self; that is, a self is partial or fragmented insofar as it is a fraction composed of a numerator and a denominator, as in $\frac{1}{2}$ or, in the verbal cipher, $\frac{Euripe}{desjoindre}$. In the world of syllogism, relations of mathematics and logic are intimate. In a different context that leads to a similar conclusion, Robert Cottrell notes how Montaigne puts standard vertical oppositions (male over female; strength over weakness, etc.) in "geometrical" structures. The terms are squared in order to lose their usu-

ally oppositional attributes. The text thus "unfolds" and transvaluates sexual difference. See his "Gender Imprinting in Montaigne's Essais," *L'Esprit Créateur* 30, no. 4 (1991): 85–96. Louise does the same by the patently visual means of the rectangular "aspect ratio" of the sonnet.

6. The sonnet uses vocables to produce a visual form, like a painting, that invests a power in its relation of center and circumference. The poem can be studied from the standpoint of Rudolph Arnheim's remarks on "Centers and their Rivals" and "The Viewer as Center," chaps. 2 and 3 of *The Power of the Center: A Study of Composition in the Visual Arts* (Berkeley: University of California Press, 1988), 13–50.

7. Louise Labé appears to share a supremely graphic, material sense of the medium that has connections with other women poets who cipher their words with elements that fragment the discourse. In the first decades of the fifteenth century Christine de Pisan begins the *Cent balades damant et de dame* in an almost identical fashion, when she writes in superscription, "Cy commence les cen balades d'aman et de dame." The line can not only be taken thematically, as an incipit, but it can also be read in its mathematical and figural dimensions that square the dialogue of the male and female, the lover and the lady, into a spatial conflict on a *damier* or chessboard. In this perspective, the first letter would be a pawn but also an inscription that finishes the work where it is begun: "Cy [$C = 100$] commence les cen [100] balades. . . ." In the same fashion Louise's sigh, *O,* announces the work, initiates the myriad copulation of letters within the text, and sums it up as well. On the tension of calligraphy and discourse, see Jacqueline Cerquiglini, "Histoire, image, raccord et désaccord du sens à la fin du Moyen Age," *Littérature* 74 (May 1989): 124 ff.

8. This strategy is almost a trait of Louise's paraph. Unwarranted reiterations are everywhere calling attention to subgrammatical linkages that throw the course of reading into multifarious directions. In sonnet IV, the first line invokes, "Clere Venus, qui erres par les Cieus . . ." (Clear Venus, you, erring in the heavens . . .) such that the clear skies that go with the name of the goddess also engender a vagabond movement—*errance*—that goes in all directions. The limpid, diurnal perspective becomes what the speaker wishes to flee when she bathes herself in "mon lit mol de larmes" (my soft mattress of tears) in the nocturnal areas of the text. And the shifter "nous" seems to waver between its grammatical function in lines 6 and 8 ("us") and its iconic figure as a knot, or a "noud," of the kind Ronsard twists his fantasy of self-containment into the buckles of Cassandre's hair: "Ou soit qu'un *noud* diapré tortement / De maintz rubiz, & maintes perles rondes" (Or that a knot, deftly diapered, / Studded with many rubies) in the *Amours* (XC).

9. Presentation, in his *Poètes du XVIe siècle* (Paris: Gallimard-Pléiade, 1953), 272. This and other sonnets studied above are taken from this edition. In a terse and elegant preface to a more recent edition of the same sonnets, Françoise Charpentier implies that by ventriloquizing the male voice, Louise produces effects lacking typical "reverberations; to dare to say, 'I desire you' has a different resonance in the mouth of a man than that of a woman. Louise pushes this logic to its extreme by stealing away male expressions," in her preface to Louise Labé, *Oeuvres poétiques* (Paris: Gallimard/Poésie, 1983), 29. It is noteworthy that the substitution of one voice in the place of another resembles "postsynch" or "voice-over" construction in cinema; in fact, the gap between the "image" and "sound" tracks in film appear to have their initial—and strongly feminist—experiment in Louise Labé's sonnets.

10. Citing Nina Catach's history of orthography, Yves Citton and André Wyss show that he printed letter or grapheme has been construed to belong to a "substitutive code, and that graphic signs signify phonic traits" (un code substitutif et que les graphies signifient les phonies) in *Les Doctrines orthographiques du XVIe siècle en France* (Geneva: Droz, 1989), 10. By questioning the substitutive model of speech and writing, they approach the very sensibility hat also seems to inspire Louise.

11. Pierre Francastel, *La Figure et le lieu* (Paris: Gallimard, 1967), 176.

CHASTITY AND THE MOTHER-DAUGHTER BOND
Odet de Turnèbe's Response
to Catherine des Roches

৶ৣ

Anne R. Larsen

Aussi Madame, estant si celeste et si belle,
N'ayme pourtant jamais, et ne veult poinct aymer.

Madame, therefore, as divine and beautiful as she is,
Never loves, and does not want to love.
—Sonnet, "Contre Amour," to Catherine des Roches

[Elle est] resolue de vivre et mourir avec sa mere.

(She is) resolved to live and die with her mother.
—Estienne Pasquier, *Lettres*

In his study on women in Castiglione's *Cortegiano,* José Guido highlights a dual system of values opposing and subtly overlapping each other. The one is predicated upon a Neoplatonic and Petrarchan ideal to which the lady's chastity is foundational; the other does its best to deny the practical applicability of such an ideal and proposes instead absolution for the favors the chaste lady must in the end concede.[1]

This study examines female chastity and the mother-daughter bond in Catherine des Roches's *Tragicomedie de Tobie* (1579) and Odet de Turnèbe's *Les Contens* (1584).[2] Turnèbe's allusion to Des Roches's drama, as well as his treatment of the plot, the heroine Geneviefve and her widowed mother Louyse indicate that he may have read Catherine's play and written his own with her in mind. Odet de Turnèbe, a young lawyer in the Paris Parlement, first met the learned Catherine Fradonnoit (1542–1587) and her widowed mother, Madeleine Neveu (1520–1587), during the *Grands Jours* of Poitiers in the Fall of 1579. With his cousin Estienne Pasquier and numerous other distinguished lawyers, he contributed extensively to the mock-heroic punning on the flea reportedly sighted by Pasquier on Catherine's breast.[3] Basing themselves on Turnèbe's poetic contribution to the

172

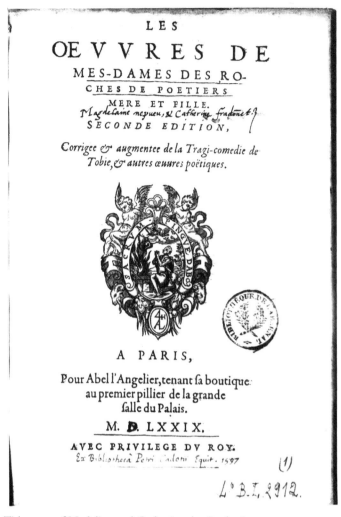

Title page of Madeline and Catherine des Roches's
Oeuvres, Paris, 1579 (courtesy of Bibl. de l'Arsenal,
Paris).

collective volume of *La Puce de Madame des Roches,* critics have called him
an "amoureux" of Catherine des Roches, without, however, giving further
thought to possible connections between their plays.[4] Turnèbe's and Des
Roches's opposing views on chastity, marriage, and the mother-daughter

bond lead me to argue that Turnèbe may be taking position with Des Roches. Establishing such a connection reinforces recent critics' judgment that *Les Contens* was written in the second half of 1580 or early 1581.[5]

Des Roches and Turnèbe dramatize antithetical approaches to thinking about female conduct, approaches previously modeled in *The Courtier*'s Book III, a work echoed at various points, as will be seen, in *Les Contens* and amply familiar to Catherine. To the latter's identification with the Neoplatonic ideal of Castiglione's Giuliano de' Medici, Turnèbe opposes the pragmatism of *The Courtier*'s cynical Gasparo and the compromising realism of Cesare. In the process, both writers raise considerably the stakes of the debate. For Turnèbe's play, considered by most critics *the* masterpiece of the genre, derives its unique interest not simply from its unusually skillful use of the conventions, as has been argued, but from its dialogical engagement with the contemporary polemics on sex, marriage, and women's nature. Catherine des Roches for her part provides, in one of the few French Renaissance female-authored plays, a powerful statement on chastity, the heterosexual couple, feminine genealogy, and the woman writer.

<hr>

Both Des Roches and Turnèbe focus on the appearances and reality of female chastity, honor, and reputation and, more crucially, the social construction and uses of chastity for women. Margaret Ferguson notes that for a Renaissance woman writer, "the fetish of chastity was a major obstacle, perhaps *the* major obstacle, to [her] ability to work as [a] writer."[6] Female chastity was founded on sexual purity, modesty, and silence. "Mulierum ornat silentium" (Silence behooves a woman) went the well-known adage. To circumvent this obstacle, Catherine defends throughout her work a concept of chastity that *safeguards* the independence of the woman as speaker and writer. She derives initially her use of chastity as device from Neoplatonism and Petrarch's *Rime sparse* where the beloved mirrors a transcendent spirituality. In Petrarch's work, however, the lady's chastity, predicated on her silence, is staged to affirm the poet-lover's identity as desiring subject. Des Roches, however, construes her speaker's chastity as a defense against male sexual desire the better to negotiate *her* writerly identity. She positions herself in a strategic gap within Neoplatonism that benefits a woman writer. As Philippa Berry points out:

> [The Neoplatonic beloved's chastity] had a disturbing habit of eluding or contradicting the significance accorded to it by the male lover as poet or philosopher. It often seemed to connote, not the negation of woman's bodily difference, of her own sexual desires, but rather the survival of a quality of feminine autonomy and self-sufficiency which could not be appropriated in the self-serving interests of the masculine subject.[7]

Throughout her writings Catherine appropriates this "quality of feminine autonomy" by grounding it in chastity, in her terms the muting of female sexuality and the speaker's ensuing evasion of male desire. She subscribes to Ficino's statements against erotic love as a valid form of reciprocity and to Giuliano de' Medici's notion that a woman's best armor against calumny is to be chaste in fact, rather than just word.[8] And she celebrates the mother-daughter bond as guarantor of poetic freedom.

While Des Roches opts for the Magnifico's position, Turnèbe is much more partial to other opposing voices in the debate. Gasparo, the leading proponent of women's incapacity to overcome her natural appetites, states that because a loose life defames a woman much more than a man, an ethics of concealment is a necessity. "The duty of every noble cavalier," he claims, "is to conceal the fault which a woman may happen to have committed, either by mischance or out of excessive love" (3:39). Cesare, who until this point has sided with the Magnifico in spinning out illustrative tales of women's heroic devotion to their chastity, now declares that "few women are capable of such great actions" and introduces a final ingredient into the debate: a *fallen* woman should be forgiven and "much compassion" bestowed on her (3:50). "For certainly," he continues, "the importunity of lovers, the arts they use, the snares they spread, are so many and so continual that it is a marvel if a tender girl manages to escape them." Her good name must be maintained at all costs. The debate ends on the practical importance for women of the *qu'en-dira-t-on* and on preserving the appearance of virtue.[9]

This divorce between word and deed, between "renommée" and "vertu" with regard to female chastity—one that Catherine des Roches emphatically denounces—reappears in treatises commenting throughout the century on *The Courtier*. Alessandro Piccolomini's *Dialogo della bella creanza delle donne,* commonly known as *La Raffaella* and written in 1538 as a carnival amusement for humanist colleagues, promotes the views of Cesare and Gasparo concerning female honor. A dramatic dialogue, *La Raffaella* is translated into French in 1577 by François d'Amboise, a close friend of Odet de Turnèbe who drew on this work in *Les Contens*.[10] The bawd Raffaella advises her pupil Margherita, a naïve *mal mariée,* on how best to locate and entertain a lover. Raffaella defends her teachings on the art of courtly love on grounds that "l'onore non è riposto in altro, se non ne la stimazione appresso a gli uomini"[11] (honor is laid up in no other thing but in repute among men) and that a lady's honor does not consist "nel fare o non fare, ché questo importa poco, ma nel credersi o non credersi" (172) (in what she does or does not [a matter of small importance] but in what she is believed to do or not) (61). Raffaella, whose name parodies that of the angel Raphael sent to Tobias to secure a happy wedding with Sarah, is mirrored in Turnèbe's *entremetteuse* Françoise. Using the same arguments as Raffaella, Françoise persuades the young heroine Geneviefve that satisfying her lover Basile's sexual desires will in no way damage her reputation: "Il n'y va en rien de vostre honneur" (I, 7) (it doesn't affect your honor in any way) she claims, because no one will ever know. Moreover, both mentors argue that Margherita's and Geneviefve's courtly virtues will protect them from their detractors. As allies in the plot of masculine desire, these maternal figures urge their young wards to buy into a discourse of play-acting chastity for the sake of *jouissance*.

La Raffaella's parody of Castiglione's *donna di palazzo* becomes, in Marie-Françoise Piéjus's words, a "texte provocateur, animé par une ironie cynique" (a provocative text, filled with cynical irony) whose message refutes a so-called hypocritical moralism in favor of carpe diem.[12] Numerous male contemporaries of Turnèbe and Des Roches contend as well that women go against nature when they repress their sexual desires and cover them under a pretence of chastity.[13] This perspective enlightens us on the obsessive manner in which Catherine des Roches's "admirers" in *La Puce*, and other unedited poems, kept returning to her "roche-" (rock-) like impenetrability to love and her unyielding chastity. How do Catherine des Roches and Turnèbe represent, then, in their respective plays, female chastity and woman's relation to marriage and the maternal figure? Knowing Des Roches's stance, what is Turnèbe's response?

———

Catherine des Roches published *Un Acte de la Tragicomedie de Tobie*, an adaptation of the Apocryphal Book of *Tobit* and her only play, in the 1579 edition of *Les Oeuvres*. Her choice of genre and subject matter includes reasons as varied as the influence of her native city's dramatists, the freedom of invention characteristic of the tragicomedy, the fact that she favored biblical paraphrase, and, especially, that the Book of *Tobit* contains a romance plot that praises female chastity and urges sexual restraint on men.[14] Even more significant, Des Roches adapts a prescriptive sacred text that acquired great popularity among theologians and conduct book writers from the thirteenth through the sixteenth centuries. As Silvana Vecchio notes, its heroine Sarah came to embody all the housewifely and conjugal virtues associated with the Good Wife.[15] Des Roches selects a well-known story whose narrative sequences were judged absolute. But far from conforming to its canonicity, she disrupts its linear unfolding: she breaks its expected sequence, subverts its message, and transforms it into a text marked by her point of view.[16]

Indeed, she condenses the original fourteen chapters of the Vulgate into one act developing Tobias's courtship of Sarah; by focusing on a single narrative element in the original tale, she brings unity of action to her drama. She also introduces two new dimensions that constitute major departures from the biblical text: the instatement of Sarah and her mother as characters of primary interest,[17] and the use of Ficinian Neoplatonic discourse.

In Des Roches's play daughter and mother openly convey ambivalence, if not outright opposition, to norms governing female conduct and the heterosexual plot. Sarah's conflicting feelings regarding her proposed marriage to Tobias are powerfully depicted in her soliloquy (scene 6), a predecessor of the Cornelian dialectic. At first, she objects to her marriage because she fears that Tobias, her platonic lover who has gained her *estime,* will die as her seven previous bridegrooms. Her eventual *mariage blanc* to Tobias ends in her boldly rewriting the marriage and erotic scripts. The Vulgate's climactic account of the successful wedding night—during which the demon who has claimed Sarah's body is exorcised—is suppressed in Des Roches's version.[18] Instead, an all-female chorus sings the praise of "chaste affection" and "amour pudique." The women denounce the unworthy lover seeking the "privautez d'un vouloir lubrique" (the intimacies of a lustful will) and focus on protecting the beloved's chastity in a sublimated love relation:

> Il n'est rien plus honorable
> Qu'une *chaste* affection:
> Il n'est rien plus agreable
> Qu'une douce passion.
>   Il n'est rien qui plus attire
> Que de se voir *estimé:*
> O que c'est un doux martire
> Que d'aymer et d'estre aymé! (183)

> There is nothing more honorable
> than a *chaste* affection:
> nor anything more agreeable
> than a sweet passion.
>   Nothing more attracts
> than knowing oneself *esteemed:*
> O what sweet martyrdom
> To love and be loved!

Tobias has merited Sarah—from the chorus's point of view—because he has vowed to preserve *her* sexual integrity by renouncing *his* carnal desire. To Raphael who insists, in the Vulgate as well, that he remain "chastement avec elle" (chastely with her) for three whole nights without desiring her and that he show himself "plus aymant de la beauté de l'ame / Que de celle du corps" (165) (more loving of spiritual than carnal beauty), Tobias promises—not in the Vulgate—that he will refrain from touching her for several years!

> Mais je desire bien de vivre plusieurs ans
> En *repos*[19] avec elle et qu'elle soit ma femme,
> La moitié de mon coeur, la moitié de mon ame:
> Je luy *obeirai,* comme un de mes ayeulx
> Obeit à la sienne. (173)

But my desire is to live with her
in *peace* and that she be my wife,
the other half of my heart, the half of my soul:
I will *obey* her, as one of my ancestors
obeyed his wife. [20]

In Tobias, Des Roches creates an idealized lover who has perfectly re-pressed his own sexuality and then only can live "en repos" with his be-loved. She gives a new twist to the heterosexual contract by requiring chas-tity for both partners.

In addition to forging *à la lettre* a sexless union entirely suited to leaving the woman in charge of her life, Sarah's virginity/chastity empow-ers her to express ambivalence concerning yet another norm governing fe-male conduct: separation from the mother. Whereas the Vulgate lauds pro-creative marriage as a divinely ordained institution that necessitates a new form of exclusive bonding between spouses, Catherine's play problema-tizes it by depicting a mother—another Ceres—and her daughter—an-other Proserpina—grieving at their loss of each other and unable or un-willing to justify its cause. Others must do that for them, namely the servant girl whose concluding prediction of happy days ahead and a large offspring willed by God functions as an utterly hollow concession to com-munal norms. Upon taking her leave of her parents, Sarah unexpectedly mourns the loss of her home ("nostre terre"), her childhood ("le temps de ma petite enfance"), and especially her mother:

Vous m'avez pourveüe
De mari et de bien, mais vous perdant de veue,
Je pers *tout* mon tresor, et vous laisse mon coeur
Pour vous porter amour, reverence, et honneur.
Je prends congé de vous, he mon Dieu je me pasme
Dans vostre *sein aimé*. (187)

You provided me
with a husband and wealth, but in the loss of seeing you,
I lose *all* my treasure, and leave you my heart
to bear witness to you of my love, reverence, and honor.
I take my leave of you, O God, I faint
on your *beloved breast*.

The preoedipal phase of the mother-child dyad irrupts into the text, as-serting itself above all other attachments: the daughter oscillates back to the mother as primary object of her love. The mother, for her part, cloaks the expression of her passion for her daughter in the poeticized rhetoric ordinarily used by the male poet to address his mistress:

O face, cler miroir de la Sainte nature,
Qui pourrois illustrer une prison obscure!

O esprit enrichi des ornemens des Cieux!
O ris tant agreable! o propos gracieux!
O chaste, sage, douce et Angelique grace!
Qui par tes doux attrais si doucement enlace:
Las que mes jours sans toy seront briefs et mauvais! (188)

O face, transparent mirror of holy Nature,
who but you can depict such a dark prison!
O spirit adorned with heavenly ornaments!
O laughter so agreeable to one's ear!
O chaste, wise, sweet and angelic grace
that through such gentle charms so sweetly entwines:
Alas, how brief and sad my days will be without you!

The mother applies the lexicon of heterosexual courtship to female-identified love, a strategy of disruption that occurs in several other instances of Catherine des Roches's oeuvre.

Mother and daughter daringly supplant the love-relation between Tobias and Sarah with their own private economy of creative exchange. But their attempt is already doomed. Immediately prior to the mother's impassioned response, the father steps in to assert cultural norms: "Ma femme laissez la, il luy faut arracher: Sarra, retirez vous" (188) (Wife, leave her, she must be torn away: Sarah, go away.) The mother is violently forced back into her appointed role as sustainer, not of her daughter, but of patriarchy. The daughter's once powerful voice is muted. By "breaking the sequence" of the original tale, however, Des Roches makes it known that marriage, sexual consummation, and separation from the Mother, all destined ends of the chaste "jeune fille," lead to great unhappiness, the destruction of the mother/daughter bond, and the end of *parole féminine*. This message is radically at odds with the biblical source and the culture at large.

The denouement also emotionally reflects Catherine des Roches's situation as unmmarried daughter/writer of the middle gentry. Separation from her mother, occasioned through either her own marriage or the death of Madeleine, would clearly work against her writerly interests. Without her widowed and financially independent mother, she could not evade marriage; nor could she write or publish as much. For Madeleine as well, the loss of her daughter threatens her very life and writing. She states in her liminary epistle to Catherine, "Le tout puissant à qui j'eu mon recours, / A faict de toy naistre mon *seul* secours" (*Les Oeuvres*, 1579) (The Almighty to whom I turned made you my *only* source of help). In Catherine she found "Amour, conseil, support" (Love, advice, support), the inspiration to write "m'eslevant l'ame et le coeur à quelque loüable entreprise" (*Les Missives*, "Epistre à sa fille") ([you] raise my spirit and heart to laudable deeds) and the legitimation to publish: "voicy la troisiesme fois que ta force m'encourage de parler en public" (*Les Missives,* "Epistre à sa fille") (this is the third time your strength enables me to speak in public). Madeleine's authorship is rooted in maternal experience. Catherine incorporates the myth of Ceres and Proserpina—a plot of a bereaved mother claiming back her daughter—into the conclusion of her play because it mirrors her anguish of separation.[21] This myth also crystallizes a key concept in her writing: that of feminine genealogy. In Luce Irigaray's words, feminine genealogy is founded on "la relation mère-fille et le respect de la parole et de la virginité féminines" (the mother-daughter relation and respect for feminine speech and virginity), basic rights that "ne laisseraient pas (les femmes) dans une perpetuelle revendication de mineures sociales"[22] (protect women from a constant assessment of themselves as social minors).

Des Roches uses the virginal heroine of Neoplatonic and biblical texts to resist literary tradition and sociosexual norms imposed on women of her time. Sarah's chastity undermines erotic and married love by calling for relationships founded on male *estime* for women and on nurturance enabling mothers and daughters to become subjects of their own narrative.

Could Turnèbe have had in mind Catherine des Roches and her widowed mother for Louyse and her daughter Geneviefve, the leading characters of *Les Contens?*[23] And could he be undermining the role of the inaccessibly chaste, learned woman that Catherine carefully created for herself throughout her works and in life? Is he playing out, to her rhetoric of self-protection in the collective volume of *La Puce,* a fantasy of seduction actualizing the voyeurism and sexual aggression so pervasive in his earlier *blason* on the flea as well as the others written by the men in the Poitiers coterie?[24] Just as Piccolomini had composed *La Raffaella* as an amusing joke for his circle, Turnèbe wrote his play as an in-house "divertissement" for his lawyer-friends of the *Grands Jours.* Like Des Roches, Turnèbe addresses the Lady's place. But unlike her, he draws on a widespread literary stratagem that authorizes the Lady the fulfillment of (her) sexual desires while maintaining all along a reputation for virtuous living.[25] The "joke" is on the Lady writer. As Kathryn Gravdal points out, "the text (the dirty joke), according to Freud himself, *constitutes* an act of sexual aggression performed by the teller on behalf of one listener and at the expense of another (the woman)."[26]

Critics have remarked consistently on the originality of Louyse and Geneviefve. Robert Aulotte underscores the novelty of the character of Louyse, a wealthy widow from the Parisian gentry, who plays the role of the "opposant," normally alloted to the figure of the father. Madeleine Lazard notes that Geneviefve is no ordinary "jeune fille" and that "il est malaisé d'[en] préciser les sources" (it is not easy to locate her sources).[27]

Geneviefve reveals traits not customarily associated with the type: in addition to her training in the usual domestic skills, she has received a good education.[28] The play's treatment of the standard comedic theme of "the successful assailment of a respectable young lady's virtue," in Norman Spector's words, is also unusual. *Les Contens*'s primary interest is its ambiguity regarding Geneviefve's chastity. Did she consent to her seduction/rape, or didn't she?[29] I would argue that Turnèbe's focus away from male aggression, a staple of Renaissance comedy, onto the heroine's ambiguous motives can be seen as a move to counter Des Roches's problematizing of male lust and unambiguous stance on female chastity.

How does Turnèbe develop the social consequences attendant to the seduction of a chaste learned heroine of the middle-gentry, should she, in Cesare's words, be "overcome by the assaults of love" (*The Courtier*, 3: 50)?

To justify the chaste young woman who follows the dictates of her lover and (he would claim) her heart, Turnèbe centers his play on the typical preoccupations of a middle-class neighborhood: his comedy revolves around a basic misunderstanding concerning the marriageable prospects of the "jeune fille" who loses her virtue. Two views are pitted against each other. Louyse argues a view promoted by moralists and writers of conduct books that once her honor is blemished, the young girl will no longer be marriageable. Basile and most of the other characters adopt Cesare's view that love covers a multitude of sins. The dynamic of the plot lies in the development of these antithetical positions and its resolution aims at establishing the moral, practical, narrative, and natural imperative of Basile's view.

Louyse's obsession with preserving her daughter's reputation for unblemished chastity is established in the play's exposition (I, 1). Her rejection of Basile as a suitable son-in-law seems motivated by her distrust of his dependability in matters of love.[30] She scolds Geneviefve for her naïveté in thinking Basile really loves her: "Ne vois-tu pas bien qu'il salue ainsi toutes les filles de la paroisse?" (ll. 54–55) (Can't you see he greets all the girls in the parish like that?) She asserts that she chose Eustache over Basile and would have married Geneviefve to the former a lot sooner if Basile had not dallied and held her in suspense for so long (ll. 63–64). She suspects that Basile is a philanderer rather than an *honnête homme*. She prefers Eustache to Basile because in her view he represents the ideal husband to ensure her daughter's honor. Hence she is horrified when she catches Geneviefve and whom she thinks is Eustache *en flagrant délit*. In spite of the protests of Eustache's father that his son most likely promised to marry Geneviefve before seducing her (IV, 4, l. 2225), Louyse refuses the marriage: "Pourrois-je endurer qu'Eustache fust mon gendre apres avoir ainsi *deshonoré* ma maison?" (ll. 2247–49) (How could I endure to have Eustache for a son-in-law after he has so dishonored my house?) She intends on dragging Eustache to court for judicial reparation. Discovering her mistake, and thinking now that the man she caught with her daughter was in reality a woman in disguise, she seeks hurriedly to marry off her daughter to Geneviefve's laughable third suitor, Rodomont, before "le monde soit abruvé de ceste histoire" (V, 2, l. 2732) (before the whole world gets wind of this story). Even when Rodomont reveals that Geneviefve is no longer "fille" (V, 5, l. 3028) and that Basile is now her legal husband because he consummated the marriage, Louyse is more convinced than ever that Basile will no longer want her daughter for "il en a fait à sa volonté" (V, 5, l. 3097) (he's had his way with her).

Louyse represents moralist doctrine on the enforcing of female virtue. She places on her daughter the full responsibility of defending the honor of her house. She equates Geneviefve with Vives's depiction of the dutiful daughter who resists books of chivalry and poems by a Ronsard or a Desportes to tend to her *ménage* and her prayers (III, vii, ll. 1670–74). She firmly believes that she has sealed off Geneviefve from illicit male desire by the protective walls of her religious oratory. When told the truth, she brutally disavows her, claiming her misfortune for having had to "[nourir] une fille qui sera la cause de ma mort" (V, v, l. 3090) ([nourish] a daughter who will be the cause of my death). Ironically, in Louyse, Turnèbe inverts the model of the "good mother" who defends a normative code of honor into that of a "bad mother" who opposes her daughter's sexual fulfillment. The play enacts a deep wedge between mother and daughter. Geneviefve discovers more in common and to her liking in the bawd Françoise, Louyse's maternal rival, who exploits the daughter for her own personal advancement. The mother-daughter dyad so powerfully integral to Catherine des Roches's *Tobie*, as well as to the lives of the Dames des Roches, is deliberately broken up in *Les Contens*.

Louyse's fetishizing of female chastity is further undercut and mocked by Basile's and other male characters' interpretation of the "seduction" of Geneviefve. From the start, Basile assumes that if he were to seduce Geneviefve, he would lose her. Louyse would never agree to a marriage. After conceding to Françoise that Geneviefve might not give him a hard time if he were to try the solution of the "fait accompli," he reveals his real anxiety: "je crains la mere" (II, 7, l. 1336) (I'm afraid of her mother). Then, while reporting to his valet Antoine the successful result of his "enterprise," he again refers to Louyse: "Mais encore ne veux-je *abandonner* [Geneviefve] que premierement je ne sçache le moyen d'apaiser sa mere" (III, 9, ll. 1856–58) (But yet I don't want to *abandon* her until I'm sure I can appease her mother). He feels himself in an insoluble quandary. He wants to continue as Geneviefve's lover for a while because he would never dream of rewarding her "faveur si segnalée" (l. 1876) (such a notable favor) with a betrayal. Yet at the same time he disavows all lovers who, in Antoine's words, "ne voudroient pour rien espouser une femme de qui ils auroient jouy auparavant le jour des nopces, quand bien elle les aymeroit uniquement" (ll. 1880–82) (would refuse to marry a woman who had granted him favors before marriage, even if he were the only one). Echoing Cesare, he declares such men "meritent d'espouser une potence ou un pi-lory" (l. 1883) (deserve to be married to the gibbet or the stocks). But to continue as Geneviefve's sexual partner, which at bottom is all he wants, he needs to marry her. In order to marry her, he must win over Louyse. In the play's economy, Basile is transformed into an honorable lover whose moral scruples over ravishing Geneviefve distinguish him from the tra-ditional "jeune amoureux" of Renaissance comedy. Basile is an "honor-able" seducer.

As well as opposing Louyse and Basile over the consequences of Gene-viefve's loss of her honor, Turnèbe has the male characters justify on two counts the rape qua seduction of the daughter. First, they interpret it as an act of marriage and so reflect canon law in which rape was construed as a way to contract a legal marriage. Second, they laud the seduction as ulti-mate proof of Geneviefve's love. Eustache praises her for putting her love above blind obedience to a moral code (IV, 2, ll. 1995–2000). Basile re-interprets the rape not as a fall on her part but as a mark of esteem for him. So much so that if he were to betray her for another, *his* "sin" would go unwashed (III, 9, ll. 1873–77). Moreover, he never goes back over his once-declared belief that Geneviefve is above all "chaste." To his valet An-toine's suggestion that he should "consommer le mariage avec Geneviefve, prenant gentilement un pain sur la fournée" (I, 4, ll. 361–62) (consum-mate a marriage with Geneviefve by gallantly taking a loaf from the oven), he replies that she would never consent for she is "si craintive et si chaste que pour rien au monde elle ne s'y voudroit accorder" (l. 368) (so timid and chaste that she wouldn't consent to it for anything in the world), a line echoed a scene later by Françoise when approached for her help in the matter (I, 5, ll. 438–39).

Geneviefve's consent, of course, is at stake. The play's valets, Antoine and Nivelet, voice the traditional naturalistic Gaulois view on the hypocrisy of women's intentions. While Basile is pursuing his "conversation" with Geneviefve,[31] Antoine indulges in rhetorical voyeurism with the complete conviction that "une fille ne veut jamais accorder de parolle ce qu'elle laisse prendre de fait, et est bien aise d'estre ravie" (III, 6, ll. 1621–23) (a woman would never agree in word what she allows to be taken from her in deed, and she loves being ravished). To Basile's revealing admission that what he did manage to get from Geneviefve until he heard someone spying on them through the keyhole was "plus de force que de son bon gré" (III, 9, l. 1867) (more by force than by consent), Antoine skeptically asserts that Basile would have never managed without Geneviefve's "consentement" (l. 1870).

Making plausible the heroine's role in her own seduction/rape cleverly discredits the Neoplatonic notion of female purity. Likewise Basile's willingness to assume responsibility and to absolve Geneviefve from all wrongdoing enforces not only the image of the good chaste daughter that Geneviefve is eager to maintain all along but also Basile's *beau rôle*.

Justifying the illusion of the chaste beloved is, finally, the point of Basile and Geneviefve's celebrated *duo amoureux*. Humanist comedy focused on the triumph of love, not its psychological motivation. Turnèbe brings both a psychological and an ideological motivation to the duo. Its serious and practical bent emphasizes the moral worth of these characters. Basile shows himself a courtly lover eager to "m'employer à vostre service quand l'occasion se presentera, et qu'il vous plaira m'honorer de vos commandemens" (V, 3, ll. 2849–51) (employ myself in your service when the occasion presents itself and it pleases you to honor me with your commandments). Turnèbe presents Basile as a model lover who does his utmost to "conceal the fault which a *woman* may happen to have committed, either by mischance or out of excessive love" (*The Courtier*, 3: 39, my emphasis). The love duet highlights as well Geneviefve's dual ability to engage in love casuistry *and* arrange for her marriage. From a male view, she is made to seem the winner. She has had her pleasure, she has kept her honor, she has won a husband. Might she not also have been made a pawn in a game in which, as Patricia Cholakian puts it, "the seduced (raped) lady's desire is the rapist's construction, a wager he wins with himself"?[32]

———

Through its treatment of a heroine who maintains a chaste reputation but makes no fetish of her chastity, *Les Contens* rejects Neoplatonic discourse on feminine libidinal purity. Its joking reference to Catherine des Roches's *Tobie* implicitly critiques the latter for attempting—in literature and especially in life—a practical application of the sexually remote, self-sufficient heroine who is above passion. To make her pliant to the male seduction plot, he would have her, like his heroine, fall in love and acknowledge sexual desire. His rupture of the mother-daughter bond indicates his awareness of how vital it was to a daughter's independence. By turning the mother into the daughter's own worst enemy, he robs the latter of her main support against the patriarchal control of body and self. The contrasting parallel with the Dames des Roches is clear: Madeleine was Catherine's most committed ally, enabling both to bypass normative authority. As such, the Des Roches anticipate succeeding generations of seventeenth-century writers like Mademoiselle de Scudéry, Madame de Villedieu, and Madame de Lafayette whose heroines rescript the love and marriage plots.[33]

Read within the context of the salacious *La Puce* and the century-long controversy originating in *The Courtier* over "renommée" and "vertu," Turnèbe's play takes on a new density. Yet, even more revealingly, it sharpens our understanding of the response to, and ambiguous status of, a Renaissance woman writer who kept her lovers at a distance and her mother at her side to defend her scholarly autonomy.

NOTES

1. José Guido, "De l'Amour courtois à l'amour sacré: la condition de la femme dans l'oeuvre de Baldassar Castiglione," in *Images de la femme dans la littérature italienne de la Renaissance: prégujés misogynes et aspirations nouvelles,* ed. André Rochon (Paris: Université de la Sorbonne Nouvelle, 1980), 28. I wish to thank JoAnn DellaNeva, Erica Harth, Marian Rothstein, and Colette Winn for their insightful comments on an earlier version of this essay.

2. Des Roches's *Un Acte de la Tragicomedie de Tobie, où sont representées les Amours et les Noces du jeune Tobie et de Sarra fille de Raguel* first appeared in *Les Oeuvres de Mes-Dames des Roches de Poetiers mere et fille, seconde edition corrigée et augmentée de la Tragi-comedie de Tobie et autres oeuvres poëtiques* (Paris: Abel L'Angelier, 1579). The page references to this edition are to the annotated copy of the Bibliothèque de l'Arsenal (4° B.L. 2912). The translations are my own. Turnèbe's play was published posthumously in 1584 by Pierre de Ravel (Paris: Felix le Mangnier). The page references are to Norman B. Spector's edition of *Les Contens* (Paris: Nizet, 1983). The translations are from Donald Beecher's *Satisfaction All Around* (Ottowa: Carleton University Renaissance Center, 1979). All emphases added are mine.

3. Turnèbe's poem, "La Puce d'Odet de Tournebu, Advocat en la cour de Parlement," his three Petrarchan sonnets, one each in French, Spanish, and Italian, and his twelve sonnets entitled "Sonets sur les ruines de Luzignan," all dedicated to Catherine, were printed in *La Puce de Madame des Roches* (Paris: Abel L'Angelier, 1582, 1583). Des Roches's two "responces" to Turnèbe cleverly conform to the conduct required of Castiglione's court lady. See the excellent analyses of Ann Rosalind Jones in *The Currency of Eros: Women's Love Lyric in Europe, 1540–1620* (Bloomington: Indiana University Press, 1990), 54–59, and Cathy Yandell in "Of Lice and Women: Rhetoric and Gender in *La Puce de Madame des Roches*," *Journal of Medieval and Renaissance Studies* 20 (1990): 123–135.

4. George Diller notes that "Turnèbe déclare surtout le fatal amour que Catherine lui inspire" (Turnèbe posits especially the fatal love that Catherine inspired in him) in *Les Dames des Roches: Etude sur la vie littéraire à Poitiers dans la deuxième moitié du XVIᵉ siècle* (Paris: Droz, 1936), 72, and Robert Aulotte comments on Turnèbe as an "amoureux" of Des Roches in *La Comédie française de la Renaissance et son chef d'oeuvre "Les Contens" d'Odet de Turnèbe* (Paris: SEDES, 1984), 39. In an enlightening footnote to which this study owes its origins, Robert Aulotte explains that the comparison that Eustache, one of Geneviefve's three suitors, makes of the bawd Françoise to the angel Raphael is a reference to the biblical Book of *Tobit*. "Comme l'ange à Tobie" (Just as the angel [warned] Tobias), Françoise warns Eustache of a supposed canker on Geneviefve's breast in order to get rid of him—cankers were thought to be caused by "l'acte vénérien," see N. de Cholières, *Les Matinées,* ed. Tricotel, 2 vols. (Paris: Librairie des Bibliophiles, 1789) 1: 151–152. Aulotte then adds in a note that Catherine des Roches had adapted the biblical story and that "nous avons peut-être ici *un coup de chapeau* de Turnèbe à celle qu'il avait célébrée à Poitiers. . . . On voit de quelle richesse signifiante se charge ici l'allusion à Tobie" (61, n. 31) (we have here a hats off on Turnèbe's part to she whom he had celebrated at Poitiers. . . . One can see how rich in meaning this allusion to Tobias is). I would further argue that the pointed reference to a canker on the heroine's breast ("le sein" [the breast] being the most frequently cited portion of the female body in the *blason* poems of *La Puce de Madame des Roches*) *coupled with* an equally parodic linking of the bawd to the angel Raphael are not accidental: rather, they function as a mnemonic device destined to bring a smile of recognition to the play's first—and perhaps only—

private audience, Turnèbe's lawyer-friends, who also attended the *Grands Jours* of Poitiers and contributed to the erotic punning on Catherine's flea.

5. The exact dating of *Les Contens* is still uncertain. The consensus is that it was written between 1577 and July 1581 when Turnèbe died of a fever at the age of twenty-eight. In the last two decades, critics have leaned toward late 1580 or early 1581 as a more likely date. See Aulotte, *La Comédie*, 44, Spector, *Les Contens*, xiii, and Marina Nickerson Eaton, *"Les Contens" of Odet de Turnèbe: A Critical Edition*, Ph. D. diss., University of Oklahoma, 1973. Most recently, Géralde Nakam in "A propos des *Contens* d'Odet de Turnèbe," *Littératures* 8 (1983): 9, and Enéa Balmas in "A propos des *Contens* d'Odet de Turnèbe," in *Saggi e ricerche sul teatro francese del Cinquecento* (Florence: Leo Olschki, 1985), 137, have subscribed to a 1580–1581 dating.

6. Margaret W. Ferguson, "A Room Not Their Own: Renaissance Women as Readers and Writers," in *The Comparative Perspective on Literature. Approaches to Theory and Practice*, ed. Clayton Koelb and Susan Noakes (Ithaca: Cornell University Press, 1988), 98.

7. Philippa Berry, *Of Chastity and Power: Elizabethan Literature and the Unmarried Queen* (London: Routledge, 1989), 18. Ann R. Jones writes: "Quasi-religious, defined in opposition to both erotic and married love, Neoplatonism leaves the woman poet free to represent herself and her lover according to a system of rules that rewrites gender relations as defined in the society at large," *The Currency of Eros*, 76.

8. Castiglione, *The Book of the Courtier*, trans. Charles Singleton (Garden City, N.Y.: Anchor Books, 1959), 3: 4.

9. Jean-Louis Carron notes that honor for a woman was wholly dependent upon public opinion for its confirmation because women, unlike men, were barred from public acts of courage and magnanimity, masculine virtues *par excellence*. Hence, "la renommée, dépendant de la parole qui la fait ou la défait, prend la place de la vertu, cette 'chose' que le mot est censé désigner" (reputation, depending on hearsay which can sustain or undo it, takes the place of virtue, the 'thing' that the word is supposed to point to); see "Les Noms de l'honneur féminin à la Renaissance. Le Nom tu et le non dit," *Poétique* 67 (1986): 270.

10. François d'Amboise's translation appeared under two different titles: *Instruction aux jeunes dames, en forme de dialogue, par laquelle les dames apprendront comme elles doivent se bien gouverner en amour* (Lyon, ca. 1577) and *Dialogues et devis des demoiselles, pour les rendre vertueuses et bienheureuses en la vraye et parfaicte amitié* (Paris, 1581, 1583). The *Catalogue général des livres imprimés* of the Bibliothèque Nationale, as well as other bibliographers, attribute concurrently to the Dames des Roches and to Marie de Romieu the translation of a 1597 version of *La Raffaella* entitled *Instruction pour les jeunes dames, par la Mere et Fille d'alliance* (Paris, 1597). Such (apparently unconscious) attributions of "ownership" to women writers known for their moral conformism perpetuate the originary inscription of *La Raffaella* as an amusement destined for private male consumption.

11. Piccolomini, *La Raffaella. Dialogue de la gentille éducation des femmes*, ed. and trans. Alcide Bonneau (Paris: Liseux, 1884), 170; English trans. John Nevinson, *Raffaella of Master Alexander Piccolomini or the Fair Perfectioning of Ladies* (Glasgow: R. MacLehose, 1968), 61.

12. M.-F. Piéjus, "Vénus Bifrons: le double idéal dans 'La Raffaela' d'Alessandro Piccolomini," in *Images de la femme dans la littérature italienne de la Renaissance*, 147.

13. Gabriel Pérouse aptly sums up this view when he describes Ronsard's concept of feminine "honnesteté" in the *Sonnets pour Hélène* (1578) as: "une résistance absurde à la loi de l'amour, un obstacle insupportable à la jouissance" (an absurd resistance to the law of love, an unbearable obstacle to "jouissance"), "'L'honneste' dans *Les Amours* de Ronsard," in *La Catégorie de l'Honneste dans la culture du XVIe siècle*, Actes du colloque international de Sommières II, 1983 (Université de Saint-Etienne, 1985), 190. See also Jacqueline Boucher, *La Cour de Henri III* (Editions Ouest-France, 1986), 165–173, and Jean-Claude Carron on this naturalistic strain in narrative and lyric literature of the second half of the century.

14. On Poitiers's numerous dramatists, see Henri Clouzot, *L'Ancien Théâtre en Poitou* (Niort: Clouzot, 1901), Chap. 4; on the tragicomedy, see Henry Lancaster, *The French Tragicomedy: Its Origin and Development from 1552 to 1628* (1907; reprint, New York: Gordian Press, 1966). Des Roches adapted Proverbs 31:10–31, which contains an emblematic portrait of the Good Wife, a text dear to moralists and reformers alike.

15. Silvana Vecchio writes: "Modèle de ce que l'épouse devrait être plus que ce qu'elle est effectivement—belle-fille respectueuse, conjointe fidèle, mère empressée, maîtresse de maison avisée, femme irréprochable sous tous rapports—, Sarra incarne l'ensemble des devoirs au sein duquel les clercs ont pensé et décrit la vie des femmes mariées" (Modeling what the wife ought to be more than what she is—a respectful daughter-in-law, a faithful spouse, a devoted mother, a thrifty housekeeper, irreprochable in every way—Sarah embodies the totality of those duties clerics thought about and described for married women), "La Bonne Epouse," in *Histoire des femmes en Occident,* ed. Georges Duby and Michelle Perrot, 5 vols. (Paris: Plon, 1991), 2: 118.

16. "Breaking the sequence," according to Rachel Blau Du Plessis, is to enact "a critique of narrative, restructuring its orders and priorities precisely by attention to specific issues of female identity and its characteristic oscillations," *Writing Beyond the Ending: Narrative Strategies of Twentieth-Century Women Writers* (Bloomington: Indiana University Press, 1985), x. A summary of the tale helps locate the changes that Des Roches brings to her adaptation. Tobit, his wife Anna, and their son Tobias (Tobit in the Vulgate) are taken captive to Nineveh. On one of his errands, Tobit becomes blind. Meanwhile, in faraway Media, his kinswoman Sarah's seven bridegrooms are murdered during the wedding night by Asmodeus, a demon of lust who is in love with Sarah. When Tobias is sent to collect some money left with a friend in Sarah's hometown, the angel Raphael, disguised as a traveler, accompagnies him. Raphael reveals a magic potion that will exorcise Sarah's demon-lover, thereby allowing Tobias to marry Sarah. Tobias completes his mission and is safely married to Sarah.

17. In the Vulgate, however, Sarah and her mother appear infrequently; Sarah is not asked whether she wishes to marry Tobias as in Des Roches's plot, nor does she express her feelings about him; Sarah's mother is an appendage of her husband. On the absence of reference in the early modern period to women's feelings concerning the marriage pact, see Benoît L'Hoest, *L'Amour enfermé: sentiment et sexualité à la Renaissance* (Paris: Olivier Orban, 1990), 178–179.

18. Des Roches appears to brush aside the issue of woman's carnal link to the demonic. Bypassing the exorcism, however, denies the validity of the belief that occasioned it and constitutes a critique of the demonizing of woman's body. It displaces the focus from the female body to male lust.

19. Meaning the contrary of sexual stimulation, as in the term "reposé," which Cotgrave defines as "reposed, rested, lyen fallow a greatwhile." Des Roches foreshadows the ideal of "repos" in seventeenth-century women's writings.

20. The anonymous annotator of the copy of the Bibliothèque de l'Arsenal makes this ironic marginal comment: "L'autheur desiroyt pour soy pareille fortune" (The author desired the same fortune for herself). He mocks Des Roches's construction of the ideal (in his view chimerical) lover who renounces sexual desire to marry and remain faithful to the beloved. Gabriel Pérouse suggests that it is for lack of such a model in real life that Catherine refused marriage, *La Nouvelle française du XVIᵉ siècle. Images de la vie du temps* (Geneva: Droz, 1977), 225, n. 158.

21. Des Roches returns to a full treatment of the Ceres/Proserpina myth in her translation of Claudian's *De raptu Proserpina* which she published in her *Missives* (Paris: Abel L'Angelier, 1586). See Tilde Sankovitch's essay in this volume. See also Marianne Hirsch's *The Mother-Daughter Plot: Narrative, Psychoanalysis, Feminism* (Bloomington: Indiana University Press, 1989) for the story of Demeter and Persephone as an alternate woman-centered mythology offering a "female family romance."

22. Luce Irigaray, *Le Temps de la différence* (Paris: Livre de Poche, 1989), 123, 95–96.

23. Norman Spector indicates that he has found no prototype for Louyse and is puzzled as to why Turnèbe made her a widow rather than having her conform to the traditional figure of the irascible wife: "C'est un trait que je n'ai jusqu'ici pas réussi à retrouver dans les comédies italiennes" (I have yet to locate this trait in Italian comedies), *Les Contens,* lv.

24. In his "Sonets sur les ruines de Luzignan," which he dedicates to Catherine (*La Puce* ff. 71–r to 75–r), Turnèbe is more subtle but just as intent on poetic seduction. There he plays on the meanings of the word "fort" (castle) and "rocher" (Luzignan was built on a high rocky hill), the latter integral to Catherine's matronym, Des Roches. At times the ruined fort is an image for war-torn France; at others, a metonymy for the poet-lover's broken heart (f. 74–r). In her "responce" to Turnèbe (f. 75–v), Catherine sidesteps innuendo by praising him for his poetic skill in building instead a new "fort" to which he has brought "la sage Logistille, / Les Muses, les vertus, les graces et l'Amour: / Je dy l'Amour venu de la Venus celeste" (wise Logistille, / The Muses, the virtues, the graces and love: / I mean the love of the celestial Venus). She corrects his rhetoric of earthly love with her emphasis on the celestial Venus to maintain the self-protection that guarantees her independence.

25. Ronsard's anti-Petrarchan poem "A son livre" exemplifies the stratagem in question. The poet-lover asserts that Petrarch was no "sot" (fool): of his mistress "Laurette," "il en jouissait, puis l'a faitte admirable, / Chaste, divine, sainte" (he enjoyed her, then made her admirable, / Chaste, divine, holy), *Oeuvres complètes,* ed. Paul Laumonier et al. (Paris: Hachette, 1914–1967), ll. 317–18, ll. 52–56. My thanks to JoAnn DellaNeva for this reference.

26. Kathryn Gravdal, *Ravishing Maidens: Writing Rape in Medieval French Literature and Law* (Philadelphia: University of Pennsylvania Press, 1991), 109.

27. Aulotte, *La Comédie,* 97; Lazard, *La Comédie humaniste au XVIᵉ siècle et ses personnages* (Paris: Presses Universitaires de France, 1978), 73, 98. For Raymond Lebègue, the characters of Genefvieve and Louyse are telling signs of Turnèbe's skill: "Dans la comédie française du XVIᵉ siècle, je ne connais pas de personnages qui soient dessinés avec autant de soin" (In French comedies of the sixteenth century, I know of no other characters drawn with such care); see *Le Théâtre comique en France de Pathelin à Mélite* (Paris: Hatier, 1972), 107.

28. Concerning the typical "jeune fille," see Lazard, *La Comédie humaniste,* 73. Robert Aulotte argues that Geneviefve's preference for Basile is owing to her desire for "la tranquillité nécessaire à son développement humaniste de jeune fille cultivée et bonne ménagère" (the tranquillity necessary to her humanist development as a cultivated and skilled housekeeper), traits that apply well to Catherine des Roches, "Visages du théâtre comique de la Renaissance: deux jeunes filles vieilles de quatre cents ans," in *Crossroads and Perspectives: French Literature of the Renaissance: Studies in Honor of Victor Graham,* ed. Catherine Grise and C. D. Tolton (Geneva: Droz, 1986), 155.

29. Another ambiguity exists in the term seduction. As Patricia Francis Cholakian writes, male Renaissance authors fictionalized rape as seduction; women writers such as Marguerite de Navarre subverted this fiction to tell the truth; see *Rape and Writing in the Heptameron of Marguerite de Navarre* (Carbondale: Southern Illinois University, 1991), 16.

30. Critics have remarked that Louyse's motivation for turning down Basile is nowhere stated in the play. N. Spector, calling her refusal "le point faible de l'intrigue" (the weak point in the plot), offers the intriguing notion that Louyse may have been in love with Basile (*Les Contens,* lvi, n. 1). This notion accentuates the impurity of Louyse's motives.

31. Turnèbe literalizes the term "conversation," which in conduct and courtesy books of the period links women's speech to promiscuity; see Jones, *The Currency of Eros,* 17–18.

32. Cholakian, *Rape and Writing,* 122.

33. Scudéry praises the Des Roches for their perfect "amitié" for each other that allowed them to refuse "cent partis avantageux," *De la Poésie françoise à Henry Quatrième* (1684) (Paris: Sansot, 1907), 53.

"Les Puissances de Vostre Empire"
Changing Power Relations in Marie de Gournay's
Le Proumenoir de Monsieur de Montaigne
from 1594 to 1626

ℒℰ

Cathleen M. Bauschatz

In the dedicatory epistle to its first reader, Montaigne, before the original 1594 edition of her moralistic novel *Le Proumenoir de Monsieur de Montaigne* (*Monsieur de Montaigne's Walk*), Marie de Gournay stated that she hoped Montaigne would correct some of the errors in her book and also that in the process she might take pleasure in experiencing the power the essayist had over her: "C'est tout un, encore ne sçay-je si je ne prends pas volontiers *plaisir* à faire quelque niaiserie exprez, pour vous mettre, en me chastiant mon pere, à l'exercice de *l'Empire que vous avez en moy*"[1] (It's all the same, but still I'm not sure whether I don't take pleasure in doing some sort of foolishness on purpose in order to goad you, in chastising me, my father, to exercise the power which you have over me). The power of men over women was a central theme in the *Proumenoir* of 1594—both Montaigne's power as writer, reader, and adoptive father over Gournay, and the power exerted by various male characters over the novel's heroine, Alinda. Her father, the Persian Satrape, and her lover, Léontin, left Alinda very little control over her own destiny. But when Gournay revised this novel thirty years later for publication in the first volume of her complete works, *L'Ombre* (*The Shadow*) (1626),[2] we see that issues of power, among others, have been rethought. Gournay addresses these issues directly in her statements about the novel in its various prefaces and other "paratextes," as well as indirectly in the revisions she makes to the novel itself.

When Gournay reprinted the *Proumenoir* in 1626, she made many changes in the book, partly in response to reactions by specific readers, but more important as well, through her developing sense of herself as a

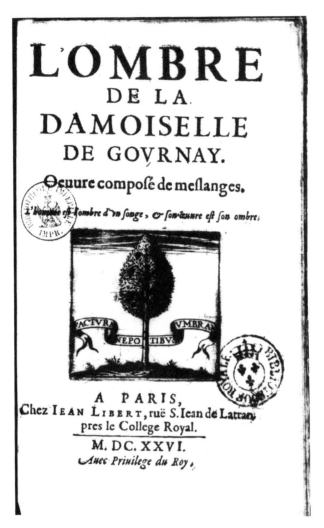

Title page of Marie Le Jars de Gournay's *L'Ombre*,
Paris, 1626 (courtesy of Bibl. Nationale, Paris).

woman writer treating a woman character and writing for a general reader
who might well also be female. Although the novel was originally written
for Montaigne to read, in 1626 this is obviously no longer the case. While
at the time of the 1594 *Proumenoir,* as in the 1595 "Préface" to Montaigne's *Essais,* she felt inhibited from taking on a strong narrative persona

because she was a novice and a woman, by 1626 she has come to terms
with this conflict. It is no accident that the *Proumenoir* is revised soon
after the writing of the "Egalité" (Equality) and the "Grief" (Grievance),
Gournay's best known feminist works. Rather than hiding or apologizing
for her identity as a woman writer, Gournay now uses this identity as a
source of strength and in some surprising ways.

——

In publishing her complete works, *L'Ombre,* Gournay wrote an introduction to the entire collection, "Advis au Lecteur" (Advice to the
Reader), which gives us a sense of the identity she has developed as a
woman writer, in the thirty years separating the volume from her first forays
into literature, the *Proumenoir* and the *Préface.* The very existence of a
collection of her complete works makes a statement about her vocation as
a writer. We find in this "Advis" confident assertions that the book is a
portrait of herself. Such a statement would have been impossible thirty
years earlier, when she saw her career and her writing as totally subordinate
to Montaigne's.

The "Advis au Lecteur" does contain many statements about the expected hostility of the reader, as we find in most of her work.[3] She begins
the "Advis" by squaring off with this imaginary reader: "c'est que sentant
que tu es poinctilleux en chois d'Escrits, & que je suis poinctilleuse en
chois de lecteurs; je cognois qu'on ne nous peut mieux accorder qu'en
nous separant" (ij) (for sensing that you are particular in your choice of
writings, and that I am particular in choosing readers; I know that no one
can find a better way to make us agree than by separating us). Her readers
may not like her, but then she does not like them, either! No longer apparently overwhelmed by their criticisms, she even suggests that these critics
might be wrong, as she did earlier but only in defending Montaigne's
Essais against critics. This self-confidence about her own work, despite opposition, would have been impossible in 1594, when she relished the
"Empire" that her first reader and critic, Montaigne, had over her.

As she earlier hoped for Montaigne's *Essais,* she tells us that like herself, its mother, her book will try to "plaire à tous les sages, & desplaire à
tous les fols" (please the wise, and displease the foolish) (ijv). Whether or
not people like it, the book will present her as she is: "Ce volume est en
fin d'un air tout particulier & tout sien: comme aussi *suis-je moy-mesme*"
(This volume finally has a very particular appearance all its own, as I do)
(ijv). But most readers do not value a woman writer: "qui daignast priser
une *femme* qui se fust efforcée d'arriver à cet excez" (who would not deign
to value a woman who endeavored to go to these lengths) (ijv–iij). Despite
the defensiveness of her tone, Gournay does state her identity and purpose
here in a new, forceful manner.

While the title of the book, *L'Ombre,* appears to be a negative one—

still the image of the shadow also suggests the idea that the book reflects her as she is: "d'autant qu'il exprime *la figure de mon esprit maistresse piece de mon estre*" (so much so that it conveys the image of my mind, mistress of my being) (iij). She has learned from Montaigne that a book can represent its author, and she now dares to apply this principle to herself because she is now able to call herself an author. Furthermore, she states that the image of a young pine tree on her title page prefigures the favor her book hopes to find in the future. The strength Gournay and her book appear to have drawn from surviving the negative reactions of their readers will carry over to many of the forceful essays and translations in the volume, as well as to the revised novel, the *Proumenoir.*

———

Gournay also wrote an "Advis" or Preface to the revised *Proumenoir* itself, in 1626, in which she once again responds to criticisms, while she also shows that the book has had some measure of success, especially with aristocratic women readers. Whether or not Montaigne ever read the novel, apparently these women readers liked the story of Alinda and asked Gournay to reprint it, although they also asked for some changes:

> Le Proumenoir ayant esté mis au jour dés ma jeunesse, je croirois avoir autant de tort de refuser *quelques Dames du premier rang, qui me commandent de luy faire revoir la lumiere à present,* que j'en aurois de le composer en l'aage où je suis aujourd'huy—bien que son histoire soit assaisonée d'advertissements *exemplaires,* & qu'elle represente *la peine en suitte de la coulpe.*[4]

> The *Proumenoir* having come to light in my youth, I would believe myself to be equally wrong to refuse several Ladies of the first rank, who have asked me to bring it back to light now, as I would have been to compose it at the age I am today—even though the story is seasoned with exemplary warnings, as well as showing punishment following guilt.

She is reprinting the story in middle age, despite the fact that it treats love, an immoral topic. But, it is seasoned with exemplary warnings and shows pain followed by punishment. The first objection by women readers (that the story is immoral) is one that Gournay had already answered in the first edition of the *Proumenoir,* where it was evident that negative exemplarity was the moral of the story.

But in 1626 Gournay defends her daring to write on the topic of love, now with more than negative exemplarity as a justification. She lists ancient authors, including Plutarch, who treated the theme. As in the "Egalité des Hommes et des Femmes" (Equality of Men and Women), Gournay uses the authority of ancient male authors here to support her writing on a woman's topic—the subject of love.[5] Of Plutarch, she cites, "son propre *exemple* en tant de *divers accidens & discours de l'amour,* qu'il a traictez

jeune & vieil" (645) (his own example in so many anecdotes and discourses on love, which he treated as both a young and old man).[6] Virgil is
another author she mentions, for his treatment of Dido, a woman to whom
Gournay frequently compares her heroine, Alinda. In citing Plutarch, Virgil, and others, Gournay now takes the topic of love more seriously than
she did in 1594, when she felt obliged to apologize for it. She also connects the topic of love with her developing feminism. This connection becomes more explicit in the novel itself, where she discusses the rivalry
between male and female conceptions of love.

A second readerly objection to which Gournay responds in the 1626
"Advis" provides us with more information about reception in the early
seventeenth century, as well as its role in the evolving definition of the
novel genre (646):

> Une autre querelle, que *le nouveau goust de ceste saison* dresse à ce petit Livre,
> ou pour mieux dire à tous mes Escrits, mais à luy plus qu'aux autres, veu ce
> charactere de *roman* qu'il porte, c'est d'inserer en son texte quelque *ornement
> en langue estrangere, & de citer les Autheurs par leurs noms.*

> Another quarrel, which the new taste of this season addresses to my little
> book, or rather to all my writings, but to this one more than to the others,
> given the character of a novel which it takes on, is that I insert into the text
> some ornamentation in foreign languages, and that I cite authors by name.

As we have just seen in Gournay's use of male authorities to justify writing
on the topic of love, the sort of argument from authority described here
has always been one of her favorite rhetorical techniques. Most of the re-
mainder of the "Advis," however, is taken up with a response to readers
who felt that she should *not* quote in a novel and especially that she should
not quote Latin passages (as she did in 1594) or give the names of authors
she cites. Gournay's real readers were no longer humanists like Montaigne
(or like herself), but they were now frequently women or nobles who had
not learned Latin or studied the classics.[7] The Latin quotations in her text
would have been perfectly appropriate in a humanist narrative of the sixteenth century, as they were in Montaigne's *Essais*. But Gournay witnesses
in the early seventeenth century what John Lyons describes as "the transition from heavy reliance on textual authority to emphasis on observation
and introspection."[8] This textual authority is no longer viewed by Gournay's readers as bearing any relationship to her story or application to their
own lives.

In this quotation from the "Advis" we also see the first reference
to Gournay's book as novel ("roman"), rather than story ("histoire" or
"conte"), as it was characterized in 1594. In describing the book in this
new way, she now appears to take the *Proumenoir* more seriously as a literary work in its own right, rather than simply as an anecdote she had told

Montaigne and wanted to remind him of. But in defining her book as "roman," she needs to come to terms with both contemporary expectations
about this genre and its readers, most of them women. While these readers
do not have the power ("Empire") over her that Montaigne did, still they
represent a force to be reckoned with. A few pages later she explains why
she disagrees with some seventeenth-century readers, who do not want
quotations in a novel. Gournay believes that the novel is just as prestigious
("glorieux") as the more lofty genres of philosophy, politics, and so on.
And, in her opinion, it needs to rely on authority as much as they do. In
other words, she sees the novel as a rhetorical genre, rather than solely as
an imaginative fictional creation. The exemplary nature of her story places
it in the tradition of the ancient works she quotes, rather than in the lighter
vein of the romance. The novel's goal, in her eyes, is still much closer to
teaching ("instruire") than to amusement ("plaire"). But readers do not
seem to agree with her. The defense of the Latin quotations in the book,
then, also entails a defense of the author's serious, moral intentions in writing it. These intentions are maintained in spite of the apparently more frivolous tastes of her contemporary public.

Gournay answers a third and related criticism of her book: to defend
the many digressions found in the first edition of the *Proumenoir,* which
readers did not like. Gournay herself (and here we see her close affinity to
Montaigne) thought the digressions were the *best* part of the story (652):

> Je puis justement representer . . . la brute & lourde humeur de ces gens icy,
> soient-ils Autheurs ou lecteurs, qui s'en vont *si seichement* apres leur narration
> toute crue, quoy qu'elle ouvre la carriere à tant *de beaux & florissans discours,*
> soit en la chose mesme, soit aupres d'elle tendant *une favorable main à la*
> *digression.*

> I can justly represent . . . the brutal and heavy humor of these people, whether
> they be authors or readers, who march along so dryly after their raw narrative,
> even though it could open the way to so many beautiful and flourishing dis-
> courses, either on the subject itself or on a closely related one, lending a favor-
> able hand to digression.

We see in the ensuing discussion that Gournay in fact is familiar with the
evolution of the novel genre in the early seventeenth century, and that she
has read many of the popular, especially Spanish, models. She proudly
points out that *Don Quixote,* the *Argenis,* the *Diana,* the *Arcadia,* and
others do use digression, as much as she does. Only the French taste (and
here we must understand frivolous court and "salon" taste) refuses the serious, reflective side of the novel.

Although the "Advis" to the *Proumenoir* began by giving women readers credit for encouraging her to reprint the novel, it ends by showing these
same readers as severe critics and expresses disappointment that they have

not been able to appreciate the style and didactic goals of the book. She asks at the end of the "Advis": "Demandes-tu si ce degoust qu'elle [la jeunesse de la Cour] a pour moy, *provient de sa faute, ou de la mienne?* Vrayement je ne sçay, mon bon amy" (655) (Do you ask whether the distaste which the young people at Court have for me comes from their fault, or from my own? Really I couldn't say, my good friend) Despite the antagonism toward readers expressed here, Gournay does seem to have moved beyond the earlier "power which you have over me" ("Empire que vous avez sur moy") as a depiction of her relationship to one of them. Rather, she is now able to throw out a challenge to her presumably hostile reader: "toutesfois je sçay bien, que *celle* de nous deux qui a tort en cela, n'en daigneroit avoir pour un peu" (still I know perfectly well, that whichever of us women is wrong about this, will not deign to be so for very long) (655). The use of the feminine "celle" in this last quotation suggests one reason why Gournay now feels more equality with her reader than she did earlier: many of her current readers are women, and so do not intimidate her as Montaigne and other male humanist readers tended to do.

———

A third piece of the "paratexte" to the *Proumenoir* of 1626 is the letter to Montaigne that originally provided the novel's frame. Surprisingly, the "Epistre sur le Proumenoir de Monsieur de Montaigne—à luy-mesme" (Letter on *Montaigne's Walk* addressed to himself) retained in the 1626 edition, also contains some changes, and it inserts a new fictitious date of 1589 (rather than the original l588). Despite the fact that Montaigne has been dead since 1592, Gournay in 1626 still maintains the pretense that the book is addressed to him. The letter begins, as before, with a description of the walk they took together (in 1588) during which they discussed the "tragiques accidents de l'amour recitez par Plutarque" (tragic accidents of love related by Plutarch) (655). She also repeats, in a slightly different form, the hope that Montaigne will send the book back to her with corrections (despite the fact that he is now deceased). Interestingly, she takes out the earlier statement that, although the topic of the book may appear inappropriate for a woman writer, still its purpose is to warn women to stay away from men ("l'utilité d'advertir les dames de se tenir en garde"). Negative exemplarity may no longer be her major objective in the book, now that its *real* readers are women. While the *fiction* of negative exemplarity for women was useful in promoting the book to *men* (and especially to Montaigne), Gournay no longer needs to maintain this fiction.

Instead of talking in this earlier way about her relationship to the *reader,* she now develops an apology or excuse for having taken the story from another *author* (Taillemont).[9] In responding to this criticism, Gournay now underlines her own role as adapter of Taillemont and departs from the earlier convention of the short story ("nouvelle"); she acknowledges that she did make many changes in the story, rather than just repeating it verbatim. She underlines her importance as writer/narrator, which is a new direction in 1626. As she begins to throw off Montaigne's "empire" over her, she also asserts her own power over the previous (male) sources or authors she has drawn from.

In developing this response, Gournay paraphrases something which she has stated in the "Advis" to the *Proumenoir*—that a story is not just a series of events, but rather consists in what an author does with them:

> Ce que je ne dis nullement pour relever le merite de mon ouvrage en cecy: mais seulement contre *la simplesse de ceux* qui presument qu'un conte ne consiste principalement qu'au *fil de ses accidens:* & qu'il ne peut appartenir ny faire honneur *qu'à celuy qui l'auroit escrit le premier.* (658)

> I say this not to point out the value of my own work here: but just against the simplicity of those who think that a story only consists in the series of events it contains: and that it cannot belong or give honor to anyone other than the person who wrote it in the first place.

This argument moves away from Gournay's more usual reliance on the authority of the past to stress the possibility of modern invention. Like most new discoveries in the "paratexte" to the *Proumenoir* of 1626, this one seems to respond to negative reactions by readers ("la simplesse de ceux"). Gournay's identity as an author has emerged almost in spite of her readers.

Not surprisingly, a final change, in the 1626 "Epistre," is the omission of the playful invitation from 1594 to Montaigne, to the effect that she hopes he will find fault with the book and demonstrate "l'Empire que vous avez en moi." Since his death this statement is neither realistic nor appropriate. But its omission may also indicate, in fact, that Gournay is beginning to assume power over both herself and her readers, as a writer.

The 1626 "Epistre" concludes however with an affectionate address of Montaigne, which was in fact *not* found in the more formal 1594 "Epistre": "Recevez quand à vous, un million de bons jours de *vostre fille;* aussi *glorieuse* de ce tiltre, qu'elle la seroit d'estre *mere des Muses mesmes*" (658) (As for you, please receive a million "Good Days" from your daughter; as proud of that title, as she would be to be mother of the Muses themselves). Written at the age of sixty, this is a surprisingly emotional expression of her continuing love for Montaigne and pride in their relationship. But this closing also expresses her sense that she has grown up and accomplished a significant artistic creation ("mere des Muses mesmes").[10] She has grown from literary daughter to literary mother.[11] In expressing her friendship for Montaigne in a direct way, here, Gournay in fact takes control of these emotions herself and begins to move away from his "empire" over her. Rather, she expresses her *own* feelings and point of view, toward him.

Gournay is much less influenced by her imaginary reader Montaigne, in this "Epistre," than she was in 1594. She is more interested, however, in defining her own role—her authority—as writer of the book. This change is understandable, as she places the book alongside the considerable number of her other writings. This new authorial voice will be even more evident when we look at the revised version of the *Proumenoir* itself.

When we turn to the text of the novel itself in 1626, we see that Gournay does make many changes in the story, despite her stated resistance to doing so, in the "Advis." Most obviously, she translates into French all the Latin quotations, which salon readers apparently did not like. This fact is all the more surprising, in that the "Advis" defended the use of Latin and did not even mention that she had made the translations! It is important to evaluate the significance of this change for Gournay's role as author in 1626.

Early in the 1626 version, Gournay explains, as she did not in 1594, that she is applying the experience of Ariadne and Dido, by these quotations, to that of her heroine, Alinda (660): "*J'applique* icy & partout ce Livret avec trop de miserable correspondance, les vers d'Ariadne & de Didon à ceste Princesse" (I am applying here and throughout this little book, with almost too wretched a resemblance, the verses of Ariadne and Dido to this Princess). This statement, which follows in 1626 eight lines of French poetry describing Alinda's upbringing, stresses the relevance of the poetry to the story. This relevance has been provided by its author, Gournay ("*J'applique*"), whose literary training has allowed her to enrich Taillemont's story with classical parallels, as she did in 1594. A few pages later, after another added line of French verse, she adds another explanation to the reader: the poetry in the book is only hers through translation (667): "Voicy les recits de l'histoire Poetique: & *je declare icy,* qu'en quelque lieu que *j'insere* des vers en *ma prose,* ils ne sont *miens* que par la version" (Here is the account of the poetic story, and I declare here, that wherever I insert verses into my prose, they are only mine through translation). Although she appears to apologize for these translations, still the apologies throw her own role as translator into relief, with a repetition of the first-person singular rare in her work before *L'Ombre*.[12] The translations give Gournay a stronger role as narrator than did the Latin quotations. The French passages substitute a contemporary woman's voice for those of the ancient male authors she originally quoted. In this way the translations help to resolve the conflict between humanism and feminism in the book. They make the parallels with ancient literary works accessible to contemporary women readers.[13] The translations, however, are not the only changes made in the text of 1626.

Almost every section of the 1626 *Proumenoir* contains major revisions. Although the action of the story remains the same, the scenes of real interest to Gournay are those she adapts: conversations, monologues, and digressions—talk rather than action. The first section to be revised is the initial conversation between father (the "Sattrappe")[14] and daughter Alinda, which treats not only her obligation to marry the "Roy de Parthes" as part of a peace treaty but also lengthy considerations about political theory and the relationship between monarch and subject, which may not seem appropriate for a young woman of twenty. The changes in 1626 show a closer relationship between father and daughter than was found in the 1594 version, which stressed Alinda's relationship to her mother;[15] but also the 1626 version takes Alinda more seriously as a member of the royal family (her father is the King of Persia's uncle) and laments the fact that now she will never be able either to rule or to provide an heir to the throne. The Sattrappe describes the way in which he has raised her ("à l'esperance de perpetuer en ma maison la Grandeur & la vertu des premiers Roys du monde" (in the hope of perpetuating in my family the greatness and virtue of the first kings of the world) and exhorts her to remember her worth. He then discourses on the art of being a good king but downplays the notion of power while stressing instead equality between subject and ruler (661): "Il faut quitter *l'Empire sur les hommes,* ou que nos passions & nos interests particuliers le quittent sur nous. *Apprenons, apprenons, m'amie, le mestier de commander*" (We must leave behind power over men, or our passions and particular interests will leave this behind for us. Let us learn, my dear, the true profession of ruling). Gournay seems to be developing here an egalitarian model of leadership, based on consensus between ruler and subject and proposed, surprisingly, to a young woman. The phrase, "l'Empire sur les hommes," reverses in a striking way the relationship of power between Gournay and Montaigne, expressed in 1594 as "l'Empire que vous avez en moy." While Gournay suggests here that a young woman may rule over men, she already begins to move beyond power to suggest equality between classes as well as between genders.[16] In the ensuing pages, the Sattrappe addresses his daughter with remarkably republican ideas such as: "Orgueil à part, ma fille, tes subjets, le masque levé, sont tes compagnons" (All pride aside, my daughter, your subjects, once the mask is removed, are your equals); and "De plus, *tous les hommes estans nais soubs les loix de l'égalité,* chacun de ceux qui vivent soubs ton sceptre estoit capable d'estre ce que tu es" (Furthermore, because all men are born under the laws of equality, each of those who live beneath your scepter was capable of being what you are) (663). In concluding this development, Gournay has him add a reflection on the singularity of telling Alinda all this, despite the fact that she is a woman (664):

Tu m'as porté, *m'amie,* outre les termes du suject present: neantmoins c'est tout un, ces instructions te pouvans servir ailleurs: & ne me desplaist pas de t'avoir entretenüe de chose si serieuse, *quoy que jeune & femme:* car puisque ces qualitez *ne te desrobent point la hardiesse & l'authorité de regir les hommes, il seroit hors de raison qu'elles t'en desrobassent la science.* (664–665)

You have brought me, my dear, beyond the limits of the present subject: still it's all the same, since these instructions can serve you elsewhere: and it doesn't displease me to have talked with you on such a serious topic, even though you are young and a woman: for since these qualities do not deny you the boldness and the authority to rule over men, it would be wrong for them to deny you the knowledge of how to do this.

In the context of the much debated French Salic law, this suggestion that women may be able to rule is surprising (and new in 1626).[17] This digression also makes a case for women's education ("la science") and suggests ideas already contained in Gournay's "Egalité," about the theoretical equality of men and women. None of this discussion was contained in the 1594 version of the novel, and it may show us that Gournay is now more in tune with the political and social thought of her time than she explicitly admits in the "Advis." Feminism may have brought her to consider equality between ruler and subject, as well as between men and women: her consciousness has now been raised on all questions of power.[18]

Alinda, Mlle de Gournay, and their women readers emerge in 1626 as intelligent, responsible citizens, fully able to comprehend the intricacies of political power and even, if need be, capable of wielding it themselves. Gournay shows us that her feminism has led her to consider the nature of political power itself and to question the authoritarian, patriarchal model for it inherited from the sixteenth century. None of this, perhaps wisely, was suggested in the "Advis" or the "Epistre" to the *Proumenoir* of 1626.

A second and very different major development added in 1626 is a long digression on the nature of love: particularly, what causes it, and whether true love is primarily physical or spiritual. This digression is added as a sort of gloss to the original scene where the novel's heroine, Alinda, en route to meet her fiancé (the King of Parthia), falls in love instead with Léontin, the son of a gentleman at whose home they are lodged. Significantly, the additions stress primarily the process by which Alinda (rather than Léontin) falls in love, and they address the difference between male and female conceptions of love. Gournay also adds some new French verse passages, not in the original, which highlight Léontin's beauty, grace, and articulateness.

One interesting feature of this development, when one is aware of Gournay's fascination with language, is her statement that Léontin wins

Alinda over by his beautiful speech ("beau langage") as well as by his grace
and good manners ("graces & gentillesses") (668), *not* just through his
beauty. As in all her rhetorical work, Gournay quotes several ancient and
modern authorities, this time to the effect that love (at least for women) is
not only physical. The principal arguments of this digression seem to be:
that although we don't really know where love comes from, still it is clearly
not just a result of physical beauty; and that Neoplatonic views of love are
more appropriate. She explicitly states that women are more capable of this
spiritual love than men are and that women need to encourage men to
understand spiritual love. Just as Gournay has begun the 1626 *Proumenoir*
by redefining the nature of political power along what could be called a
feminist model, she continues in the book to redefine love as a spiritual
power, which view she explicitly labels as feminist. Because she cannot
eliminate the subject of love completely from the book, she substitutes a
feminist *version* of love.

   She continues to develop the rivalry between male and female conceptions of love, with a repetition of the word "empire," which we have seen
to be central in the 1626 edition (673):

> & puis encores que le sexe masculin y [à la beauté] vise plus que l'autre en ses
> desirs, estant neantmoins tous deux jettez en mesme moule, elle [la beauté]
> n'a pas consequemment de juste & naturel *empire sur les coeurs:* les choses
> vrayement naturelles, estans universelles & necessitées. Tel est l'*empire des
> graces* qui s'estend par tout, bien que plus & moins, selon la disposition,
> capacité ou incapacité, des objects qu'elles rencontrent pour spectateurs.

> And then since the male sex is more attracted to beauty than is the female,
> even though both are made from the same mold, beauty, therefore, does not
> have a just and natural power over our hearts: for the truly natural tendencies
> are universal and necessary. Such is the power of grace which extends every-
> where, although a little more or less, according to the disposition, capacity or
> incapacity, of the observer.

The word "empire," repeated in this passage, is significant in the context
of Gournay's definition of political power in 1626, as well as her earlier
treatment of Montaigne's power over her, in 1594. The topic of love is tied
to these other discussions because it, too, is a question of power. The fact
that Alinda now falls in love with Léontin's "beau langage" shows her to
be making in part a rational choice rather than only succumbing to a fatal
physical attraction, which is more the case in his fleeting love for her. There
is also a feminist argument contained here: because the female conception
of love based on grace rather than only beauty is more universal, it is therefore truer: it has, in fact, more power ("empire").

———

A third major area of change in 1626 comes during Léontin's tirade, as
he realizes that he is in love with Alinda and tries to persuade her not to

marry the King of Parthia. Gournay adds some new arguments here by showing the power Alinda has over Léontin, which he even describes himself.

While the 1594 edition contained a short (three-line) and economical Latin quotation, describing the fact that Léontin noticed her ("spectat & audit"), the l626 version substitutes a twelve-line French passage translated from Sappho. This passage is much more passionate than the earlier Latin verse, and it highlights Léontin's subjugation to Alinda. Like all the French verse in l626, this selection is more immediate and more closely linked to the text than was the earlier Latin quotation. It brings into focus the emotional and psychological impact of the scene, rather than the narrator's moralistic conclusions to it. The passage also throws the heroine's power over the hero (described as weak, enslaved, and transported) into relief.

The 1626 version of the story then repeats a scene from l594, where Leontin approaches Alinda to reveal his passion for her. But the later version stresses Alinda's role in this scene, and particularly, once more, her power: "Alinda *le veid vaciller*, le prevint doucement: comme les personnes vrayement *naies à dominer, dominent leur Grandeur* mesme, pour se rendre affables & benignes" (678) (Alinda saw him hesitate, and encouraged him gently as those who are really born to lead, overcome even their greatness, to make themselves gracious and kindly). The l626 version also adds a much more declamatory conclusion by Léontin, stating that the proposed marriage prostitutes Alinda, violating Cupid and his mother, and finally addresses Alinda herself:

> Miserable beauté! miserable jeunesse! miserable fleur de toutes les graces & delices! vous n'aurez donc jamais le plaisir de recognoistre & de contempler en l'ardeur d'un gentil esprit quelles sont *les puissances de vostre empire:* & renoncerez pour le reste de vostre vie, à vous enrichir d'une si douce obligation, que seroit celle *d'une belle ame qui vous possederoit!* (681)

> Wretched beauty! Wretched youth! Wretched flower of all the graces and delights! You will never, then, have the pleasure of recognizing and contemplating in the ardor of a pleasing spirit what the strengths of your power are: and you will give up for the rest of your life the possibility of enriching yourself with such a sweet obligation, as that of a beautiful soul which would possess you!

In the 1594 version of this argument Léontin stressed military ethics and Alinda's responsibility to provide a male heir; this addition turns our attention once again to Alinda's power ("empire") through love: if she consents to an arranged marriage, she will never be able to experience this power. Passages like this one may contain the key to Gournay's surprising interest in love, in this version of the novel, written at the age of sixty, soon after publishing two feminist tracts. Love is a feminist topic, for her, because it can demonstrate the power of women over men. But this power, like the political power described earlier, should be democratic or reciprocal, with respect to "une belle ame qui vous possederoit." By eventually following Léontin, Alinda will choose the "Empire" of love rather than that of political power. In 1626 this is a conscious choice, while in 1594 it was simply a result of blind passion.

In the 1626 version, Gournay as author feels much freer than in 1594 to express Alinda's emotions and physical sensations, when she falls in love with Léontin. Although these additions may be reception driven, part of an attempt to imitate the genre of the "roman sentimental," still it would be hard to deny that the narrator seems to enjoy the more subtly erotic aspects of the description of the storm ("orage") of emotions that comes over Alinda as well as a certain shivering ("quelque frisson") (682). While the 1594 text described feelings contained within her breast, in 1626 this becomes "en son beau sein pantelant du ressentiment de ses infortunes" (in her beautiful breast heaving with resentment against her misfortunes). While 1594 relates that a glance ("oeillade") was exchanged, 1626 elaborates on this and, although condemning the exchange, admits that sensual pleasure ("volupté") was as significant a result as the misery stressed in 1594. Gournay also translates a short Latin passage into French, in 1626, expanding metaphors describing the flame of love. She no longer hides behind Latin quotations to express things she may hesitate to say in French, as she did in 1594, perhaps following Montaigne's example in "Sur des vers de Virgile."

The "tête à tête" between Alinda and Léontin is interrupted, as Gournay repeats an earlier statement from 1594: her goal is not to describe their love, but to bemoan it. She reminds us that she is only describing all this because punishment followed the guilty actions (684). In 1626 these excuses hardly still seem true, however. Rather, Gournay now has the courage to describe romantic love from a woman's point of view and even to enjoy this description. She also adds ten lines of French poetry (replacing the earlier five lines of Latin), which in fact do paint the fiery progress of love, in detail. The description of love in all its fury now predominates over its ostensible condemnation. Surely this change is owing in part to Gournay's sense as a woman writer of what women readers *really* want, as opposed to what male writers think women *should* read.

A fourth scene that undergoes extensive transformation in 1626 contains a description of Alinda's turmoil, as she eventually decides to give in to Léontin, with a declamatory speech (as in 1594) in which she bemoans the bad example that she sets to future generations of women. Despite Gournay's determination to keep the "lesson" in this part of the book, still the 1626 version seems more positive, adds extenuating factors (Alinda's upbringing and inexperience), delves into Alinda's psyche more extensively,

and now speaks of the young lovers' flight as hidden under the veil of clandestine marriage ("soubs un voile de nopces clandestines") (686). Like the
other discussions of love in 1626, this one presents Alinda's experience in
a more accepting manner, rather than condemning it as the earlier version
consistently did.

While the first edition stated that Alinda did not give in to Léontin
without great mental conflict, the 1626 *Proumenoir* analyzes that conflict
in terms of divisions within the self. The 1626 version acknowledges that
this passion has become part of herself ("si sa passion & elle se peuvent
distinguer icy"), whereas 1594 saw it as foreign to her and largely owing to
Leontin's manipulations. This change conforms to what we see as greater
emphasis on Alinda's responsibility, control, autonomy, in 1626. She is no
longer just a victim, as she was earlier, but she now has some control over
her feelings and actions. Issues of power over herself are now as important
as those of power over others.

The central scene in the book contains Alinda's tragic lament on what
her family, friends, and future generations will think and say about her
actions. This is largely the same as in 1594, although 1626 adds a few
sentences underlining her importance as a woman to the Persian Empire—
her exemplarity is not only negative, here:

> Est-il dit que je precipite ce precieux honneur: rendu si souverainement *im-
> portant en moy, par dessus toutes les femmes, par l'importance de ma personne;*
> heritiere du diademe de Cyrus, *rançon du Roy des Roys, rançon de l'Empire?*
> (686)

> Will it be said that I have thrown away this precious honor, which has become
> so supremely important to me, above all women, by the importance of my
> person; inheritor of the crown of Cyrus, ransom of the King of Kings, ransom
> of the Empire?

In this passage the use of "Empire" as a noun to refer to the Persian Empire makes explicit the connection, already latent in the text, between notions of power of various kinds and that of empire, the ultimate source of
power for Alinda as a member of the royal family.

While the 1594 version stressed her horror at what she had done
("l'horreur de mon exemple"), the later version questions whether she really does regret her actions because they have now become part of her.
Although Gournay ostensibly still criticizes this tendency in Alinda, it is
obvious that she is also swept away by the description of a strong and over-
whelming passion to see her heroine's point of view as well as the moralizing stance she must adopt as narrator (and which earlier supported only
Alinda's self-flagellation and self-denial). Gournay as narrator now identifies much more closely with Alinda the character than she did earlier.

Although Alinda states that she would like to be "cured" of this passion, if necessary, through death, the narrator questions how sincere this desire is: "si les amans vrayement picquez, c'est à dire insensez, *peuvent vrayement desirer de s'y mettre:* & s'ils ne prenoient plaisir, *d'enflammer exprés les amorces de leur propre passion"* (687) (as if lovers who are really stung, that is who have lost their senses, can really desire to be cured, and as if they don't take pleasure in purposely inflaming the beginnings of their own passion). In fact, it is useless for Alinda to try to "root out" ("déraciner") Léontin from her mind because her mind has become the image of Léontin himself ("la figure mesme de Leontin").

What we take away from this scene is a strong sense of Alinda's love for Léontin, which is presented in this later version as an active, conscious part of her identity—not a result of passive victimization. As in the previous example, the passages of poetry added here continue to belie or subvert Gournay's stated purpose to bemoan and condemn Alinda's actions.[19] These striking visual metaphors strengthen our picture of Alinda's passion as something larger than an excuse for moralizing. The novel has become more literary and less exemplary than it was in 1594.

———

The action of the novel in 1626 unfolds essentially as it did in 1594, although there are additions by the narrator in almost every scene, which make the descriptions more vivid. Toward the end of the story, the 1594 version added (in Latin) a quotation of Ariadne's lament (by Catullus) and a long (eighteen page) digression on women's education, beginning with the opinion that "Ces vers de la chetive Ariadné devroient estre escrits par tout dans les heures des dames" (These verses by the wretched Ariadne should be written everywhere in ladies' books of hours) (41–41v). In 1626, this entire development (as well as the Latin verse) is gone. While the 1594 version stressed the negative exemplarity of Ariadne's and Alinda's stories, which illustrated the principle that women should read in order to learn what kinds of behavior to *avoid,* in 1626 this entire moral lesson has disappeared! No doubt Gournay's women readers found the digression boring and irrelevant, out of place at the moment of the heroine's death. The defense of digressions in the 1626 "Advis au Proumenoir" seemed to imply as much, although Gournay did not reveal there that she had in fact *eliminated* the major digression from the book. But when we see this omission in the light of the additions in 1626, it is possible to speculate about what other reasons Gournay may have had for removing the digression. Her narrative project in the *Proumenoir* seems to have changed— from a moralistic demonstration of negative exemplarity to a much more positive exploration of the psychology of love, which has value in itself as a form of experience and as one step in the formation of a woman's identity. In 1626 Gournay allows herself to express these views, which have in addition the advantage of appealing to the literary taste of her time. Rather than impose her earlier belief, largely inherited from humanist authors like Vives, that women should read to receive chastisement and moral instruction, Gournay now has learned through experience that women, like men, may also read for pleasure, escapism, and emotional catharsis. The 1626 poetic passages that partially displace the digression of 1594 bear out our sense that Gournay now outlines a different role for her reader than she did earlier, more in line with the appreciation of metaphor than with the absorption of a moral lesson. She has moved closer to "plaire" and further from "instruire," on the aesthetic continuum.

   In the light of Gournay's defensive statements about her novel in the "Advis au *Proumenoir*" of 1626, the actual changes made to it are surprising and even at times astonishing. They involve nothing less than a revolution in the genre of the book, the depiction of its heroine, and, most important, in the role it outlines for its author and her relationship to the reader. These changes follow some metamorphosis in social and literary climate from the late sixteenth to the early seventeenth centuries. But they also mirror some internal developments on the part of Gournay herself, who seems to have undergone a transformation between 1594 and 1626, paralleling the transformation undergone by her heroine, Alinda.[20]
   The word "Empire," repeated throughout the 1626 version of the *Proumenoir*, contains a key to Gournay's preoccupations at this time and also links the seemingly disparate elements of the book to each other and to Gournay's development as a woman writer. While "Empire" was originally defined as the power Montaigne as father-figure had over Gournay, his adoptive daughter, in 1626 this definition has changed. "Empire" now refers to not only the Persian Empire but also issues of political and personal power, which Gournay links in anticipation of the twentieth-century feminist realization that "the personal is political." Throughout the book she now struggles to understand the nature of the relationship between ruler and subject, as well as the nature of the power that men and women exert over each other. Both kinds of power, spiritual as well as physical in 1626, should ideally involve reciprocity rather than only dominance and coercion.
   The exploration of "les puissances de vostre Empire" also extends to a new understanding of the relationship between reader and writer, for Gournay as well as between Gournay as author and her sources or "authorities." Although she earlier invested her readers with excessive power over her, Gournay now is able to express herself forcefully as a writer and as a woman. The "Advis au Proumenoir" seemed to imply that her relationship with readers was largely negative: she had won her right to be called an author through a battle with these inconsiderate slanderers ("calomniateurs"). But the *Proumenoir* itself, in 1626, actually demonstrates a much

more positive relationship with readers than the two "Advis" imply. Gournay transforms her novel in part through responsiveness to the requests of readers and comes part way from "instruire" to "plaire" to meet their desire for a love story expressed in French, rather than a moralistic tract laced with Latin quotations. Gournay's role as translator and adaptor of earlier material shows us another facet of her "Empire," which now involves integration and interpretation of her sources rather than only quotation and citation.

The final "Empire" that Gournay may still need to master, in 1626, is power over her own emotions, a central concern for "Cartesian women" of her time.[21] Although the objectives of her book are defined in the "Advis" with rationalism and objectivity, the changes she actually makes in the story reveal her own emotionalism and physicality.[22] In allowing this second version of the novel to be published, however, Gournay may move "beyond power" to an acceptance of herself as a woman as well as a writer. This acceptance is partially expressed in the statement found in her "Advis au Lecteur," that the book reflects her as she is: "maistresse piece de mon estre." Like Montaigne, Gournay comes toward the end of her life to accept her physical and emotional traits as a human being, even when they may conflict with her moral and rational program as a writer. In moving away from the "Empire" that Montaigne had over her in 1594, Gournay has nonetheless internalized his message by now disengaging the "Empire" of self-repression and moving instead toward self-acceptance.

NOTES

1. Marie de Gournay, *Le Proumenoir de Monsieur de Montaigne,* ed. Patricia Francis Cholakian (Delmar, N.Y.: Scholars' Facsimiles & Reprints, 1985), 4. Emphasis mine, as is the case throughout this study.

2. Marie de Gournay, *L'Ombre de la Damoiselle de Gournay* (Paris: Jean Libert, 1626). This volume was consulted at the Houghton Library, Harvard University. Although Gournay revised the *Proumenoir* again in the later volumes of her collected works, *Les Advis* (1634 and 1641), I have selected the 1626 edition because it illustrates most dramatically the emergence of her authorial voice after the death of Montaigne. A separate study of each of the other two revised versions requires more space than I have here.

3. See for example the 1595 "Préface" to Montaigne's *Essais,* which complained: "Tu devines ja, Lecteur, que je me veux plaindre du froid recueil, que nos hommes ont fait aux *Essais*" (You already guess, Reader, that I want to complain about the cold reception that people have given our *Essays*), "Préface sur les Essais de Michel Seigneur de Montaigne, par sa fille d'alliance," ed. François Rigolot, in *Montaigne Studies* 1 (1989): 22–54; citation at 23.

4. Marie de Gournay, "Advis sur la nouvelle édition du Proumenoir de Monsieur de Montaigne," *L'Ombre* (644).

5. In his *Etudes sur la littérature féminine au XVIIᵉ siècle: Mademoiselle de Gournay, Mademoiselle de Scudéry, Madame de Villedieu, Madame de Lafayette* (Birmingham, Ala.: Summa Publications, Inc., 1990), Constant Venesoen comments on the use of male authorities to make feminist arguments in the *Egalité*: "Mais, soit qu'elle passe outre la leçon 'antiféministe', soit qu'elle préfère l'ignorer et brandir des références qui prouveraient le contraire, toujours est-il que la sagesse antique, de tradition gréco-latine ou judéo-chrétienne, lui sert

de solide rempart contre le mépris du mérite féminin" (2: 27) (But, whether she glosses over the "anti-feminist" lesson, or whether she prefers to ignore it and brandish references that seem to prove the contrary, still it remains that ancient wisdom, of the greco-latin or judeo-christian tradition, serves her as a solid rampart against scorn at feminine merit).

6. Citations from "L'Egalité des Hommes et des Femmes" and "Grief des Dames" are from *Marie de Gournay: Fragments d'un discours féminin*, ed. Elyane Dezon-Jones (Paris: Librairie José Corti, 1988).

7. In his *Naissance de l'écrivain: sociologie de la littérature à l'âge classique* (Paris: Les Editions de Minuit, 1985), Alain Viala describes the "para-scholarly" education received by most young girls, from tutors, which did not include Latin: "De plus, l'instruction restreinte donnée aux filles, ne passant pas par les collèges, ignorait en général les lettres, la tâche des précepteurs se bornant à l'apprentissage de la lecture et de l'écriture, en laissant la plus large place à l'éducation morale, à la civilité et à la religion" (138) (Furthermore, the limited instruction given to girls, who did not go to school, generally left out literature, while the task of tutors was limited to teaching, reading, and writing, leaving the greatest role to moral instruction, to manners, and to religion).

8. See John Lyons, *Exemplum: The Rhetoric of Example in Early Modern France and Italy* (Princeton, N.J.: Princeton University Press, 1989), 238.

9. She claims her story to be from Claude de Taillemont, *Discours des champs faëz à l'honneur, et exaltation de l'amour, et des dames* (Lyon: Michel Du Bois, 1553): "Ny ne suis pas de ceux qui croyent, que celuy qui prend l'argument d'un conte quelque part, ne puisse avoir autant de merite, s'il le recite de bonne grace, que si l'argument mesme estoit sien" (657) (Nor am I one of those who believes, that the person who takes the argument of a story from somewhere else, cannot have as much merit, if he tells it with grace, as if the argument itself were his own).

10. Tilde Sankovitch notes that Gournay does not publish anything until after Montaigne's death: "After Montaigne's death, Marie de Gournay finds it possible to become her own champion, and to complete, once and for all, her journey toward her constantly pursued and constant self." See "Marie le Jars de Gournay: The Self-Portrait of an Androgynous Hero," in *French Women and the Book: Myths of Access and Desire* (Syracuse, N.Y.: Syracuse University Press, 1988), 83.

11. See Philippe Desan's treatment of Gournay's transition from daughter to mother of the *Essais* in "'Cet orphelin qui m'estoit commis': la préface de Marie de Gournay à l'édition de 1635 des *Essais*," *Montaigne Studies* 2, no. 2 (1990): 58–67.

12. Dezon-Jones shows that not only does Gournay refer to herself as "sa fille d'alliance" on the title page of the 1594 edition of the *Proumenoir* as well as on that of the 1595 edition of Montaigne's *Essais,* but that she also wrote an autobiographical sketch of herself, "Copie de la Vie de la Demoiselle de Gournay," entirely in the third person. See "Marie de Gournay: le je/u/ palimpseste," *L'Esprit Créateur* 23, no. 2 (1983): 26–36.

13. On the role of women as writers and readers of translation in the English Renaissance, see *Silent But for the Word: Tudor Women as Patrons, Translators and Writers of Religious Works,* ed. Margaret Patterson Hannay (Kent, Ohio: Kent State University Press, 1985); and Suzanne W. Hull, *Chaste, Silent and Obedient: English Books for Women, 1475–1640* (San Marino, Calif.: Huntington Library, 1982).

14. The spelling of "Satrape" in 1594 becomes "Sattrappe" in 1626.

15. See Patricia F. Cholakian's discussion of the importance of Alinda's mother to the story, in her introduction to the 1594 *Proumenoir* (21–22).

16. On this subject see Marilyn French, *Beyond Power: On Women, Men and Morals* (New York: Summit Books, 1985).

17. Ian Maclean suggests that debate over the Salic Law was part of the "Querelle des Femmes" in the seventeenth century. See his *Woman Triumphant: Feminism in French Literature, 1610–1652* (Oxford: Clarendon Press, 1977), 259.

18. See Carolyn Lougee's discussion of the connections between feminism and other social movements in the seventeenth century in *'Le Paradis des Femmes': Women, Salons, and*

Social Stratification in Seventeenth-Century France (Princeton, N.J.: Princeton University Press, 1976).

19. The poetic passages describe Alinda variously as a doe fleeing with an arrow in her side, then as a Bacchante, and then (as frequently) engulfed in "une si belle flamme" (688–689).

20. Tilde Sankovitch sees this transformation as an analog to the process of alchemical transformation, which also interested Gournay (83).

21. See Erica Harth, *Cartesian Women: Versions and Subversions of Rational Discourse in the Old Regime* (Ithaca: Cornell University Press, 1992).

22. See Constant Venesoen's statement that: "L'histoire d'Alinda et de Léontin, sirupeuse ou naïve, si on veut, révèle un rêve et un destin. Elle lève aussi le voile sur la sensibilité de Mlle de Gournay" (22) (The story of Alinda and of Léontin, syrupy or naïve, if you will, reveals a dream and a destiny. It also discloses Mlle de Gournay's sensitivity).

Appendix
CHRONOLOGICAL CHART
૪ᴐ

Historical Events		French Letters & Translations	
1492	Birth of Marguerite de Navarre		
1494–1550	Italian Wars		
		1497	Christine de Pisan: *Tresor de la cité des dames* (+1503, 1536)
		1503	Champier: *La Nef des dames vertueuses*
1515–1547	Reign of Francis I	ca. 1515	Vigneulles: *Les Cent Nouvelles Nouvelles*
1515	Marignan		
1519	Charles V, Emperor		
1520	Wars against Charles V		
		1521	Anne de France: *Enseignemens* (+1535); Anne de Graville: *Palamon et Arcita*
		1523	Lesnauderie: *La Louange de mariage*
		1524	Anne de Graville: *La Belle Dame sans mercy*
1525	Pavie; Francis I made prisoner; Louise de Savoie, Regent		
1526	Treaty of Madrid; Francis I freed		
1529	Collège de France	1529	Tory: *Champ fleury*
1530	Lefèvre translates the Bible into French		
		1531	Marguerite de Navarre: *Miroir de l'âme pécheresse*
		1532	Finé: *Protomathesis;* Marot: *Adolescence clémentine;* Rabelais: *Pantagruel*

209

1534	Affaire des Placards	1534	Jeanne de Jussie: *Le Levain du Calvinisme;* Rabelais: *Gargantua;*
		1536	Marie Dentière: *La Guerre et delivrance de la ville de Genesve*
		ca. 1537	Jeanne Flore: *Contes amoureux;* Boccaccio: *Le Livre de la louange et vertu des nobles et cleres dames* (trans.)
		1538	Hélisenne de Crenne: *Les Angoysses douloureuses qui procedent d'amours*
1539	Ordonnance de Villers-Cotterêts	1539	Crenne: *Les Epistres familieres et invectives;* Dentière: *Epistre tres utile*
		1540	Des Essarts: *Amadis* (trans.)
1541– 1564	Calvin in Geneva	1541	La Borderie: *L'Amye de court;* Crenne: *Quatre Livres des Eneydes;* Fontaine: *La Contr'Amye de court;* Vivès: *Institution de la femme chrestienne* (trans.)
		1542	Héroët: *La Parfaicte Amye*
		1544	Scève: *Délie*
1545	Council of Trent (1549, 1551–1552, 1562–1563)	1545	Boccaccio: *Decameron* (trans. Antoine le Maçon); Crenne: *Songe;* Pernette du Guillet: *Rymes*
		1546	Rabelais: *Tiers Livre*
1547	Death of Francis I	1547	Du Fail: *Propos rustiques et facetieux;*
1547– 1559	Reign of Henri II		Marguerite de Navarre: *Les Marguerites de la Marguerite des Princesses; Les Prisons; La Navire*
		1548	Marguerite de Navarre: *Comédie de Mont-de-Marsan;* Rabelais: *Quart Livre* (first eleven chapters); Sébillet: *Art poétique françois*
1549	Death of Marguerite de Navarre	1549	Du Bellay: *Deffence et illustration; Olive;* Marguerite de Navarre: *Pieces mystiques;* Tyard: *Erreurs amoureuses*
		1550	Ronsard: *Odes*
		1551	Leone Ebreo: *De L'Amour* (trans. Tyard)
		1552	Rabelais: *Quart Livre* (second ed.); Ronsard: *Amours;* Tyard: *Solitaire premier*
		1553	Postel: *Les Très Merveilleuses Victoires des femmes du nouveau monde;* Ronsard: *Amours, Folastries;* Taillemont: *Discours des champs faëz*
		1555	Louise Labé: *Oeuvres;* Peletier:

			Art poétique; Ronsard: *Continuation des amours*
		1556	Ronsard: *Nouvelle Continuation; Hymnes*
		1558	Des Périers: *Nouvelles Récréations et joyeux devis;* Du Bellay: *Antiquités, Regrets;* Marguerite de Navarre: *Histoire des amants fortunez* (ed. Boaisteau)
1559–1560	Reign of Francis II	1559	Marguerite de Navarre: *Heptaméron* (ed. Gruget)
1560–1574	Reign of Charles IX	1560	Pasquier: *Recherches de la France*
1562	Massacre at Wassy; Wars of Religion	1562	Anne de Marquets: *Sonets, prières et devises en forme de pasquins*
1566	Death of Louise Labé (born ca. 1524)		
		1568	Marquets: *Les Divines Poesies de Marc Antoine Flaminius* (+1569)
		1570–1573	D'Aubigné:*Printemps* (unpubl.)
		1571	Marie de Costeblanche: *Trois Dialogues de M. Pierre Messie;* Georgette de Montenay: *Emblemes*
1572	St. Bartholomew's Day Massacres (August 23–24)	1572	Yver: *Le Printemps*
1574–1589	Reign of Henri III		
		1577	D'Amboise: *Instruction aux jeunes dames* (trans. of *La Rafaella* by Piccolomini)
		1578	Madeleine and Catherine des Roches; *Oeuvres;* Ronsard: fifth collective ed. of the *Oeuvres* (first publ. of *Sur la mort de Marie* and *Sonnets pour Hélène*)
		1579	Des Roches: *Oeuvres* (2d ed.)
		1580	Montaigne: *Essais* (I, II)
		1581	Marie de Romieu: *Premières Oeuvres poétiques*
		1581	D'Amboise: *Dialogues et devis des demoiselles* (+1583)
		1582	Des Roches: *La Puce de Madame des Roches* (+1583)
		1583	Des Roches: *Secondes Oeuvres;* Poissenot: *L'Eté*
		1584	Bouchet: *Les Serées* (I); D'Amboise: *Les Néapolitaines;* La Croix du Maine: *Bibliothèque;* Marie Le Gendre: *Cabinet des saines affections;* Turnèbe: *Les Contens*

		1584–	Brantôme: *Vie des dames galantes*
		1614	(ed. 1666); *Vie des dames illustres* (ed. 1666)
		1585	Du Fail: *Contes d'Eutrapel;* Du Verdier: *Bibliothèque françoise*
1586–	Marguerite de Valois's imprison-	1586	Des Roches: *Missives*
1605	ment at the Château of Usson		
		1587	Cholières: *Après-Dînées;* Nicole Estienne, dame Liébault: *Les Miseres de la femme mariée;* Le Poulchre: *Le Passe-temps;* Ronsard: 7th collective ed. of the *Oeuvres* (posth.)
		1588	Montaigne: *Essais* (I, II, III)
1589	Death of Catherine of Medicis		
1589–	Reign of Henri IV		
1610			
		1592	Montaigne: *Essais* (Bordeaux ed.)
		1594	Marie Le Jars de Gournay: *Le Proumenoir*
		1594	Gabrielle de Coignard: *Oeuvres chrestiennes* (+1595)
		1595	Gournay: *"Préface" aux Essais de Montaigne;* Montaigne: *Essais* (posth. ed.; M. de Gournay, ed.)
		1596	Marie Le Gendre: *L'Exercice de l'âme vertueuse*
		1597–	Bouchet: *Les Serées* (II and III)
		1598	
1598	Edict of Nantes		
		1600	Artus Thomas: *Qu'il est bienséant que les filles soient sçavantes*
		1602	Jacqueline de Miremont: *Apologie pour les dames*
		1604	Charlotte de Brachart: *Harengue*
		1605	Marquets: *Sonets spirituels*
1610	Assassination of Henri IV; Marie of Medicis, Regent		
		1616	D'Aubigné: *Tragiques*
		1622	Gournay: *Egalité des hommes et des femmes*
		1626	Gournay: *L'Ombre*

Bibliography
ℬ

INDIVIDUAL AUTHORS

HELISENNE DE CRENNE

Sixteenth-Century Editions

Crenne, Hélisenne de. *Les Angoysses douloureuses qui procedent d'amours.* Paris: Denys Janot, 1538.

———. *Les Epistres familieres et invectives.* Paris: Denys Janot, 1539.

———. *Les Quatre Premiers Livres des Eneydes du treselegant poete Virgile, traduictz de latin en prose Francoyse par ma dame Hélisenne, à la traduction desquelz y a pluralité de propos qui par maniere de phrase y son adjoustez: ce que beaucoup sert à l'elucidation et decoration desdictz livres, dirigez à tresillustre et tresauguste Prince Françoys, premier de ce nom invictissime Roy de France.* Paris: Denys Janot, 1541.

———. *Les Oeuvres de Ma Dame Helisenne de Crenne. A Sçavoir, Les Angoysses douloureuses qui procedent d'amours. Les Epistres familieres & invectives. Le Songe de ladicte Dame, le tout reveu & corrigé de nouveau par elle.* Paris: Estienne Grouleau, 1560.

Modern Editions

———. "*Les Angoysses douloureuses qui procedent d'amours* (1538). A Critical Edition based on the Original Text with Introduction, Notes, and Glossary." Ed. Harry Rennell Secor, Jr. Ph. D. diss., Yale University, 1957.

———. *Les Angoysses douloureuses qui procedent d'amours. Première partie.* Ed. Paule Demats. Paris: Belles Lettres, 1968.

———. *Les Angoysses douloureuses qui procedent d'amours. Première Partie.* Ed. Jérôme Vercruysse. Paris: Lettres Modernes, 1968.

———. *Les Oeuvres de Madame Helisenne de Crenne.* Paris: Estienne Grouleau, 1560. Reprint. Geneva: Slatkine, 1977.

English Translation

A Renaissance Woman: Hélisenne's Personal and Invectives Letters. Ed. and trans. Marianna M. Mustacchi and Paul J. Archambault. Syracuse, N.Y.: Syracuse University Press, 1986.

Selective Bibliography

Baker, M. J. "*Fiammetta* and The *Angoysses douloureuses qui procedent d'amours.*" *Symposium* 27, no. 4 (1973): 303–308.

———. "France's First Sentimental Novel and Novels of Chivalry." *Bibliothèque d'Humanisme et Renaissance* 36 (1974): 33–45.

Beaulieu, Jean-Philippe. "Erudition and Aphasia in Hélisenne de Crenne's *Angoysses douloureuses qui procedent d'amours.*" *L'Esprit Créateur* 29, no. 3 (Fall 1989): 36–42.

Bergal, Irène. "Hélisenne de Crenne: A XVIth-Century Novelist." Ph. D. diss., University of Minnesota, 1968.

Charasson, Henriette. "Les Origines de la sentimentalité moderne: d'Hélisenne de Crenne à Jean de Tinan." *Mercure de France* 86 (1910): 193–216.

Conley, Tom. "Feminism, 'Ecriture,' and the Closed Room: The *Angoysses douloureuses qui procedent d'amours.*" *Symposium* 27, no. 4 (1973): 322–331.

Cottrell, Robert D. "Female Subjectivity and Libidinal Infractions: Hélisenne de Crenne's *Angoysses douloureuses qui procedent d'amours.*" *French Forum* 16 (1991): 5–20.

Debaisieux, Martine. "'Des dames du temps jadis': fatalité culturelle et identité féminine dans *Les Angoysses douloureuses.*" *Symposium* 4, no. 1 (1987): 28–41.

Delle Robbins-Herring, Kittye. "Hélisenne de Crenne: Champion of Women's Rights." In *Women Writers of the Renaissance and Reformation.* Ed. Katharina Wilson. Athens: University of Georgia Press, 1987. 177–218.

Guillerm, Luce. "La Prison des textes ou *Les Angoysses douloureuses qui procedent d'amours.*" *Revue des Sciences Humaines* 196 (1984): 9–32.

Larsen, Anne. "The Rhetoric of Self-Defense in *Les Angoysses douloureuses qui procedent d'amours.*" *Kentucky Romance Quarterly* 29, no. 3 (1982): 235–243.

Nash, Jerry. "'Exerçant oeuvres viriles': Feminine Anger and Feminist (Re)Writing in Hélisenne de Crenne." *L'Esprit Créateur* 30, no. 4 (1990): 38–48.

Neubert, Fritz. "Hélisenne de Crenne und ihr Werk." *Zeitschrift für französische Sprache und Literatur* 80 (December 1970): 291–322.

Walstein, Helen. "A Woman of the Renaissance." Ph. D. diss., Wayne State University, 1965.

Winn, Colette H. "Perception spatiale dans *Les Angoysses douloureuses* d'Hélisenne de Crenne." *Degré Second* 9 (September 1985): 1–14.

———. "La Symbolique du regard dans *Les Angoysses douloureuses qui procedent d'amours.*" *Orbis Litterarum* 40 (1985): 207–227.

———. "R-écrire le féminin: *Les Angoysses douloureuses qui procedent d'amours* d'Hélisenne de Crenne (1ère partie): autour des notions de transgression et de 'jouyssance'." *Renaissance et Réforme*, 16, no. 1 (1992): 39–55.

Wood, Diane. "Literary Devices and Rhetorical Techniques in the Works of Hélisenne de Crenne." Ph. D. diss., University of Wisconsin-Madison, 1975.

MADELEINE DES ROCHES AND CATHERINE DES ROCHES

Sixteenth-Century Editions

Des Roches, Madeleine, and Catherine des Roches. *Les Oeuvres de Mes-dames des Roches de Poëtiers mere et fille.* Paris: Abel L'Angelier, 1578.

———. *Les Oeuvres de Mes-dames des Roches de Poëtiers mere et fille. Seconde édition. Corrigée et augmentée de la Tragi-comédie de Tobie et autres oeuvres poëtiques.* Paris: Abel L'Angelier, 1579.

———. *Les Secondes Oeuvres.* Poitiers: Chez Nicolas Courtoys, 1583.

———. *Les Missives de Mes-dames des Roches de Poitiers mere et fille. Avec le Ravissement de Proserpine prins du Latin de Clodian. Et Autres Imitations et meslanges poëtiques.* Paris: Chez Abel L'Angelier, 1586.

Des Roches, Catherine, et al. *La Puce de Madame des Roches. Qui est un recueil de divers poemes Grecs, Latins et François, composez par plusieurs doctes Personnages aux Grands Jours tenus à Poitiers l'an M.D.LXXIX.* Paris: Chez Abel L'Angelier, 1582, 1583.

English Translations

Madeleine des Roches's "Ode première" and "Réponse à sa fille." In *The Defiant Muse: French Feminist Poems from the Middle Ages to the Present —A Bilingual Anthology.* Ed. Domna C. Stanton. New York: Feminist Press, 1985. 40–41, 46–47.

———. Catherine des Roches's "L'Agnodice" and "A ma quenouille." In *The Defiant Muse* 62–63, 70–71.

"Catherine des Roches's *Epistre à sa mere* (1579)." Annotated translation by Anne R. Larsen. *Allegorica* 7 (1982): 58–64.

"Catherine des Roches's *Femme Forte décrite par Salomon.*" Annotated translation by Anne R. Larsen. *Allegorica* 12 (1991): 43–52.

Translation of a Sampling of Madeleine and Catherine des Roches's works. Trans. Anne R. Larsen. In *Women Writers of the Renaissance and Reformation.* Ed. Katharina Wilson. 232–259.

Selective Bibliography

Berriot-Salvadore, Evelyne. "Les Femmes dans les cercles intellectuels de la Renaissance: de la fille prodige à la précieuse." *Etudes Corses, Etudes Littéraires—Mélanges offerts au Doyen François Pitti-Ferrandi.* Le Cerf, Publications du Centre des Langues et de la Communication de l'Université de Corse, 1989. 210–237.

Diller, George E. *Les Dames des Roches: Etude sur la vie littéraire à Poitiers dans la deuxième moitié du XVIe siècle.* Paris: Droz, 1936.

Jones, Ann Rosalind. "Nets and Bridles: Early Modern Conduct Books and Sixteenth-Century Women's Lyrics." In *The Ideology of Conduct.* Ed. Nancy Armstrong and Leonard Tennenhouse. New York: Methuen, 1987. 39–72.

———. "Writing to Live: Pedagogical Poetics in Isabella Whitney and Catherine des Roches." In her *Currency of Eros: Women's Love Lyric in Europe, 1540–1620.* Bloomington: Indiana University Press, 1990. 36–78.

Kupisz, Kazimierz. "Dans le sillage de Louise Labé (Louise Labé et Catherine des Roches)." In *Il Rinascimento a Lione.* 2 vols. Ed. Antonio Possenti and Giulia Mastrangelo. Rome: Dell'Ateneo, 1988. 2: 529–547.

Larsen, Anne R. "Les Dames des Roches: The French Humanist Scholars." In *Women Writers of the Renaissance and Reformation.* Ed. Katharina Wilson. 232–259.

———. "Catherine des Roches (1542–1587): Humanism and the Learned Woman." *The Journal of the Rocky Mountain Medieval and Renaissance Association* 8 (1987): 97–117.

———. "Reading/Writing and Gender in the Renaissance: The Case of Catherine des Roches (1542–1587)." *Symposium* 41, no. 4 (Fall 1987): 292–308.

———. "Legitimizing the Daughter's Writing: Catherine des Roches's Proverbial Good Wife." *The Sixteenth Century Journal* 21, no. 4 (1990): 559–574.

Sankovitch, Tilde A. *French Women Writers and the Book: Myths of Access and Desire.* Syracuse: Syracuse University Press, 1987. 43–71.

Schutz, A. H. "The Group of the Dames des Roches in XVIth-Century Poitiers." *Publications of the Modern Language Association* 48 (1933): 648–654.

Winn, Colette H. "Mère/fille/femme/muse: maternité et créativité dans les oeuvres des Dames des Roches." *Travaux de Littérature* 4 (1991): 55–68.

Yandell, Cathy. "Of Lice and Women: Rhetoric and Gender in *La Puce de Madame des Roches.*" *Journal of Medieval and Renaissance Studies* 21 (1990): 123–135.

PERNETTE DU GUILLET
Sixteenth-Century Editions

Du Guillet, Pernette. *Rymes de gentile, et vertueuse dame, D. Pernette du Guillet, Lyonnoise.* Lyon: Chez Jean de Tournes, 1545.
————. *Rithmes et poesies.* Paris: Chez Jeanne de Marnef, 1546, 1547.
————. *Rymes.* Lyon: Chez Jean de Tournes, 1552.

Modern Editions

Du Guillet, Pernette. *Rymes.* Ed. Victor Graham. Geneva: Droz, 1968.
————. *Rymes.* Ed. Françoise Charpentier. Paris: Gallimard, 1983. (In the same volume with *Oeuvres poétiques* of Louise Labé.)

English Translations

Epigrams 2, 4, 5, 8, 13, 17, 24, 26, 31; Chansons 5, 7, 9; Elegy 2. Trans. Ann Rosalind Jones. In *Women Writers of the Renaissance and Reformation.* 224–231.
Epigrams 2, 21, 22, 24, 48; Chansons 2 and 3. Translated into prose. In *Penguin Book of French Verse.* Ed. Geoffrey Brereton. Harmondsworth: Penguin, 1958. 2: 20–24.

Selective Bibliography

Aynard, Joseph. *Les Poètes lyonnais, précurseurs de la Pléiade.* Paris: Ed. Bossard, 1924.
Ardouin, Paul. *Maurice Scève, Pernette du Guillet, Louise Labé: l'amour à Lyon au temps de la Renaissance.* Paris: Nizet, 1981.
————. *Pernette du Guillet, l'heureuse Renaissante—Miracle de l'amour, de la lumière et de la poésie.* Paris: Nizet, 1991.
Bots, W.J.A. "Maurice Scève, Pernette du Guillet, ou la victoire de deux voix sur les escarpements de la syntaxe." *L'Information Littéraire* 39, no. 3 (1987): 102–106.
Buche, Joseph. "Pernette du Guillet et la *Délie* de Maurice Scève." In *Mélanges de philologie offerts à Ferdinand Brunot.* Paris, 1904. Reprint. Geneva: Slatkine, 1972. 33–39.
Cottrell, Robert D. "Pernette du Guillet's 'Rymes': An Adventure in Ideal Love." *Bibliothèque d'Humanisme et Renaissance* 31 (1969): 553–571.
DellaNeva, Joann. "Mutare/Mutatus: Pernette du Guillet's Actaeon Myth and the Silencing of the Poetic Voice." In *Women in French Literature.* Ed. Michel Guggenheim. Saratoga, Calif.,: Anma Libri, 1988. 47–55.
Donaldson-Evans, Lance. "The Taming of the Muse: The Female Poetic Voice in Pernette du Guillet's 'Rymes.'" In *Pre-Pléiade Poetry.* Ed. Jerry Nash. Lexington: French Forum Publishers, 1985. 84–96.
Griffin, Robert. "Pernette du Guillet's Response to Scève: A Case for Abstract Love." *L'Esprit Créateur* 5, no. 2 (1965): 110–116.
James, Karen Simroth. "Pernette du Guillet: Spiritual Union and Poetic Distance." *French Literature Series* 16 (1989): 27–37.
Jones, Ann Rosalind. "Assimilation with a Difference: Renaissance Women Poets and Literary Influence." *Yale French Studies* 62 (1981): 135–153.
————. "Pernette du Guillet: The Lyonnais Neoplatonist." In *Women Writers of the Renaissance and Reformation.* 219–231.
————. "The Poetics of Group Identity: Self-Commemoration through Dialogue in Pernette du Guillet and Tullia d'Aragona." In her *Currency of Eros: Women's Love Lyric in Europe, 1540–1620.* 79–117.

Mathieu-Castellani, Gisèle. "La Parole chétive: les *Rymes* de Pernette du Guillet." *Littérature* 73 (1989): 47–60.

———. "Parole d'Echo? Pernette au miroir des *Rymes*." *L'Esprit Créateur* 30, no. 4 (1990): 61–71.

Miller, Joyce. "Convention and Form in the *Rymes* of Pernette du Guillet." Ph. D. diss., University of Pennsylvania, 1977.

Perry, Theodore Anthony. "Pernette du Guillet's Poetry of Love and Desire." In his *Erotic Spirituality*. Birmingham: University of Alabama Press, 1980. 53–67.

Saulnier, V. L. "Etude sur Pernette du Guillet." *Bibliothèque d'Humanisme et Renaissance* 4 (1944): 7–119.

Winn, Colette H. "Le Chant de la nouvelle née: les *Rymes* de Pernette du Guillet." *Poétique* 78 (1989): 208–217.

MARIE LE JARS DE GOURNAY
Sixteenth-Century Editions

Gournay, Marie le Jars de. *Le Proumenoir de Monsieur de Montaigne, par sa fille d'alliance.* Paris: Abel L'Angelier, 1594.

———. "Preface" to Montaigne's *Essais.* Paris: Abel L'Angelier, 1595. Reprinted with revisions in the 1598, 1600, 1604, 1611, 1617, 1625, and 1635 editions of the *Essais.*

———. *Bienvenue de Monseigneur le Duc d'Anjou (Abrégé d'institution pour le prince souverain).* Paris: Fleury Bourriquant, 1608.

———. *Adieu de l'Ame du Roy de France et de Navarre, Henry le Grand à la Royne, avec la Défence des Pères Jesuites.* Paris: Fleury Bourriquant, 1610.

———. *Version de quelques pièces de Virgile, Tacite et Saluste, avec l'Institution de Monseigneur, frère unique du Roy, par la Damoiselle de Gournay et M. Bertaut, évêque de Séez.* Paris: Fleury Bourriquant, 1619.

———. *Egalité des hommes et des femmes. A la Reyne.* Paris, n. p., 1622.

———. *Remerciement au Roy.* Dédicace signed Gournay. n. p., 1624.

———. *L'Ombre de la Damoiselle de Gournay. Oeuvre composée de meslanges.* Paris: Jean Libert, 1626.

———. *Les Advis ou les Presens de la Demoiselle de Gournay.* Paris: Toussainct-Du-Bray, 1634.

———. *Les Advis ou les Presens de la Demoiselle de Gournay* (With *Apologie pour celle qui escrit*). Paris: Jean Du-Bray, 1641.

Modern Editions

Gournay, Marie le Jars de. *Le Proumenoir de Monsieur de Montaigne.* Ed. Patricia Francis Cholakian. Delmar, N.Y.: Scholars' Facsimiles & Reprints, 1985.

———. "L'Egalité des Hommes et des Femmes" (1622). Ed. Mario Schiff. Paris: Champion, 1910. Reprint. Geneva: Slatkine, 1978.

———. "L'Egalité des Hommes et des Femmes" (1622) and "Grief des Dames." In *Marie de Gournay: Fragments d'un discours féminin.* Ed. Elyane Dezon-Jones. Paris: Librairie José Corti, 1988.

———. "Préface sur les Essais de Michel Seigneur de Montaigne, par sa fille d'alliance." Ed. François Rigolot. *Montaigne Studies* 1 (1989): 22–54.

English Translation

"Of the Equality of Men and Women" and "The Complaint of the Ladies." Trans. Eva M. Sartori. *Allegorica* 9 (Winter 1987): 135–164.

Selective Bibliography

Bauschatz, Cathleen. "Marie de Gournay's 'Préface de 1595': A Critical Evaluation." *Bulletin de la Société des Amis de Montaigne* 3–4 (1986): 73–82.

———. "'L'horreur de mon exemple' in Marie de Gournay's *Proumenoir de Monsieur de Montaigne (1594)*." *Ecrire au féminin à la Renaissance.* Ed. François Rigolot. *L'Esprit Créateur* 30, no. 4 (Winter 1990): 97–105.

———. "Marie de Gournay and the Crisis of Humanism." In *Humanism in Crisis. The Decline of the French Renaissance.* Ed. Philippe Desan. Ann Arbor: University of Michigan Press, 1991. 279–294.

———. "Imitation, Writing, and Self-Study in Marie de Gournay's 1595 'Preface' to Montaigne's *Essais.*" In *Contending Kingdoms: Historical, Psychological, and Feminist Approaches to the Literature of Sixteenth-Century England and France.* Ed. Marie-Rose Logan and Peter Rudnytsky. Detroit: Wayne State University Press, 1991. 346–364.

Boase, Alan. *The Fortunes of Montaigne: A History of the Essays in France (1580–1669).* London: Methuen, 1935. Chapters 4 and 5.

Casevitz, Thérèse. "Melle. de Gournay et le féminisme." *Revue Bleue* 63 (December 1925): 768–771.

Chenot, Anna Adèle. "Marie de Gournay, Feminist and Friend of Montaigne." *Poet Lore* 34 (1923): 63–71.

Desan, Philippe. "'Cet orphelin qui m'estoit commis': la préface de Marie de Gournay à l'édition de 1635 des *Essais.*" *Montaigne Studies* 2, no. 2 (1990): 58–67.

Dezon-Jones, Elyane. "Marie de Gournay: le je/u/ palimpseste." *L'Esprit Créateur* 23, no. 2 (1983): 26–36.

———. *Marie de Gournay: fragments d'un discours féminin.* Paris: Corti, 1988.

Holmes, Peggy. "Marie de Gournay's Defense of Baroque Imagery." *French Studies* (April 1954): 122–131.

Horowitz, Maryanne Cline. "Marie de Gournay, Editor of the *Essais* of Michel de Montaigne: A Case-Study in Mentor-Protégée Friendship." *The Sixteenth Century Journal* 17, no. 3 (1986): 271–284.

Ilsley, Marjorie. *A Daughter of the Renaissance: Marie le Jars de Gournay, Her Life and Works.* The Hague: Mouton, 1963.

Insdorf, Cecile. *Montaigne and Feminism.* Studies in the Romance Languages and Literatures, no. 194. Chapel Hill: University of North Carolina Press, 1977.

Maclean, Ian. "Marie de Gournay et la préhistoire du discours féminin." In *Femmes et pouvoirs sous l'ancien régime.* Ed. Danielle Haase-Dubosc and Eliane Viennot. Paris: Rivages, 1991. 120–133.

Regosin, Richard L. "Montaigne's Dutiful Daughter." *Montaigne Studies* 3 (1991): 103–127.

Sankovitch, Tilde. "Marie Le Jars de Gournay: The Self-Portrait of an Androgynous Hero." In her *French Women Writers and the Book.* 73–99.

Schiff, Mario. *La Fille d'alliance de Montaigne, Marie de Gournay.* Paris: Champion, 1910.

Stanton, Domna. "Women as Object and Subject of Exchange: Marie de Gournay's *Le Proumenoir.*" *L'Esprit Créateur* 23 (Summer 1983): 9–25.

———. "Autogynography: The Case of Marie de Gournay's *Apologie pour celle qui escrit.*" *French Literature Series* 12 (1985): 18–31.

Uildricks, Anne. *Les Idées littéraires de Mlle de Gournay.* Gröningen, 1962.

Venesoen, Constant. *Etudes sur la littérature féminine au XVIIe siècle: Mademoiselle de Gournay, Mademoiselle de Scudéry, Madame de Villedieu, Madame de Lafayette.* Birmingham, Ala.: Summa Publications, Inc., 1990.

Louise Labé

Sixteenth-Century Editions

Labé, Louise. *Euvres de Louize Labé Lionnoize.* Lyon: Jean de Tournes, 1555.
———. *Euvres de Louize Labé Lionnoize.* ("Revues et corrigées par la dite Dame.") Lyon: Jean de Tournes, 1556.
———. *Euvres de Louize Labé Lionnoize.* Lyon: Jean de Tournes, 1556.
———. *Euvres de Louyse Labé Lionnoise.* Rouen: Jean Garou, 1556.

Modern Editions

Labé, Louise. *Euvres de Louize Labé Lionnoize.* Ed. N. F. Cochard and Breghot de Lut. Lyon: Drant and Perrin, 1824.
———. *Oeuvres de Louise Labé.* Ed. Prosper Blanchemain. Paris: Librairie des Bibliophiles, 1875.
———. *Oeuvres de Louise Labé.* Ed. Charles Boy. 2 vols. Paris: A Lemerre, 1887. Reprint. Geneva: Slatkine, 1968.
———. *Oeuvres complètes.* Ed. Enzo Guidici. Geneva: Droz, 1981.
———. *Oeuvres de Louise Labé, précédées des Rymes de Pernette du Guillet.* Ed. Françoise Charpentier. Paris: Gallimard, 1983.
———. *Oeuvres complètes.* Ed. François Rigolot. Paris: Flammarion, 1986.

English Translations

Labé, Louise. *The Debate Betweene Follie and Love.* Trans. Robert Greene, Maister of Artes. 4th ed. London: H. Lownes, 1608.
———. *Débat.* Ed. and trans. Edwin Marion Cox. London: Williams and Morgata, 1925.
———. *Sonnets of Louise Labé, "La Belle Cordière".* Trans. Alta Lind Cook. Toronto: University of Toronto Press, 1950.
———. *Twenty-Four Love Sonnets.* Trans. Frances Lobb. London, 1950.
———. *The Sonnets.* Ed. and trans. Bettina L. Knapp. Paris: Minard, 1964.
———. *Sonnets.* Trans. Graham Dunstan Martin. With an Introduction and Commentaries by Peter Sharratt. Austin: University of Texas Press, 1972.

Selective Bibliography

Baker, M. J. "The Sonnets of Louise Labé: A Reappraisal." *Neophilologus* 60, no. 1 (January 1976): 20–30.
Berriot, Karine. *Louise Labé. La Belle Rebelle et le François nouveau, suivi des Oeuvres complètes.* Paris: Seuil, 1985.
Chan, Andrea. "Petrarchism and Neoplatonism in Louise Labé's Concept of Happiness." *Australian Journal of French Studies* 14 (1977): 213–232.
———. "The Function of the Beloved in the Poetry of Louise Labé." *Australian Journal of French Studies* 17 (1980): 46–57.
Charpentier, Françoise. "Les Voix du désir: le *Débat de Folie et d'Amour* de Louise Labé." *Le Signe et le texte: Etudes sur l'écriture au XVIe siècle en France.* Ed. Lawrence D. Kritzman. Lexington, Ky.: French Forum Publishers, 1990. 27–38.
Cottrell, Robert D. "The Problematics of Opposition in Louise Labé's *Débat de Folie et d'Amour.*" *French Forum* 12 (1987): 27–42.
Donaldson-Evans, Lance. *Love's Fatal Glance: A Study of Imagery in the Poets of the Ecole Lyonnaise.* University, Miss.: Romance Monographs, 1980.
Demerson, Guy, ed. *Louise Labé: les voix du lyrisme.* Saint-Etienne: Institut Claude Longeon.

Paris: Editions du CNRS, 1990. (Articles by Berriot-Salvadore, Charpentier, and Mathieu-Castellani, among others).

Freadman, Anne. "Poeta (1st. decl., n., fem.)." *Australian Journal of French Studies* 16 (1979): 152–165.

Guidici, Enzo. *Louise Labé e l'"Ecole lyonnaise": Studi e ricerche con documenti inediti.* Intro. Jean Tricou. Naples: Liguore, 1964.

———. *Louise Labé.* Paris: Nizet, 1981.

Guillot, Gérard. *Louise Labé.* Paris: Seghers, 1962.

Hanish, G. S. *Love Elegies of the Renaissance: Marot, Louise Labé and Ronsard.* Saratoga, Calif.: Anma Libri, 1979.

Harvey, Lawrence E. *The Aesthetics of the Renaissance Love Sonnet: An Essay on the Art of The Sonnet in the Poetry of Louise Labé.* Geneva: Droz, 1962.

Jondorf, Gillian. "Petrarchan Variations in Pernette du Guillet and Louise Labé." *Modern Language Review* 71, no. 4 (October 1976): 766–778.

Jones, Ann Rosalind. "Assimilation with a Difference: Renaissance Women Poets and Literary Influence." *Yale French Studies* 62 (1981): 135–153.

———. "Surprising Fame: Renaissance Gender Ideologies and Women's Lyric." In *The Poetics of Gender.* Ed. Nancy K. Miller. New York: Columbia University Press, 1986. 74–95.

———. "City Women and Their Audiences: Louise Labé and Veronica Franco." In *Rewriting the Renaissance.* Ed. Margaret W. Ferguson, Maureen Quilligan, Nancy J. Vickers. Chicago: University of Chicago Press, 1986. 299–316.

———. "Eros Equalized: Literary Cross-Dressing and the Defense of Women in Louise Labé and Veronica Franco." In her *Currency of Eros. Women's Love Lyric in Europe, 1540–1620.* 155–200.

Kupisz, Kazimierz. "L'Epître dédicatoire de Louise Labé à Mlle de Bourges." *Le Lingue straniere* 13 (1964): 17–28.

Larnac, Jean. *Louise Labé, la belle cordière de Lyon (1522?–1566).* Paris: Firmin-Didot et Cie, 1934.

Larsen, Anne R. "Louise Labé's *Débat de Folie et d'Amour:* Feminism and the Defense of Learning." *Tulsa Studies in Women's Literature* 2, no. 1 (Spring 1983): 43–55.

Logan, Marie-Rose. "La Portée théorique du *Débat de Folie et d'Amour* de Louise Labé." *Saggi e ricerche di letteratura francese* 16 (1977): 9–25.

Mathieu-Castellani, Gisèle. "Les Marques du féminin dans la parole amoureuse de Louise Labé." In *Louise Labé: les voix du lyrisme.* Ed. Guy Demerson. Saint-Etienne: Institut Claude Longeon. Paris: Editions du CNRS, 1990. 189–205.

Nash, Jerry C. "Louise Labé and Learned Levity." *Romance Notes* 21 (1980): 227–233.

———. "'Ne veuillez point condamner ma simplesse': Louise Labé and Literary Simplicity." *Res Publica Litterarum* 3 (1980): 91–100.

O'Connor, Dorothy. *Louise Labé, sa vie et son oeuvre.* Paris: Les Presses françaises, 1926.

Petry, Sandy. "The Character of the Speaker in the Poetry of Louise Labé." *French Review* 43, no. 4 (March 1970): 588–596.

Poliner, S. M. "'Signes d'amante' and the Dispossessed Lover: Louise Labé's Poetics of Inheritance." *Bibliothèque d'Humanisme et Renaissance* 46, no. 2 (1984): 323–342.

Prine, Jeanne. "Louise Labé: Poet of Lyon." In *Women Writers of the Renaissance and Reformation.* 132–157.

Rigolot, François. "Louise Labé et la redécouverte de Sappho." *Nouvelle Revue du XVIᵉ siècle* 1 (1983): 19–31.

———. "Signature et signification: les baisers de Louise Labé." *Romanic Review* 75, no. 1 (January 1984): 10–24.

———. "Gender vs. Sex Difference in Louise Labé's Grammar of Love." In *Rewriting the Renaissance.* 287–298.

———. "Les 'Sutils ouvrages' de Louise Labé, ou: quand Pallas devient Arachné." *Etudes littéraires* 20, no. 2 (1987): 43–60.

———. "Louise Labé et les 'Dames Lionnoises': les ambiguités de la censure." In *Le Signe et le texte: Etudes sur l'écriture au XVIe siècle en France*. Ed. Lawrence D. Kritzman. Lexington, Ky.: French Forum, 1990. 13–25.

———— and Julianne Jones Wright. "Les Irruptions de Folie: fonction idéologique du porteparole dans les *Oeuvres* de Louise Labé." *Ecrire au féminin à la Renaissance*. Ed. François Rigolot. *L'Esprit Créateur* 30 (1990): 72–83.

Schulze-Witzenrath, Elisabeth. *Die Originalität der Louise Labé. Studien zum weiblichen Petrarkismus*. Munich: Fink, 1974.

Tricou, Georges. "Louise Labé et sa famille." *Bibliothèque d'Humanisme et Renaissance* 5 (1944): 60–104.

Varty, Kenneth. "The Life and Legend of Louise Labé." *Nottingham Medieval Studies* 3 (1959): 78–108.

Wheatley, Katherine E. "A Woman of the Renaissance (Louise Labé)." *Forum* 9 (Spring 1971): 55–63.

Wiley, Karen F. "Louise Labé's Deceptive Petrarchism." *Modern Language Studies* 9 (1981): 51–60.

Zamaron, Fernand. *Louise Labé, dame de franchise*. Paris: Nizet, 1968.

Marguerite de Navarre

Principal Sixteenth-Century Editions

Navarre, Marguerite de. *Le Miroir de l'âme pécheresse*. Alençon: Chez Simon Du Bois, 1531.

————. *Le Miroir de tres chrestienne princesse Marguerite de France*. Paris: Chez Antoine Augereau, 1533.

————. *Les Marguerites de la Marguerite des Princesses très illustre royne de Navarre*. Lyon: Chez Jean de Tournes, 1547. 2 vols.

————. *Les Marguerites de la Marguerite des Princesses très illustre royne de Navarre*. Ed. Pierre de Tours. Lyon, 1549.

————. *Histoires des Amans fortunez, dédiées à très illustre princesse, Madame Marguerite de Bourbon, duchesse de Nivernois*. Ed. Pierre Boaistuau, dit Launay. Paris: Gilles Robinot, 1558.

————. *L'Heptaméron des Nouvelles de très illustre et très excellente Princesse Marguerite de Valois, Royne de Navarre, remis en son vray ordre, confus auparavant en sa première impression et dédié à très illustre et très vertueuse Princesse Jeanne de Foix, Royne de Navarre*. Ed. Claude Gruget, parisien. Paris: Jean Caveiller, 1559.

————. *L'Heptaméron. Paris: Chez Gilles Robinot, 1576*.

Modern Editions

Navarre, Marguerite de. *Dialogue en forme de vision nocturne*. Ed. Pierre Jourda. Paris: Champion, 1926. Extrait de la *Revue du seizième siècle* 13 (1926): 177–204.

————. *Théâtre profane*. Ed. V.-L. Saulnier. Geneva: Droz, 1946.

————. *La Navire, ou Consolation du Roi François Ier à sa soeur Marguerite*. Ed. Robert Marichal. Paris: Champion, 1956.

————. *L'Heptaméron. Ed. Pierre Jourda. Conteurs français du XVIe siècle*. Paris: Gallimard, coll. Bibl. de la Pléiade, 1956. 70–113.

————. *L'Heptaméron*. Ed. Michel François. Paris: Garnier, 1967.

————. *L'Heptaméron*. Ed. Simone de Reyff. Paris: Flammarion, 1982.

————. *Les Marguerites de la Marguerite des Princesses*. Ed. Félix Frank. 4 vols. Paris; Jouaust, 1873. Reprint. Geneva: Slatkine, 1970.

————. *Suyte des Marguerites de la Marguerite des Princesses, très illustre Royne de Navarre*. Lyon: Jean de Tournes, 1547. Facsimile Reprint, ed. Ruth Thomas. The Hague: Johnson Reprint Corporation, Mouton, 1970.

———. *Chansons spirituelles.* Ed. Georges Dottin. Geneva: Droz, 1971.

———. *La Coche.* Ed. Robert Marichal. Geneva: Droz, 1971.

———. *Le Miroir de l'âme pécheresse.* Ed. Joseph L. Allaire. Munich: Fink, 1972.

———. *Les Prisons.* Ed. Simone Glasson. Geneva: Droz, 1978.

———. *Guillaume Briçonnet-Marguerite d'Angoulême. Correspondance (1521–1524).* Ed. Christine Martineau, Michel Veissière, and Henry Heller. 2 vols. Geneva: Droz, I, 1975; II, 1979.

English Translations

The Fortunate Lovers. Trans. Arthur Machen. London: George Redway, 1887.

The Heptameron; or, Tales and Novels. Trans. Arthur Machen. London: G. Routledge, 1905.

The Heptameron. Trans. P. A. Chilton. Harmondsworth: Penguin Books, 1984.

Selective Bibliography

Ahmed, Esham. "Marguerite de Navarre's *Chansons spirituelles* and the Poet's Passion." *Bibliothèque d'Humanisme et Renaissance* 52, no. 1 (1990): 37–52.

Atance, Félix R. "Les Religieux de l'*Heptaméron:* Marguerite de Navarre et les novateurs." *Archiv für Reformationsgeschichte* 64 (1974): 185–210.

———. "Les Comédies profanes de Marguerite de Navarre: aspects de la satire religieuse en France au XVIᵉ siècle." *Revue d'histoire et de philosophie religieuse* 66 (1976): 289–313.

———. "Marguerite de Navarre et ses activités en faveur des novateurs." *Neophilologus* 60 (1976): 505–524.

Auld, Louis E. "Music as Dramatic Device in the Secular Theatre of Marguerite de Navarre." *Renaissance Drama* 7 (1976): 192–217.

Bideaux, Michel. '*L'Heptaméron*': *de l'enquête au débat.* Paris: Editions Inter Universitaires, 1992.

Cazauran, Nicole. *L'Heptaméron de Marguerite de Navarre.* Paris: C.D.U. & SEDES, 1976. Reprint, 1991.

Cholakian, Patricia Francis. *Rape and Writing in the Heptameron of Marguerite de Navarre.* "Ad Feminam" Series. Carbondale: Southern Illinois University Press, 1991.

Cottrell, Robert D. *The Grammar of Silence: A Reading of Marguerite de Navarre's Poetry.* Washington, D.C.: Catholic University of America Press, 1986.

Dassonville, Michel. "Le Testament spirituel de Marguerite de Navarre." In *From Marot to Montaigne. Essays on French Renaissance Literature.* Ed. Raymond La Charité. Suppl. of *Kentucky Romance Quarterly* 19, no. 1 (1972): 109–124.

Davis, Betty J. *The Storytellers in Marguerite de Navarre's Heptameron.* Lexington, Ky.: French Forum Publishers, 1978.

Delègue, Yves. "La Présence et ses doubles dans l'*Heptaméron*." *Bibliothèque d'Humanisme et Renaissance* 52 (1990): 269–291.

Febvre, Lucien. *Amour sacré, amour profane: autour de l'Heptaméron.* Paris: Gallimard, 1944.

Freccero, Carla. "Marguerite de Navarre and the Politics of Maternal Sovereignty." *Cosmos* 7. Special Issue on *Rethinking Queenship,* ed. Louise Fradenburg. Forthcoming.

———. "Rewriting the Rhetoric of Desire in the *Heptameron*." In *Contending Kingdoms: Historical, Psychological, and Feminist Approaches to the Literature of Sixteenth-Century England and France.* Detroit: Wayne State University Press, 1991. 298–312.

Gelernt, Jules. *World of Many Loves: The Heptameron of Marguerite de Navarre.* Chapel Hill: University of North Carolina Press, 1966.

Heller, Henry. "Marguerite de Navarre and the Reformers of Meaux." *Bibliothèque d'Humanisme et Renaissance* 33 (1971): 271–310.

Jourda, Pierre. *Marguerite d'Angoulême, Duchesse d'Alençon, Reine de Navarre (1492–1549):*

Etude biographique et littéraire. 2 vols. Paris: Champion, 1930. Reprint. Geneva: Slatkine, 1978.

Kritzman, Lawrence. "Verba erotica: Marguerite de Navarre and the Rhetoric of Silence." In his *The Rhetoric of Sexuality and the Literature of the French Renaissance.* Cambridge: Cambridge University Press, 1991. 45–56.

Kupisz, Kazimierz. "Autour de la technique de l'*Heptaméron.*" In *La Nouvelle française à la Renaissance.* Ed. Lionello Sozzi and V.-L. Saulnier. Geneva: Slatkine, 1981. 379–395.

Lajarte, Philippe de. "*L'Heptaméron* et le ficinisme: rapports d'un texte et d'une idéologie." *Revue des Sciences Humaines* 37 (1972): 339–371.

————. "*L'Heptaméron* et la naissance du récit moderne." *Littérature* 17 (1975): 31–42.

————. "Le Prologue de l'*Heptaméron* et le processus de production de l'oeuvre." In *La Nouvelle française à la Renaissance.* 397–424.

————. "Modes du discours et formes d'altérité dans les 'Nouvelles' de Marguerite de Navarre." *Littérature* 55 (1984): 64–73.

————. "Des Nouvelles de Marguerite de Navarre à la *Princesse de Clèves:* notes sur quelques transformations de l'écriture narrative de la Renaissance à l'âge classique." *Nouvelle Revue du seizième siècle* 6 (1988): 45–56.

Lebègue, Raymond. "Marguerite de Navarre et le théâtre." *Humanisme et Renaissance* 5 (1938): 330–333.

————. "Le Cuyder avant Montaigne et dans les *Essais.*" *Cahiers de l'Association Internationale des Etudes Françaises* 14 (1962): 275–284.

————. "La Fidélité conjugale dans l'*Heptaméron.*" In *La Nouvelle française à la Renaissance.* Ed. L. Sozzi and V.-L. Saulnier. Geneva: Slatkine, 1981. 425–433.

Lefranc, Abel. *Les Idées religieuses de Marguerite de Navarre.* 1898. Reprint. Geneva: Slatkine, 1969.

————. "Marguerite de Navarre et le Platonisme de la Renaissance." *Bibliothèque de l'Ecole des Chartes* 58 (1897): 259–292; 59 (1898): 712–757. Reprint. In his *Grands Ecrivains de la Renaissance.* Paris: Champion, 1914. 139–249.

Losse, Deborah N. "Distortion as a Means of Reassessment: Marguerite de Navarre's *Heptameron* and the 'Querelle des Femmes.'" *Journal of the Rocky Mountain Medieval and Renaissance Association* 3 (1982): 75–84.

————. "The Representation of Discourse in the Renaissance French *Nouvelle:* Bonaventure des Périers and Marguerite de Navarre." *Poetics Today* 3 (1985): 585–595.

————. "Authorial and Narrative Voice in the *Heptameron.*" *Renaissance and Reformation* 11 (1987): 223–242.

Lyons, John D. "The *Heptameron* and Unlearning from Example." In his *Exemplum: The Rhetoric of Example in Early Modern France and Italy.* Princeton: Princeton University Press, 1989. 72–117.

Martineau-Génieys, Christine. "Le Platonisme de Marguerite de Navarre?" *Réforme, Humanisme, Renaissance* 4 (1976): 12–35.

Masters, G. Mallary. "Structured Prisons, Imprisoned Structures: Marguerite de Navarre's *Prisons.*" *Renaissance Papers* 1973. Ed. Dennis G. Donavan and A. Leigh Deneef. Artes Gráficas Soler, S. A.-Jávea, 28. Valencia 8, 1974. 11–22.

Mathieu-Castellani, Gisèle. *La Conversation conteuse: les nouvelles de Marguerite de Navarre.* Paris: Presses Universitaires de France, 1992.

Parturier, E. "Les Sources du mysticisme de Marguerite de Navarre." *Revue de la Renaissance* 5 (1905): 1–16, 49–62. Reprint. Geneva: Slatkine, 1968.

Reynolds, Régine. *Les Devisants de l'Heptaméron: dix personnages en quête d'audience.* Washington, D.C.: University Press of America, 1977.

Sage, Pierre. "Le Platonisme de Marguerite de Navarre." *Travaux de Linguistique et de Littérature* 7, no. 2 (1969): 65–82.

Saulnier, V. L. "Marguerite de Navarre: art médiéval et pensée nouvelle." *Revue Universitaire* 63 (1954): 154–162.

————. "Marguerite de Navarre au temps de Briçonnet." *Bibliothèque d'Humanisme et Renaissance* 39 (1977): 437–478.

————. "Marguerite de Navarre au temps de Briçonnet. 2ᵉ et 3ᵉ parties." *Bibliothèque d'Humanisme et Renaissance* 40 (1978): 7–47, 193–237.

Sckommodau, Hans. *Die religiosen Dichtungen Margaretes von Navarra*. Koln: Westdeutscher Verlag, 1955.

Sommers, Paula. *Celestial Ladders: Readings in Marguerite de Navarre's Poetry of Spiritual Ascent*. Geneva: Droz, 1989.

Telle, Emile. *L'Oeuvre de Marguerite d'Angoulême, Reine de Navarre et la querelle des femmes*. Toulouse: Lion, 1937.

Tetel, Marcel. "Marguerite de Navarre et Montaigne: relativisme et paradoxe." In *From Marot to Montaigne: Essays on French Renaissance Literature*. Ed. Raymond C. La Charité. *Kentucky Romance Quarterly* 19, Suppl. 1 (1972): 125–135.

————. *Marguerite de Navarre's Heptameron: Themes, Language, and Structure*. Durham, N.C.: Duke University Press, 1973.

————. "The *Heptameron*, a Simulacrum of Love." In *Women Writers of the Renaissance and Reformation*. Ed. Katharina M. Wilson. 99–108.

Winandy, André. "Piety and Humanistic Symbolism in the Works of Marguerite de Navarre." *Image and Symbol in the Renaissance. Yale French Studies* 47 (1972): 145–169.

Winn, Colette H. "La Loi du silence dans *L'Heptaméron* de Marguerite de Navarre." *Romance Quarterly* 33, no. 2 (May 1986): 157–168.

————. "Gastronomy and Sexuality: Table Language in the *Heptameron*." *Journal of the Rocky Mountain Medieval and Renaissance Association* 7 (1986): 209–218.

————. "L'Expérience de la mort dans *La Navire* de Marguerite de Navarre: mysticisme et création poétique." In *Love and Death in the Renaissance*. Ed. Kenneth R. Bartlett, Konrad Eisenbichler, and Janice Liedl. Ottawa, Canada: Dovehouse Editions Inc., 1991. 199–219.

————. *L'Esthétique du jeu dans l'Heptaméron de Marguerite de Navarre*. Paris: Vrin. Montréal: Institut d'Etudes Médiévales, Université de Montréal, 1993.

MARGUERITE DE VALOIS

Sixteenth-Century Editions

Valois, Marguerite de. *Discours docte et subtil envoyé à l'autheur des Secrets moraux*. In *L'Excellence des femmes, avec la Response à l'autheur de l'Alphabet*. Paris: Chez Pierre Passy, 1618.

————. *Les Memoires de la roine Marguerite*. Publiées par Mauléon de Granier. Paris: C. Chappelain, 1628.

————. *La Ruelle Mal Assortie: ou entretiens amoureux d'une dame éloquente* (1644).

Modern Editions

Valois, Marguerite de. *Mémoires*. Ed. L. Lalanne. Paris: P. Jannet, 1858.

————. *La Ruelle Mal Assortie: ou entretiens amoureux d'une dame éloquente* (1644). Ed. L. Lalanne. Paris: Auguste Aubry, 1855.

————. *Mémoires de Marguerite de Valois, La Reine Margot, suivis de Lettres et autres écrits*. Ed. Yves Cazaux. Paris: Mercure de France, 1971.

English Translation

Valois, Marguerite de. *Memoirs of Marguerite de Valois*. Ed. and trans. Liselotte Dieckmann. Paris: Papers on French Seventeenth-Century Literature, 1984.

Selective Bibliography

Babelon, Jean. *La Reine Margot*. Paris, 1965.

Bauschatz, Cathleen M. "'Plaisir et proffict' in the Reading and Writing of Marguerite de Valois." *Tulsa Studies in Women's Literature* 7, no. 1 (Spring 1988): 27–48.

Delpech, Jeanine. "L'Inoubliable Reine Margot." *Nouvelles littéraires* (21 May 1953): 1–2.

Dumas, Alexandre. *La Reine Margot*. Paris: Calmann-Lévy, 1887.

Ferrière, Hector de la. *Trois Amoureuses au seizième siècle: Françoise de Rohan, Isabelle de Limeuil, la Reine Margot*. Paris: Calmann-Levy, 1885.

Haldane, Charlotte. *The Queen of Hearts, Margaret of Valois, 'La Reine Margot,' 1553–1615*. Indianapolis: Bobbs-Merrill, 1968.

Mariéjol, Jean H. *La Vie de Marguerite de Valois, reine de Navarre et de France (1553–1615)*. Paris, 1928. Reprint. Geneva: Slatkine, 1970.

Merki, Charles. *La Reine Margot et la fin des Valois (1553–1615)*. Paris: Plon-Nourrit et Cie, 1905.

Polignac, Hedwige de Chabannes, Princesse Françoise de. *Marguerite de Valois, grande princesse, grand écrivain*. Paris: La Pensée Universelle, 1973.

Ratel, Simonne. "La Cour de la Reine Marguerite." *Revue du XVIᵉ siècle* 11 (1924): 1–29, 193–207; 12 (1925): 1–43.

Schrenck, Gilbert. "Brantôme et Marguerite de Valois: d'un genre l'autre ou les Mémoires incertains." In *La Cour au miroir des mémorialistes (1530–1682)*. Ed. Noémi Hepp. Paris: Klincksieck, 1991. 183–192.

Tilley, Arthur A. "The Literary Circle of Margaret of Navarre." In *A Miscellany of Studies in Romance Languages and Literatures Presented to Leon E. Kaster*. Ed. Mary Williams and James A. de Rothschild. Cambridge: W. Heffer & Sons, 1932. 518–531.

Vaissière, Pierre de. "La Jeunesse de la reine Margot." *Humanisme et Renaissance* 7 (1940): 7–44, 190–212.

———. "Reine sans couronne: la reine Margot à Paris." *Revue des Etudes Historiques* 105 (January-March 1938): 17–44.

Viennot, Eliane. *La Vie et l'oeuvre de Marguerite de Valois: discours contemporains, historiques, littéraires, légendaires*. Ph. D. diss., Université de Paris III, 1991.

———. "Marguerite de Valois et *La Ruelle mal assortie:* une attribution erronée." *Nouvelle Revue du seizième siècle* 10 (1992): 81–98.

Watts, Derek A. "Self-Portrayal in Seventeenth-Century French Memoirs." *Australian Journal of French Studies* 12, no. 3 (1975): 264–285.

———. "Seventeenth-Century French Memoirs: New Perspectives." *Journal of European Studies* 10 (1980): 126–144.

Other Primary Sources

Alberti, Leone Battista. *Opuscoli morali*. Trans. Cosimo Bartoli. Venice: F. Franceschi, 1568.

Alcripe, Philippe d'. *La Nouvelle Fabrique*. Ed. Françoise Joukovsky. Geneva: Droz, 1983.

Amboise, François d'. *Instruction aux jeunes dames, en forme de dialogue, par laquelle les dames apprendront comme elles doivent se bien gouverner en amour*. Lyon: Benoist Rigaud, ca. 1577.

———. *Dialogues et devis des demoiselles, pour les rendre vertueuses et bienheureuses en la vraye et parfaicte amitié*. Paris: Vincens Norment, 1581; Paris: Robert le Maignier, 1583.

Artus, Thomas. *Qu'il est bienséant que les filles soient sçavantes*. Paris: L. Breyel, 1600. In *Misères et grandeur de la femme au XVIᵉ siècle*. Ed. Ilana Zinguer. Geneva: Slatkine, 1982.

Boccaccio, Giovanni. *Opere*. Ed. Cesare Segre. Milano: U. Mursia, 1978.

——. *The Decameron.* Trans. Mark Musa and Peter Bondanella. New York: W. W. Norton, 1982.

Brantôme, Pierre de Bourdeilles. "Discours sur La Reyne de France et Marguerite de Navarre." In *Oeuvres complètes.* 11 vols. Ed. Ludovic Lalanne. Paris: Renouard, 1875. 8: 22–85.

Castiglione, Baldesar. *The Book of the Courtier.* Trans. Charles Singleton. Garden City, N.Y.: Anchor Books, 1959.

Cholières, Le seigneur de. *Les Après-disnées du Seigneur de Cholières.* Paris: Jean Richter, 1587.

——. *Les Matinées,* ed. Tricotel, 2 vols. Paris: Librairie des Bibliophiles, 1789.

Claudian. *De Raptu Proserpinae.* Ed. J. B. Hall. Cambridge: Cambridge University Press, 1969.

Des Périers, Bonaventure. *Nouvelles Récréations et joyeux devis.* Ed. Krystyna Kasprzyk. Paris: Champion, 1980.

Du Fail, Noël. *Propos rustiques de Maistre Leon Ladulfi.* Ed. Pierre Jourda. In *Conteurs français du XVIᵉ siècle.* Paris: Gallimard, 1956.

Eaton, Marina Nickerson. *"Les Contens" of Odet de Turnèbe: A Critical Edition.* Ph. D. Diss., University of Oklahoma, 1973.

Ebreo, Leone. *De L'Amour.* Trans. Pontus de Tyard. Lyon: Jean de Tournes, 1551.

Flore, Jeanne. *Contes amoureux par Madame Jeanne Flore.* Eds. Gabriel-A. Pérouse et al. Lyon: Presses Universitaires de Lyon, 1980.

Hall, J. B., ed. *Claudian. De Raptu Proserpinae.* Cambridge: Cambridge University Press, 1969.

Jodelle, Etienne. *Oeuvres complètes.* Ed. Enéa Balmas, 2 vols. Paris: Gallimard, 1965.

Le Poulchre, F., Seigneur de la Motte-Messemé. *Le Passe-temps.* Paris: Jean Leblanc, 1595.

Lesnauderie, Pierre. *La Louange de mariage.* Paris: Pierre Sargent and Paris: F. Regnault, 1523.

Montaigne, Michel de. *Essais.* Paris: Gallimard, 1962.

——. *The Complete Essays of Montaigne.* Trans. Donald M. Frame. Stanford: Stanford University Press, 1965.

Ovid. *Metamorphoses.* 3rd ed. 2 vols. Ed. and trans. Frank J. Miller. Cambridge, MA: Harvard University Press, 1977.

——. *Metamorphoses.* Trans. Rolfe Humphries. Bloomington: Indiana University Press, 1955.

Pasquier, Etienne. *Oeuvres complètes.* 2 vols. Geneva: Slatkine Reprints, 1971.

Peletier du Mans, Jacques. *L'Art poëtique.* Ed. André Boulanger. Paris: Belles Lettres, 1930.

Petrarca, Francesco. *Canzoniere e Triomfi.* Florence: Phil. di Giunta, 1515.

——. *Letters from Petrarch.* Ed. Morris Bishop. Bloomington: Indiana University Press, 1966.

Piccolomini, Alessandro. *La Raffaella. Dialogue de la gentille éducation des femmes.* Ed. and trans. Alcide Bonneau. Paris: Liseux, 1884.

——. *Raffaella of Master Alexander Piccolomini or the Fair Perfectioning of Ladies.* Trans. John Nevinson. Glasgow: R. MacLehose, 1968.

Scève, Maurice. *Délie.* Ed. I. D. McFarlane. Cambridge: Cambridge University Press, 1961.

——. *Délie.* Ed. Françoise Charpentier. Paris: Gallimard, 1984.

Scudéry, Madeleine de. *De la Poésie française à Henry Quatrième.* 1684; Paris: Sansot, 1907.

Taillemont, Claude de. *Discours des champs faëz à l'honneur, et exaltation de l'amour, et des dames.* Lyon: Michel Du Bois, 1553.

Turnèbe, Odet de. *Les Contens.* Ed. Norman B. Spector. Paris: Nizet, 1983.

——. *Satisfaction All Around.* Trans. Donald Beecher. Ottowa: Carleton University Renaissance Centre, 1979.

Vigneulles, Philippe de. *Les Cent Nouvelles Nouvelles.* Ed. Charles H. with Françoise R. Livingston and Robert H. Ivy. Geneva: Droz, 1972.

Vivès, Juan Luis. *Institution de la femme chrétienne.* Trans. Pierre de Changy. Lyon: S. Sabon, n.d [between 1541 and 1549].

Yver, Jacques. *Le Printemps d'Yver.* Anvers: Guillaume Silvias, 1572.

Secondary Sources

Ariès, Philippe. "Pourquoi écrit-on des mémoires?" In *Les Valeurs chez les mémorialistes français du XVII*ᵉ *siècle avant la Fronde.* Ed. Naomi Hepp and Jacques Hennequin. Actes et Colloques 22. Paris: Klincksieck, 1979. 13–20.

Arnheim, Rudolph. *The Power of the Center: A Study of Composition in the Visual Arts.* Berkeley: University of California Press, 1988.

Ashley, Kathleen M. "Medieval Courtesy Literature and Dramatic Mirrors of Female Conduct." In *The Ideology of Conduct.* Ed. Nancy Armstrong and Leonard Tennenhouse. New York: Methuen, 1987. 25–37.

Aulotte, Robert. *La Comédie française de la Renaissance et son chef d'oeuvre "Les Contens" d'Odet de Turnèbe.* Paris: SEDES, 1984.

———. "Visages du théâtre comique de la Renaissance: deux jeunes filles vieilles de quatre cents ans." In *Crossroads and Perspectives: French Literature of the Renaissance. Studies in Honor of Victor Graham.* Ed. Catherine Grise and C. D. Tolton. Geneva: Droz, 1986. 155–159.

Balmas, Enéa. "A propos des *Contens* d'Odet de Turnèbe." In *Saggi e ricerche sul teatro francese del Cinquecento.* Florence: Leo Olschki, 1985. 131–140.

Barkan, Leonard. *The Gods Made Flesh: Metamorphosis and the Pursuit of Paganism.* New Haven: Yale University Press, 1986.

———. "Diana and Actaeon: The Myth as Synthesis." *English Literary Renaissance* 10 (1980): 317–359.

Beasley, Faith E. *Revising Memory: Women's Fiction and Memoirs in Seventeenth-Century France.* New Brunswick: Rutgers University Press, 1990.

Berriot-Salvadore, Evelyne. "Les Femmes et les pratiques de l'écriture de Christine de Pisan à Marie de Gournay. 'Femmes sçavantes et sçavoir féminin.'" *Réforme, Humanisme, Renaissance* 16 (1983): 52–69.

———. *Les Femmes dans la société française de la Renaissance.* Geneva: Droz, 1991.

Berry, Philippa. *Of Chastity and Power: Elizabethan Literature and the Unmarried Queen.* London: Routledge, 1989.

Beugnot, Bernard. "Livre de raison, livre de retraite: interférences des points de vue chez les mémorialistes." In *Les Valeurs chez les mémorialistes français du XVII*ᵉ *siècle avant la Fronde.* Ed. Naomi Hepp and Jacques Hennequin. 47–64.

Bornstein, Diane. *The Lady in the Tower. Medieval Courtesy Literature for Women.* Hamden: Archon Books, 1983.

Boucher, Jacqueline. *La Cour de Henri III.* Editions Ouest-France, 1986.

Cameron, Alan. *Claudian, Poetry and Propaganda at the Court of Honorius.* Oxford: Clarendon Press, 1970.

Carron, Jean-Louis. "Les Noms de l'honneur féminin à la Renaissance. Le Nom tu et le non dit." *Poétique* 67 (1986): 269–280.

Catach, Nina. *Les Doctrines ortographiques du XVI*ᵉ *siècle en France.* Geneva: Droz, 1989.

Cerquiglini, Jacqueline. "Histoire, image, raccord et désaccord du sens à la fin du Moyen Age." *Littérature* 74 (1989): 110–126.

Chamard, Henri. *Histoire de la Pléiade.* Paris: Didier, 1963.

Citton, Yves, and André Wyss. *Les Doctrines orthographiques du XVI*ᵉ *siècle en France.* Geneva: Droz, 1989.

Clouzot, Henri. *L'Ancien Théâtre en Poitou.* Niort: H. Clouzot, 1901.

Cohen, Simona. *The Image of Time in Renaissance Depictions of Petrarch's 'Trionfo del tempo'.* Tel Aviv: S. Cohen, 1982.

Cottrell, Robert. "Gender Imprinting in Montaigne's *Essais.*" *Ecrire au féminin à la Renaissance. L'Esprit Créateur* 30, no. 4 (1990): 85–96.

Davis, Natalie Zemon. *Society and Culture in Early Modern France.* Stanford: Stanford University Press, 1975.

———. *Fiction in the Archives: Pardon Tales and their Tellers in Sixteenth-Century France.* Stanford: Stanford University Press, 1987.

Deleuze, Gilles. *Le Pli.* Paris: Minuit, 1988.

Duby, Georges, and Michelle Perrot, ed. *Histoire des femmes en Occident.* 5 vols. Paris: Plon, 1991.

Fanon, Frantz. *Peau noire, masques blancs.* Paris: Seuil, 1952.

———. *Les Damnés de la terre.* Paris: Maspero, 1961; reprint, 1987.

Febvre, Lucien. *Le Problème de l'incroyance au XVIᵉ siècle.* Paris: Albin Michel, 1942.

Francastel, Pierre. *La Figure et le lieu.* Paris: Gallimard, 1967.

Fumaroli, Marc. "Les Mémoires du XVIIᵉ siècle avant la Fronde." *XVIIᵉ Siècle* 94–95 (1971): 5–37.

———. "Mémoires et histoire: le dilemme de l'historiographe humaniste au XVIIᵉ siècle." In *Les Valeurs chez les mémorialistes français du XVIIᵉ siècle avant la Fronde.* Ed. Naomi Hepp and Jacques Hennequin. 21–45.

Giudici, Enzo. *Spiritualismo e carnascialismo.* Naples: Edizione Scientifiche Italiane, 1968.

Goux, Jean-Joseph. *Symbolic Economies: After Marx and Freud.* Trans. Jennifer Curtis Gage. Ithaca: Cornell University Press, 1990.

Grafton, Anthony. *Joseph Scaliger: A Study in the History of Classical Scholarship.* Oxford: Clarendon Press, 1983.

Greene, Thomas M. *The Light in Troy: Imitation and Discovery in Renaissance Poetry.* New Haven: Yale University Press, 1982.

Guggisberg, R., Frank Lestringant, and Jean-Claude Margolin, ed. *La Liberté de conscience (XVIᵉ–XVIIᵉ siècles).* Geneva: Droz, 1991.

Guido, José. "De l'Amour courtois à l'amour sacré: la condition de la femme dans l'oeuvre de Baldassar Castiglione." In *Images de la femme dans la littérature italienne de la Renaissance: préjugés misogynes et aspirations nouvelles.* Ed. André Rochon. Paris: Université de la Sorbonne Nouvelle, 1980. 9–80.

Hannay, Margaret Patterson, ed. *Silent But for the Word: Tudor Women as Patrons, Translators and Writers of Religious Works.* Kent, Ohio: Kent State University Press, 1985.

Harth, Erica. *Cartesian Women: Versions and Subversions of Rational Discourse in the Old Regime.* Ithaca: Cornell University Press, 1992.

Hipp, Marie-Thérèse. *Mythes et réalités: enquête sur le roman et les mémoires (1660–1700).* Paris: Klincksieck, 1976.

Hollier, Denis, ed. *A New History of French Literature.* Cambridge: Harvard University Press, 1989.

Hull, Suzanne W. *Chaste, Silent and Obedient: English Books for Women, 1475–1640.* San Marino, Calif.: Huntington Library, 1982.

Jones, Ann Rosalind. "Surprising Fame: Renaissance Gender Ideologies and Women's Lyric." In *The Poetics of Gender.* Ed. Nancy K. Miller. New York: Columbia University Press, 1986. 74–95.

———. "Nets and Bridles: Early Modern Conduct Books and Sixteenth Century Women's Lyrics." In *The Ideology of Conduct.* Ed. Nancy Armstrong and Leonard Tennenhouse. New York: Methuen, 1987. 39–72.

Jordan, Constance. "Boccaccio's In-Famous Women: Gender and Civic Virtue in the *De mulieribus claris.*" In *Ambiguous Realities: Women in the Middle Ages and Renaissance.* Ed. Carole Levin and Jeanie Watson. Detroit: Wayne State University Press, 1987. 25–47.

Kelly-Gadol, Joan. "Did Women Have a Renaissance?" In *Becoming Visible: Women in European History.* Ed. Renate Bridenthal and Claudia Koonz. Boston: Houghton Mifflin, 1977. 137–164.

Kelso, Ruth. *Doctrine for the Lady of the Renaissance.* Urbana: University of Illinois Press, 1956; reprint, 1978.

Kleinbaum, Abbey Wettan. *The War Against The Amazons.* New York: McGraw-Hill, 1983.

Kritzman, Lawrence. *The Rhetoric of Sexuality and the Literature of the French Renaissance.* Cambridge: Cambridge University Press, 1991.

Lancaster, Henry. *The French Tragi-Comedy: Its Origin and Development from 1552 to 1628.* 1907. New York: Gordian Press, 1966.

Larsen, Anne R. "'Un honneste passetems': Strategies of Legitimation in French Renaissance Women's Prefaces." *L'Esprit Créateur* 30 (1990): 11–22.

Lazard, Madeleine. *La Comédie humaniste au XVIᵉ siècle et ses personnages.* Paris: Presses Universitaires de France, 1978.

———. *Le Théâtre en France au XVIᵉ siècle.* Paris: Presses Universitaires de France, 1980.

———. *Images littéraires de la femme à la Renaissance.* Paris: Presses Universitaires de France, 1985.

———. "Protestations et revendications féminines dans la littéraire française du XVIᵉ siècle." *Revue d'histoire littéraire de la France* 6 (1991): 859–877.

Lebègue, Raymond. *Le Théâtre comique en France de Pathelin à Mélite.* Paris: Hatier, 1972.

Levin, Carole, and Jeanie Watson, eds. *Ambiguous Realities: Women in the Middle Ages and Renaissance.* Detroit: Wayne State University Press, 1987.

L'Hoest, Benoît. *L'Amour enfermé: sentiment et sexualité à la Renaissance.* Paris: Olivier Orban, 1990.

Lougee, Carolyn. *'Le Paradis des femmes': Women, Salons, and Social Stratification in Seventeenth-Century France.* Princeton: Princeton University Press, 1976.

Maclean, Ian. *The Renaissance Notion of Woman.* Cambridge: Cambridge University Press, 1980.

———. *Woman Triumphant: Feminism in French Literature, 1610–1652.* Oxford: Clarendon Press, 1977.

Mathieu-Castellani, Gisèle. "La Figure mythique de Diane dans *L'Hécatombe* de d'Aubigné." *Revue d'Histoire Littéraire de la France* 78, no. 1 (1978): 3–18.

———. "Le Nombre et la lettre; pour une lecture du sonnet XCVI de *L'Hécatombe à Diane* de d'Aubigné." *Revue des Sciences Humaines* 51, no. 179 (1980): 93–108.

———. "Lune, Femme: l'image de Diane chez Théophile et Tristan." In *Onze Nouvelles Etudes sur l'image de la femme dans la littérature française du dix-septième siècle.* Ed. W. Leiner. Tubingen: Narr, 1984. 39–44.

May, Georges. *Autobiographie.* Paris: Presses Universitaires de France, 1979 and 1984.

Memmi, Albert. *Portrait du colonisé.* Paris: Gallimard, 1957; reprint, 1985.

Michaud, M. *Biographie universelle.* 45 vols. Paris: Desplaces. 1843–1865.

Minkowski, Eugène. *Le Temps vécu: études phénoménologiques et psychopathologiques.* Saint-Pierre de Salerne: G. Monfort, 1988.

Monter, E. William. "The Pedestal and the Stake: Courtly Love and Witchcraft." In *Becoming Visible: Women in European History.* Ed. Renate Bridenthal and Claudia Koonz. 119–136.

Norton, Glen P. *The Ideology and Language of Translation in Renaissance France, and their Humanist Antecedents.* Geneva: Droz, 1984.

Panofsky, Erwin. *Renaissance and Renascences in Western Art.* Stockholm: Almquist, 1960.

Pérouse, Gabriel. "'L'Honneste' dans les *Amours* de Ronsard." In *La Catégorie de l'Honneste dans la culture du XVIᵉ siècle.* Actes du colloque international de Sommières II, 1983. Université de Saint-Etienne, 1985. 179–193.

———. *La Nouvelle Française du XVIᵉ siècle. Images de la vie du temps.* Geneva: Droz, 1977.

Piéjus, Marie-Françoise. "Vénus Bifrons: le double idéal dans 'La Raffaella' d'Alessandro Piccolomini." In *Images de la femme dans la littérature italienne de la Renaissance.* Ed. André Rochon. Paris: Presses Universitaire de la Sorbonne Nouvelle, 1980. 81–167.

Poulet, Georges. *Mesure de l'instant.* In *Etudes sur le temps humain.* 4 vols. Monaco: Editions du Rocher, 1977.

Quinones, Ricardo. *The Renaissance Discovery of Time.* Cambridge: Harvard University Press, 1972.

Reichler, Claude. *Le Corps et ses fictions.* Paris: Minuit, 1983.

Reno, Christine. "Virginity as an Ideal in Christine de Pizan's *Cité des dames.*" In *Ideals for Women in the Works of Christine de Pizan.* Ed. Diane Bornstein. Detroit: Michigan Consortium for Medieval and Early Modern Studies, 1981. 69–91.

Reynolds-Cornell, Régine. "Madame Jeanne Flore and the *Contes amoureux.*" *Bibliothèque d'Humanisme et Renaissance.* 51, no. 1 (1989): 123–133.

Ricoeur, Paul. *Le Temps raconté.* Paris: Seuil, 1985.

Riffaterre, Michael. *Semiotics of Poetry.* Bloomington: Indiana University Press, 1978.

———. "La trace de l'intertexte." *La Pensée* 215 (1980): 4–18.

Rigolot, François, ed. "Writing in the Feminine in the Renaissance." Special Issue of *L'Esprit Créateur* 30 (Winter 1990).

———. With Kirk D. Read, "Discours liminaire et identité littéraire." *Versants* 15 (1989): 75–98.

Rochon, André, ed. *Images de la Femme dans la littérature italienne de la Renaissance: préjugés misogynes et aspirations nouvelles.* Paris: Université de la Sorbonne Nouvelle, 1980.

Ronsard, Pierre de. *Oeuvres complètes.* Ed. Paul Laumonier et al. Paris: Hachette, 1914–1967.

Rosolato, Guy. *Eléments de l'interprétation.* Paris: Gallimard, Coll. "Connaissance de l'inconscient," 1985.

Rose, Mary Beth, ed. *Women in the Middle Ages and the Renaissance. Literary and Historical Perspectives.* Syracuse: Syracuse University Press, 1986.

Saulnier, Verdun L. *Maurice Scève.* Paris: Klincksieck, 1948.

Sobol, Donald J. *The Amazons in Greek Mythology.* New York: A. S. Barnes and Co., 1972.

Spector, Norman B. "Odet de Turnèbe's *Les Contens* and the Italian Comedy." *French Studies* 13 (1959): 304–313.

Tyrell, William Blake. *Amazons: A Study in Mythmaking.* Baltimore: Johns Hopkins University Press, 1984.

Vecchio, Sylvana. "La Bonne Epouse." In *Histoire des Femmes,* ed. Georges Duby and Michelle Perrot. Vol. II: *Le Moyen Age,* ed. Christiane Klapisch-Zuber. Paris: Plon, 1991. 117–145.

Viala, Alain. *Naissance de l'écrivain: sociologie de la littérature à l'âge classique.* Paris: Les Editions de Minuit, 1985.

Vickers, Nancy J. "Diana Described: Scattered Woman and Scattered Rhyme." *Critical Inquiry* 8, no. 2 (1981): 265–279.

Weber, Henri. *La Création poétique au XVIᵉ siècle en France.* Paris: Nizet, 1955.

Wiesner, Merry E. "Women's Defense of Their Public Role." In *Women in the Middle Ages and the Renaissance: Literary and Historical Perspectives.* Ed. Mary Beth Rose. Syracuse: Syracuse University Press, 1986. 1–27.

Wilson, Katharina M., ed. *Women Writers of the Renaissance and Reformation.* Athens: University of Georgia Press, 1987.

Feminist Theory

Blau Du Plessis, Rachel. "'Perceiving the Other-Side of Everything': Tactics of Revisionary Mythopoesis." In *Writing Beyond the Ending: Narrative Strategies of Twentieth-Century Women Writers.* Bloomington: Indiana University Press, 1985. 105–122.

Cixous, Hélène. "Le rire de la méduse." *L'Arc* 61 (1975): 39–54.

———. *Entre L'Ecriture.* Paris: des femmes, 1976.

———. *The Newly Born Woman.* With Catherine Clément. Trans. Betsy Wing. *Theory and History of Literature,* 24. Minneapolis: University of Minnesota Press, 1986.

Daly, Mary. *Gyn/Ecology: The Metaethics of Radical Feminism.* Boston: Beacon Press, 1978.

Ferguson, Ann. "On Conceiving Motherhood and Sexuality: A Feminist Materialist Approach." In *Mothering: Essays in Feminist Theory.* Ed. Joyce Trebilcot. Totowa, N.J.: Rowman and Allanheld, 1984. 153–182.

Ferguson, Margaret W., Maureen Quilligan, and Nancy J. Vickers, eds. *Rewriting the Renaissance. The Discourses of Sexual Difference in Early Modern Europe.* Chicago: University of Chicago Press, 1986.

Ferguson, Margaret. "A Room Not Their Own: Renaissance Women as Readers and Writers." In *The Comparative Perspective on Literature. Approaches to Theory and Practice.* Ed. Clayton Koelb and Susan Noakes. Ithaca: Cornell University Press, 1988. 93–116.

Fisher, Sheila, and Janet E. Halley, eds. *Seeking the Woman in Late Medieval and Renaissance Writings: Essays in Feminist Contextual Criticism.* Knoxville: University of Tennessee Press, 1989.

French, Marilyn. *Beyond Power: On Women, Men and Morals.* New York: Summit Books, 1985.

Gagnon, Madeleine. "Mon corps dans l'écriture." In *La Venue à l'écriture.* Ed. Hélène Cixous, Madeleine Gagnon, and Annie Leclerc. Paris: Union Générale d'Editions, 1977.

Gaudin, Colette et al., ed. "Feminist Readings: French Texts/American Contexts." Special issue of *Yale French Studies* 62 (1981).

Gilbert, Sandra, and Susan Gubar. *The Madwoman in the Attic: The Woman Writer and the Nineteenth-Century Literary Imagination.* New Haven: Yale University Press, 1979.

Gravdal, Kathryn. *Ravishing Maidens: Writing Rape in Medieval French Literature and Law.* Philadelphia: University of Pennsylvania Press, 1991.

Heilbrun, Carolyn G. *Writing a Woman's Life.* New York: W. W. Norton, 1988.

Hirsch, Marianne. *The Mother/Daughter Plot: Narrative, Psychoanalysis, Feminism.* Bloomington: Indiana University Press, 1989.

———. "A Mother's Discourse: Incorporation and Repetition in *La Princesse de Clèves*." *Yale French Studies* 62 (1981): 67–87.

Irigaray, Luce. *Speculum de l'autre femme.* Paris: Editions de Minuit, 1974.

———. *Ce Sexe qui n'en est pas un.* Paris: Editions de Minuit, 1977.

———. *This Sex Which Is Not One.* Trans. Catherine Porter with Carolyn Burke. Ithaca: Cornell University Press, 1985.

———. *Le Temps de la différence.* Paris: Livre de Poche, 1989.

Jones, Ann Rosalind. *The Currency of Eros: Women's Love Lyric in Europe, 1540–1620.* Bloomington: Indiana University Press, 1990.

———. "Assimilation with a Difference: Renaissance Women Poets and Literary Influence." *Yale French Studies* 14 (1981): 213–232.

———. "French Theories of the Feminine." In *Making a Difference: Feminist Literary Criticism.* Ed. Gayle Greene and Coppélia Kahn. New York: Methuen, 1985. 80–112.

Jordan, Constance. *Renaissance Feminism: Literary Texts and Political Models.* Ithaca: Cornell University Press, 1990.

Kamuf, Peggy. "A Double Life (Femminism II)." In *Men in Feminism.* Ed. Alice Jardine and Paul Smith. New York: Methuen, 1987. 93–98.

Kofman, Sarah. "The Narcissistic Woman: Freud and Girard." *Diacritics* 9 (1980): 36–45.

Kristeva, Julia. *La Révolution du langage poétique.* Paris: Seuil, 1974.

Lindsay, Cécile. "Body/Language: French Feminist Utopias." *The French Review* 60 (1986): 46–55.

Marks, Elaine. "Women and Literature in France." *Signs* 3 (1978): 832–855.

Marks, Elaine, and Isabelle de Courtivron, ed. *New French Feminisms.* Amherst: University of Massachusetts Press, 1980.

Michie, Helena. *The Flesh Made Word: Female Figures and Women's Bodies.* New York: Oxford University Press, 1987.

Miles, Margaret R. *Carnal Knowing: Female Nakedness and Religious Meaning in the Christian West.* Boston: Beacon Press, 1990.

Miller, Nancy K., ed. *The Poetics of Gender.* New York: Columbia University Press, 1986.

————. "Rereading as a Woman: The Body in Practice." In *The Female Body in Western Culture. Contemporary Perspectives.* Ed. Susan Rubin Suleiman. Cambridge: Harvard University Press, 1986. 354–362.

Moi, Toril. "The Missing Mother: The Oedipal Rivalries of René Girard." *Diacritics* 12 (1982): 21–31.

Rich, Adrienne. *Of Woman Born.* New York: Norton, 1976.

————. *Of Woman Born: Motherhood as Experience and Instruction.* New York, Bantam, 1977.

Rubin, Gayle. "The Traffic in Women: Notes on the 'Political Economy' of Sex." In *Toward an Anthropology of Women.* Ed. Rayna R. Reiter. New York: Monthly Review Press, 1975. 157–210.

Ruddick, Sara. "Maternal Thinking." In *Mothering: Essays in Feminist Theory.* Ed. Joyce Trebilcot. 213–230.

————. *Maternal Thinking: Toward a Politics of Peace.* Boston: Beacon Press, 1989.

Sankovitch, Tilde. *French Women Writers and the Book: Myths of Access and Desire.* Syracuse: Syracuse University Press, 1988.

Scholes, Robert. "Uncoding Mama: The Female Body as Text." In *Semiotics and Interpretation.* New Haven: Yale University Press, 1982. 127–142.

Segal, Naomi. *The Unintended Reader: Feminism and Manon Lescaut.* Cambridge: Cambridge University Press, 1986.

Showalter, Elaine, ed. *The New Feminist Criticism.* New York: Parthenon, 1985.

Smith, Sidonie. *A Poetics of Women's Autobiography: Marginality and the Fictions of Self-Representation.* Bloomington: Indiana University Press, 1987.

Spivak, Gayatri. "French Feminism in an International Frame." In *Feminist Readings: French Texts/American Contexts.* Ed. Colette Gaudin et al. *Yale French Studies* 62 (1981): 154–184.

Stallybrass, Peter. "Patriarchal Territories: The Body Enclosed." In *Rewriting the Renaissance.* Ed. Margaret Ferguson et al. 123–142.

Suleiman, Susan Rubin. "(Re)Writing the Body: The Politics and Poetics of Female Eroticism." In *The Female Body in Western Culture: Contemporary Perspectives.* Ed. Susan Rubin Suleiman. 7–29.

Wittig, Monique. *Les Guérillères.* Paris: Minuit, 1969.

————. "The Mark of Gender." In *The Poetics of Gender.* Ed. Nancy K. Miller. New York: Columbia University Press, 1986. 63–73.

Contributors

༄

CATHLEEN M. BAUSCHATZ, associate professor of French at the University of Maine, has published numerous articles on readers and reading in the French Renaissance, in journals in the United States and Europe. She has also published in the following collections: *The Reader in the Text: Essays on Audience and Interpretation*, ed. I. Crosman and S. Suleiman (Princeton: Princeton University Press, 1980); *Contending Kingdoms: Historical, Psychological, and Feminist Approaches to the Literature of Sixteenth-Century England and France*, ed. M.-R. Logan and P. Rudnytsky (Detroit: Wayne State University Press, 1991); and *Humanism in Crisis: The Decline of the French Renaissance*, ed. P. Desan (Ann Arbor: University of Michigan Press, 1991). She is currently working on a book project, "Women as Readers in and of French Renaissance Literature."

PATRICIA FRANCIS CHOLAKIAN, associate professor of Romance Languages at Hamilton College, is the author of *Rape and Writing in the Heptameron of Marguerite de Navarre* (Carbondale: Southern Illinois University Press, 1992) and co-author of *The Early French Novella* (Buffalo: SUNY Press, 1972). She has also published on Marie de Gournay, Melle de Montpensier, and Mme de Villedieu and has contributed articles to *Arms and the Woman: Feminist Essays on War and Gender*, ed. H. Cooper, A. Munich, and S. Squier (Chapel Hill: University of North Carolina Press, 1989); and *Reading Women: Feminist Contextual Criticism and Renaissance Texts*, ed. J. Halley and S. Fisher (Knoxville: University of Tennessee Press, 1989). At present she is working on a study of self-representation in women's memoirs under the *Ancien Régime*.

TOM CONLEY, professor of French at the University of Minnesota, is the author of *The Graphic Unconscious in Early Modern French Literature* (Cambridge: Cambridge University Press, 1992); *Film Hieroglyphs: Ruptures in Classical Cinema* (Minneapolis: University of Minnesota Press, 1991); Michel de Certeau's *The Writing of History*, trans. from French (New York: Columbia University Press, 1988). He has also written on major Renaissance writers (Marot, Scève, Montaigne), film theory, and Dada and Surrealism, and has contributed articles to *Poétiques: théorie et critique littéraires* (Ann Arbor: University of Michigan, Department of Romance Languages, 1980); *1492–1992: Re/Discovering Colonial Writing*, ed. René

233

Jara (Minneapolis: Prisma Inst., 1989); *Reading Proust Now,* ed. Mary Ann Caws and Eugène Nicole (New York: Peter Lang, 1990); and *Le Signe et le texte: études sur l'écriture au XVIe siècle en France,* ed. Lawrence Kritzman (Lexington, Ky.: French Forum, 1990).

GARY FERGUSON, assistant professor of French at the University of Delaware, gained his doctorate at the University of Durham, England, before going to work in the United States. He has published articles on the development of Protestant theology in France and on Marguerite de Navarre's religious poetry. He is the author of *Mirroring Belief: Marguerite de Navarre's Devotional Poetry* (Edinburgh: Edinburgh University Press, 1992).

CARLA FRECCERO, associate professor of Literature and Women's Studies at the University of California, Santa Cruz, is the author of *Father Figures: Genealogy and Narrative Structure in Rabelais* (Ithaca: Cornell University Press, 1991) and numerous articles on Rabelais and Marguerite de Navarre. She is currently working on a monograph on the politics of maternal sovereignty in the *Heptaméron.*

ANNE R. LARSEN, associate professor of French at Hope College, has published articles on Louise Labé, Hélisenne de Crenne, and the Dames des Roches, and has contributed to *Women Writers of the Renaissance and Reformation,* ed. Katharina Wilson (Athens: University of Georgia Press, 1987). She has published a critical edition of Madeleine and Catherine des Roches's *Les Oeuvres* (Geneva: Droz, 1993), and is currently preparing an edition of the Des Roches's *Secondes Oeuvres.*

DEBORAH N. LOSSE, associate professor of French at Arizona State University, has published *Rhetoric at Play: Rabelais and Satirical Eulogy* (Utah Studies in Language and Literature, vol. 17, 1980) and numerous articles on Bonaventure des Périers, Rabelais, Marguerite de Navarre, and the Renaissance *Nouvelle.* She is presently at work on a book-length study on Montaigne and the *conteurs.*

KIRK D. READ, assistant professor of French at Bates College, has published on Louise Labé and women's prefaces in the French Renaissance. His current research interests include women authors of sixteenth-century France, and aspects of female community in the works of Louise Labé, the Dames des Roches, and Anne de Marquets.

TILDE SANKOVITCH, professor of French in the Department of French and Italian at Northwestern University, has published *Jodelle et la création du masque. Etude structurale et normative de "L'Eugène"* (York, S.C.: French Literature Publications Co., 1979); *The Poems of the Troubadour Bertran de Born,* with W. D. Paden and Patricia Stäblein (Berkeley: University of California Press, 1986); and *French Women Writers and the Book: Myths of Access and Desire* (Syracuse: Syracuse University Press, 1988). Her current research interests are in French literature of the Middle Ages and the Renaissance, with a special focus on writings by and about women.

PAULA SOMMERS, professor of French at the University of Missouri-Columbia, has published articles on major writers of the Renaissance, D'Aubigné, Bonaventure des Périers, Jacques Tahureau, Marguerite de Navarre, Ronsard, Rabelais, and Montaigne, and a book on Marguerite de Navarre, *Celestial Ladders: Readings in Marguerite de Navarre's Poetry of Spiritual Ascent* (Geneva: Droz, 1989).

COLETTE H. WINN, associate professor of French at Washington University in St. Louis, has published *La Poétique de l'accoutumance: les Sonnets de la Mort de Jean de Sponde* (Potomac, M.D.: Studia Humanitatis, 1984); *L'Esthétique du jeu dans L'Heptaméron de Marguerite de Navarre* (Montreal: Institut d'Etudes Médiévales, Université de Montréal/Vrin, 1993). She has published on Marguerite de Navarre, Hélisenne de Crenne, Pernette du Guillet, Jeanne Flore, Bonaventure des Périers, and Joachim du Bellay. She is presently working on "feminine writing in the Renaissance" and preparing a critical edition of Gabrielle de Coignard's *Oeuvres chrestiennes.*

CATHY YANDELL, professor of French at Carleton College, has published a critical edition of Pontus de Tyard's *Solitaire second* (Geneva: Droz, 1980), and articles on Tyard, Montaigne, Catherine des Roches, Tahureau, and the *Blasons du corps féminin.* Her current research interests include carpe diem, the body in sixteenth-century texts, and temporal ideology in Renaissance France and Italy.

Index